THE HISTORY OF THE REIGN OF THE EMPEROR CHARLES V

Volume III

William Robertson

This edition published by Routledge/Thoemmes Press, 1996

Routledge/Thoemmes Press
11 New Fetter Lane
London EC4P 4EE

The Works of William Robertson
12 Volumes : ISBN 0 415 13743 8

This is a reprint of the 1792 edition

Routledge / Thoemmes Press is a joint imprint
of Routledge and Thoemmes Antiquarian Books Ltd.

British Library Cataloguing-in-Publication Data
A CIP record of this set is available from the British Library

Publisher's Note

The publisher has gone to great lengths to ensure the quality of this reprint but points out that some imperfections in the original book may be apparent.

THE WORKS OF
WILLIAM ROBERTSON

Volume V

Printed and bound by
Antony Rowe Ltd., Chippenham, Wiltshire

THE
HISTORY
OF THE
REIGN
OF THE
EMPEROR CHARLES V.

VOL. III.

Titian. pinx. J. Heath. Sculp.

Published as the Act directs, Feb.1.st 1792, by T. Cadell, Strand.

THE
HISTORY
OF THE
REIGN
OF THE
EMPEROR CHARLES V.

By WILLIAM ROBERTSON, D.D.
PRINCIPAL OF THE UNIVERSITY OF EDINBURGH, AND
HISTORIOGRAPHER TO HIS MAJESTY FOR SCOTLAND.

VOLUME III.

The SEVENTH EDITION, Corrected.

LONDON:

Printed for A. STRAHAN; T. CADELL, in the Strand;
and J. BALFOUR, at Edinburgh.
M DCC XCII.

THE
HISTORY
OF THE
REIGN
OF THE
EMPEROR CHARLES V.

BOOK V.

THE account of the cruel manner in which the Pope had been treated, filled all Europe with aftonifhment or horror. To fee a Chriftian Emperor, who, by poffeffing that dignity, ought to have been the protector and advocate of the holy fee, lay violent hands on him who reprefented Chrift on earth, and detain his facred perfon in a rigorous captivity, was confidered as an impiety that merited the fevereft vengeance, and which called for the immediate interpofition of every dutiful fon of the church. Francis and Henry, alarmed at the progrefs of the Imperial arms in Italy, had, even before the taking of Rome, entered into a clofer alliance; and,

BOOK V.
1527.
General indignation excited againft the Emperor.

BOOK V.
1527.

and, in order to give some check to the Emperor's ambition, had agreed to make a vigorous diversion in the Low Countries. The force of every motive, which had influenced them at that time, was now increased; and to these were added the desire of rescuing the Pope out of the Emperor's hands, a measure no less politic, than it appeared to be pious. This, however, rendered it necessary to abandon their hostile intentions against the Low Countries, and to make Italy the seat of war, as it was by vigorous operations there they might contribute most effectually towards delivering Rome, and setting Clement at liberty. Francis being now sensible, that, in his system with regard to the affairs of Italy, the spirit of refinement had carried him too far; and that, by an excess of remissness, he had allowed Charles to attain advantages which he might easily have prevented, was eager to make reparation for an error, of which he was not often guilty, by an activity more suitable to his temper. Henry thought his interposition necessary, in order to hinder the Emperor from becoming master of all Italy, and acquiring by that means such superiority of power, as would enable him, for the future, to dictate without controul to the other princes of Europe. Wolsey, whom Francis had taken care to secure by flattery and presents, the certain methods of gaining his favour, neglected nothing that could incense his master against the Emperor. Besides all these public considerations, Henry was influenced by one of a more private nature; having begun,

begun, about this time, to form his great scheme of divorcing Catherine of Aragon, towards the execution of which he knew that the sanction of papal authority would be necessary, he was desirous to acquire as much merit as possible with Clement, by appearing to be the chief instrument of his deliverance.

BOOK V.

1527.

THE negociation, between princes thus disposed, was not tedious. Wolsey himself conducted it, on the part of his sovereign, with unbounded powers. Francis treated with him in person at Amiens, where the Cardinal appeared, and was received with royal magnificence. A marriage between the duke of Orleans and the princess Mary was agreed to as the basis of the confederacy; it was resolved that Italy should be the theatre of war; the strength of the army which should take the field, as well as the contingent of troops or of money, which each prince should furnish, were settled; and if the Emperor did not accept of the proposals which they were jointly to make him, they bound themselves immediately to declare war, and to begin hostilities. Henry, who took every resolution with impetuosity, entered so eagerly into this new alliance, that, in order to give Francis the strongest proof of his friendship and respect, he formally renounced the ancient claim of the English monarchs to the crown of France, which had long been the pride and ruin of the nation; as a full compensation for which he accepted a pension of fifty thousand crowns,

Confederacy against him. July 11.

Aug. 18.

BOOK V.
1527.

The Florentines recover their freedom.

to be paid annually to himself and his successors [a].

THE Pope, being unable to fulfil the conditions of his capitulation, still remained a prisoner under the severe custody of Alarcon. The Florentines no sooner heard of what had happened at Rome, than they ran to arms in a tumultuous manner; expelled the Cardinal di Cortona, who governed their city in the Pope's name; defaced the arms of the Medici; broke in pieces the statues of Leo and Clement; and declaring themselves a free state, re-established their ancient popular government. The Venetians, taking advantage of the calamity of their ally the Pope, seized Ravenna, and other places belonging to the church, under pretext of keeping them in deposite. The dukes of Urbino and Ferrara laid hold likewise on part of the spoils of the unfortunate Pontiff, whom they considered as irretrievably ruined [b].

The Imperial troops inactive.

LANNOY, on the other hand, laboured to derive some solid benefit from that unforeseen event, which gave such splendour and superiority to his master's arms. For this purpose he marched to Rome, together with Moncada, and the marquis del Guasto, at the head of all the troops which they could assemble in the kingdom of Naples.

[a] Herbert, 83, &c. Rym. Fœd. xiv. 203.
[b] Guic. l. xviii. 453.

Naples. The arrival of this reinforcement brought new calamities on the unhappy citizens of Rome; for the foldiers envying the wealth of their companions, imitated their licence, and with the utmoft rapacity gathered the gleanings, which had efcaped the avarice of the Spaniards and Germans. There was not now any army in Italy capable of making head againft the Imperialifts; and nothing more was requifite to reduce Bologna, and the other towns in the ecclefiaftical ftate, than to have appeared before them. But the foldiers having been fo long accuftomed, under Bourbon, to an entire relaxation of difcipline, and having tafted the fweets of living at difcretion in a great city, almoft without the controul of a fuperior, were become fo impatient of military fubordination, and fo averfe to fervice, that they refufed to leave Rome, unlefs all their arrears were paid; a condition which they knew to be impoffible. At the fame time, they declared, that they would not obey any other perfon than the prince of Orange, whom the army had chofen general. Lannoy, finding that it was no longer fafe for him to remain among licentious troops, who defpifed his dignity, and hated his perfon, returned to Naples; foon after the marquis del Guafto and Moncada thought it prudent to quit Rome for the fame reafon. The prince of Orange, a general only in name, and by the moft precarious of all tenures, the good-will of foldiers, whom fuccefs and licence had rendered capricious, was obliged to to pay more attention to their humours, than they did to his commands. Thus the Emperor, instead of reaping any of the advantages which he might have expected from the reduction of Rome, had the mortification to see the most formidable body of troops that he had ever brought into the field, continue in a state of inactivity from which it was impossible to rouse them [c].

The French army marches into Italy.

This gave the King of France and the Venetians leisure to form new schemes, and to enter into new engagements for delivering the Pope, and preserving the liberties of Italy. The newly-restored republic of Florence very imprudently joined with them, and Lautrec, of whose abilities the Italians entertained a much more favourable opinion than his own master, was, in order to gratify them, appointed generalissimo of the league. It was with the utmost reluctance he undertook that office, being unwilling to expose himself a second time to the difficulties and disgraces, which the negligence of the King, or the malice of his favourites, might bring upon him. The best troops in France marched under his command; and the King of England, though he had not yet declared war against the Emperor, advanced a considerable sum towards carrying on the expedition. Lautrec's first operations

[c] Guic. l. xviii. 454.

rations were prudent, vigorous, and succefsful. By the affiftance of Andrew Doria, the ableft sea-officer of that age, he rendered himself mafter of Genoa, and re-eftablifhed in that republic the faction of the Fregofi, together with the dominion of France. He obliged Alexandria to surrender after a fhort fiege, and reduced all the country on that fide of the Tefino. He took Pavia, which had fo long refifted the arms of his fovereign, by affault, and plundered it with that cruelty, which the memory of the fatal difafter that had befallen the French nation before its walls naturally infpired. All the Milanefe, which Antonio de Leyva defended with a fmall body of troops, kept together, and fupported by his own addrefs and induftry, muft have foon fubmitted to his power, if he had continued to bend the force of his arms againft that country. But Lautrec durft not complete a conqueft which would have been fo honourable to himfelf, and of fuch advantage to the league. Francis knew his confederates to be more defirous of circumfcribing the Imperial power in Italy, than of acquiring new territories for him; and was afraid, that if Sforza were once re-eftablifhed in Milan, they would second but coldly the attack which he intended to make on the kingdom of Naples. For this reafon he inftructed Lautrec not to pufh his operations with too much vigour in Lombardy; and happily the importunities of the Pope, and the folicitations of the Florentines, the one for relief, and the other for protection, were fo urgent as to furnifh

BOOK V.

1527.
His operations.

BOOK V.
1527.

THE REIGN OF THE

furnish him with a decent pretext for marching forward, without yielding to the intreaties of the Venetians and Sforza, who insisted on his laying siege to Milan [d].

The Emperor sets the Pope at liberty.

WHILE Lautrec advanced slowly towards Rome, the Emperor had time to deliberate concerning the disposal of the Pope's person, who still remained a prisoner in the castle of St. Angelo. Notwithstanding the specious veil of religion, with which he usually endeavoured to cover his actions, Charles, in many instances, appears to have been but little under the influence of religious considerations, and had frequently, on this occasion, expressed an inclination to transport the Pope into Spain, that he might indulge his ambition with the spectacle of the two most illustrious personages in Europe successively prisoners in his court. But the fear of giving new offence to all Christendom, and of filling his own subjects with horror, obliged him to forego that satisfaction [e]. The progress of the confederates made it now necessary, either to set the Pope at liberty, or to remove him to some place of confinement more secure than the castle of St. Angelo. Many considerations induced him to prefer the former, particularly his want of the money, requisite as well for recruiting his army, as for paying off the vast arrears due to it. In

[d] Guic. l. xviii. 461. Bellay, 107, &c. Mauroc. Hist. Venet. lib. iii. 238.
[e] Guic. l. xviii. 457.

order

EMPEROR CHARLES V. 9

order to obtain this, he had affembled the Cortes of Caftile at Valladolid about the beginning of the year, and having laid before them the ftate of his affairs, and reprefented the neceffity of making great preparations to refift the enemies, whom envy at the fuccefs which had crowned his arms would unite againft him, he demanded a large fupply in the moft preffing terms; but the Cortes, as the nation was already exhaufted by extraordinary donatives, refufed to load it with any new burden, and in fpite of all his endeavours to gain or to intimidate the members, perfifted in this refolution [f]. No refource, therefore, remained, but the extorting from Clement, by way of ranfom, a fum fufficient for difcharging what was due to his troops, without which it was vain to mention to them their leaving Rome.

Nor was the Pope inactive on his part, or his intrigues unfuccefsful towards haftening fuch a treaty. By flattery, and the appearance of unbounded confidence, he difarmed the refentment of Cardinal Colonna, and wrought upon his vanity, which made him defirous of fhewing the world, that as his power had at firft depreffed the Pope, it could now raife him to his former dignity. By favours and promifes he gained Moronè, who, by one of thofe whimfical revo-

[f] Sandov. i. p. 814.

lutions which occur so often in his life, and which so strongly display his character, had now recovered his credit and authority with the Imperialists. The address and influence of two such men easily removed all the obstacles which retarded an accommodation, and brought the treaty for Clement's liberty to a conclusion, upon conditions hard indeed, but not more severe than a prince in his situation had reason to expect. He was obliged to advance, in ready money, an hundred thousand crowns for the use of the army; to pay the same sum at the distance of a fortnight; and, at the end of three months, an hundred and fifty thousand more. He engaged not to take part in the war against Charles, either in Lombardy or in Naples; he granted him a bull of cruzado, and the tenth of ecclesiastical revenues in Spain; and he not only gave hostages, but put the Emperor in possession of several towns, as a security for the performance of these articles [g]. Having raised the first moiety by a sale of ecclesiastical dignities and benefices, and other expedients equally uncanonical, a day was fixed for delivering him from imprisonment. But Clement, impatient to be free, after a tedious confinement of six months, as well as full of the suspicion and distrust natural to the unfortunate, was so much afraid that the Imperialists might still throw in obstacles to put off his deliverance, that he disguised himself, on the night preceding

[g] Guic. l. xviii. 467, &c.

the day when he was to be set free, in the habit of a merchant, and Alarcon having remitted somewhat of his vigilance upon the conclusion of the treaty, he made his escape undiscovered. He arrived before next morning at Orvietto, without any attendants but a single officer; and from thence wrote a letter of thanks to Lautrec, as the chief instrument of procuring him liberty [h].

During these transactions, the ambassadors of France and England repaired to Spain, in consequence of the treaty which Wolsey had concluded with the French King. The Emperor, unwilling to draw on himself the united forces of the two monarchs, discovered an inclination to relax somewhat the rigour of the treaty of Madrid, to which, hitherto, he had adhered inflexibly. He offered to accept of the two millions of crowns, which Francis had proposed to pay as an equivalent for the dutchy of Burgundy, and to set his sons at liberty, on condition that he would recall his army out of Italy, and restore Genoa, together with the other conquests which he had made in that country. With regard to Sforza, he insisted that his fate should be determined by the judges appointed to inquire into his crimes. These propositions being made to Henry, he transmitted them to his ally the French King, whom it more nearly concerned

Overtures of the Emperor to Francis and Henry.

[h] Guic. l. xviii. 467, &c. Jov. Vit. Colon. 169. Mauroc. Hist. Venet. lib. iii. 252.

to examine and to anfwer them; and if Francis had been fincerely folicitous, either to conclude peace or preferve confiftency in his own conduct, he ought inftantly to have clofed with overtures which differed but little from the propofitions which he himfelf had formerly made[1]. But his views were now much changed; his alliance with Henry, Lautrec's progrefs in Italy, and the fuperiority of his army there above that of the Emperor, hardly left him room to doubt of the fuccefs of his enterprize againft Naples. Full of thofe fanguine hopes, he was at no lofs to find pretexts for rejecting or evading what the Emperor had propofed. Under the appearance of fympathy with Sforza, for whofe interefts he had not hitherto difcovered much folicitude, he again demanded the full and unconditional re-eftablifhment of that unfortunate prince in his dominions. Under colour of its being imprudent to rely on the Emperor's fincerity, he infifted that his fons fhould be fet at liberty before the French troops left Italy, or furrendered Genoa. The unreafonablenefs of thefe demands, as well as the reproachful infinuation with which they were accompanied, irritated Charles to fuch a degree, that he could hardly liften to them with patience; and repenting of his moderation, which had made fo little impreffion on his enemies, declared that he would not depart in the fmalleft article from the conditions which he had

[1] Recueil des Traitéz, ii. 249.

now

now offered. Upon this the French and English ambaffadors (for Henry had been drawn unaccountably to concur with Francis in thefe ftrange propofitions) demanded and obtained their audience of leave [k].

NEXT day, two heralds, who had accompanied the ambaffadors on purpofe, though they had hitherto concealed their character, having affumed the enfigns of their office, appeared in the Emperor's court, and being admitted into his prefence, they, in the name of their refpective mafters, and with all the folemnities cuftomary on fuch occafions, denounced war againft him. Charles received both with a dignity fuitable to his own rank, but fpoke to each in a tone adapted to the fentiments which he entertained of their fovereigns. He accepted the defiance of the English monarch with a firmnefs tempered by fome degree of decency and refpect. His reply to the French King abounded with that acrimony of expreffion, which perfonal rivalfhip, exafperated by the memory of many injuries inflicted as well as fuffered, naturally fuggefts. He defired the French herald to acquaint his fovereign, that he would henceforth confider him not only as a bafe violator of public faith, but as a ftranger to the honour and integrity becoming a gentleman. Francis, too high-fpirited to bear fuch an imputation, had recourfe to an

They declare war againft the Emperor.

[k] Rym. xiv. 200. Herbert, 85. Guic. l. xviii. 471.

uncommon

uncommon expedient in order to vindicate his character. He instantly sent back the herald with a *cartel* of defiance, in which he gave the Emperor the lie in form, challenged him to single combat, requiring him to name the time and place of the encounter, and the weapons with which he chose to fight. Charles, as he was not inferior to his rival in spirit or bravery, readily accepted the challenge; but, after several messages concerning the arrangement of all the circumstances relative to the combat, accompanied with mutual reproaches, bordering on the most indecent scurrility, all thoughts of this duel, more becoming the heroes of romance than the two greatest monarchs of their age, were entirely laid aside [1].

The effect of this in promoting the custom of duelling.

THE example of two personages so illustrious drew such general attention, and carried with it so much authority, that it had considerable influence in producing an important change in manners all over Europe. Duels, as has already been observed, had long been permitted by the laws of all the European nations, and forming a part of their jurisprudence, were authorised by the magistrate, on many occasions, as the most proper method of terminating questions with regard to property, or of deciding those which respected crimes. But single combats being considered as solemn appeals to the

[1] Recueil des Traitéz, 2. Mem. de Bellay, 103, &c. Sandov. Hist. i. 837.

omniscience

omniscience and justice of the Supreme Being, they were allowed only in public causes, according to the prescription of law, and carried on in a judicial form. Men accustomed to this manner of decisions in courts of justice, were naturally led to apply it to personal and private quarrels. Duels, which at first could be appointed by the civil judge alone, were fought without the interposition of his authority, and in cases to which the laws did not extend. The transaction between Charles and Francis strongly countenanced this practice. Upon every affront, or injury, which seemed to touch his honour, a gentleman thought himself entitled to draw his sword, and to call on his adversary to give him satisfaction. Such an opinion becoming prevalent among men of fierce courage, of high spirit, and of rude manners, when offence was often given, and revenge was always prompt, produced most fatal consequences. Much of the best blood in Christendom was shed; many useful lives were sacrificed; and, at some periods, war itself hath hardly been more destructive than these private contests of honour. So powerful, however, is the dominion of fashion, that neither the terror of penal laws, nor reverence for religion, have been able entirely to abolish a practice unknown among the ancients, and not justifiable by any principle of reason; though at the same time it must be admitted, that, to this absurd custom, we must ascribe in some degree the extraordinary gentleness and complaisance of modern manners, and that respectful attention of one man to another, which, at present, render the

social

social intercourses of life far more agreeable and decent, than among the most civilized nations of antiquity.

Retreat of the Imperialists from Rome. February.

WHILE the two monarchs seemed so eager to terminate their quarrel by a personal combat, Lautrec continued his operations, which promised to be more decisive. His army, which was now increased to thirty-five thousand men, advanced by great marches towards Naples. The terror of their approach, as well as the remonstrances and the entreaties of the prince of Orange, prevailed at last on the Imperial troops, though with difficulty, to quit Rome, of which they had kept possession during ten months. But of that flourishing army which had entered the city, scarcely one half remained; the rest, cut off by the plague, or wasted by diseases, the effects of their inactivity, intemperance, and debauchery, fell victims to their own crimes[m]. Lautrec made the greatest efforts to attack them in their retreat towards the Neapolitan territories, which would have finished the war at one blow. But the prudence of their leaders disappointed all his measures, and conducted them with little loss to Naples. The people of that kingdom, extremely impatient to shake off the Spanish yoke, received the French with open arms, wherever they appeared to take possession; and Gaeta and Naples excepted, hardly any place of importance

[m] Guic. l. xviii. 478.

remained

remained in the hands of the Imperialists. The preservation of the former was owing to the strength of its fortifications, that of the latter to the presence of the Imperial army. Lautrec, however, sat down before Naples; but finding it vain to think of reducing a city by force while defended by a whole army, he was obliged to employ the slower, but less dangerous method of blockade; and having taken measures which appeared to him effectual, he confidently assured his master, that famine would soon compel the besieged to capitulate. These hopes were strongly confirmed by the defeat of a vigorous attempt made by the enemy in order to recover the command of the sea. The gallies of Andrew Doria, under the command of his nephew Philippino, guarded the mouth of the harbour. Moncada, who had succeeded Lannoy in the vice-royalty, rigged out a number of gallies superior to Doria's, manned them with a chosen body of Spanish veterans, and going on board himself, together with the marquis del Guasto, attacked Philippino before the arrival of the Venetian and French fleets. But the Genoese admiral, by his superior skill in naval operations, easily triumphed over the valour and number of the Spaniards. The viceroy was killed, most of his fleet destroyed, and Guasto, with many officers of distinction, being taken prisoners, were put on board the captive gallies, and sent by Philippino as trophies of his victory to his uncle[n].

French besiege Naples.

---

[n] Guic. l. xix. 487. P. Heuter. lib. x. c. 2. p. 231.

NOTWITHSTANDING this flattering prospect of success, many circumstances concurred to frustrate Lautrec's expectations. Clement, though he always acknowledged his being indebted to Francis for the recovery of his liberty, and often complained of the cruel treatment which he had met with from the Emperor, was not influenced at this juncture by principles of gratitude, nor, which is more extraordinary, was he swayed by the desire of revenge. His past misfortunes rendered him more cautious than ever, and his recollection of the errors which he had committed, increased the natural irresolution of his mind. While he amused Francis with promises, he secretly negociated with Charles; and being solicitous, above all things, to re-establish his family in Florence with its ancient authority, which he could not expect from Francis, who had entered into strict alliance with the new republic, he leaned rather to the side of his enemy than to that of his benefactor, and gave Lautrec no assistance towards carrying on his operations. The Venetians, viewing with jealousy the progress of the French arms, were intent only upon recovering such maritime towns in the Neapolitan dominions as were to be possessed by their republic, while they were altogether careless about the reduction of Naples, on which the success of the common cause depended°. The King of England, instead of being able, as had been projected, to embarrass the Emperor by attack-

° Guic. lib. xix. 491.

ing his territories in the Low-Countries, found his subjects so averse to an unnecessary war, which would have ruined the trade of the nation, that in order to silence their clamours, and put a stop to the insurrections ready to break out among them, he was compelled to conclude a truce for eight months with the governess of the Netherlands[p]. Francis himself, with the same unpardonable inattention of which he had formerly been guilty, and for which he had suffered so severely, neglected to make proper remittances to Lautrec for the support of his army.[q]

THESE unexpected events retarded the progress of the French, discouraging both the general and his troops; but the revolt of Andrew Doria proved a fatal blow to all their measures. That gallant officer, the citizen of a republic, and trained up from his infancy in the sea-service, retained the spirit of independence natural to the former, together with the plain liberal manners peculiar to the latter. A stranger to the arts of submission or flattery necessary in courts, but conscious at the same time of his own merit and importance, he always offered his advice with freedom, and often preferred his complaints and remonstrances with boldness. The French ministers, unaccustomed to such liberties, determined to ruin a man who treated them with so

Revolt of Andrew Doria from France.

[p] Herbert, 90. Rymer, 14. 258.
[q] Guic. l. xviii. 478.

little

little deference; and though Francis himself had a just sense of Doria's services, as well as an high esteem for his character, the courtiers, by continually representing him as a man haughty, intractable, and more solicitous to aggrandize himself, than to promote the interest of France, gradually undermined the foundations of his credit, and filled the King's mind with suspicion and distrust. From thence proceeded several affronts and indignities put upon Doria. His appointments were not regularly paid; his advice, even in naval affairs, was often slighted; an attempt was made to seize the prisoners taken by his nephew in the sea-fight off Naples; all which he bore with abundance of ill-humour. But an injury offered to his country, transported him beyond all bounds of patience. The French began to fortify Savona, to clear its harbour, and removing thither some branches of trade carried on at Genoa, plainly shewed that they intended to render that town, which had been long the object of jealousy and hatred to the Genoese, their rival in wealth and commerce. Doria, animated with a patriotic zeal for the honour and interest of his country, remonstrated against this in the highest tone, not without threats, if the measure were not instantly abandoned. This bold action, aggravated by the malice of the courtiers, and placed in the most odious light, irritated Francis to such a degree, that he commanded Barbesieux, whom he appointed admiral of the Levant, to sail directly to Genoa with the French fleet, to arrest Doria, and

and to seize his gallies. This rash order, the execution of which could have been secured only by the most profound secrecy, was concealed with so little care, that Doria got timely intelligence of it, and retired with all his gallies to a place of safety. Guasto, his prisoner, who had long observed and fomented his growing discontent, and had often allured him by magnificent promises to enter into the Emperor's service, laid hold on this favourable opportunity. While his indignation and resentment were at their height, he prevailed on him to dispatch one of his officers to the Imperial court with his overtures and demands. The negociation was not long; Charles, fully sensible of the importance of such an acquisition, granted him whatever terms he required. Doria sent back his commission, together with the collar of St. Michael, to Francis, and hoisting the Imperial colours, sailed with all his gallies towards Naples, not to block up the harbour of that unhappy city, as he had formerly engaged, but to bring them protection and deliverance.

His arrival opened the communication with the sea, and restored plenty in Naples, which was now reduced to the last extremity; and the French having lost their superiority at sea, were soon reduced to great straits for want of provisions. The prince of Orange, who succeeded the viceroy in the command of the Imperial army, shewed

Wretched situation of the French army before Naples.

shewed himself by his prudent conduct worthy of that honour which his good fortune and the death of his generals had twice acquired him. Beloved by the troops, who remembering the prosperity which they had enjoyed under his command, served him with the utmost alacrity, he let slip no opportunity of harassing the enemy, and by continual alarms or sallies fatigued and weakened them [r]. As an addition to all these misfortunes, the diseases common in that country during the sultry months, began to break out among the French troops. The prisoners communicated to them the pestilence which the Imperial army had brought to Naples from Rome, and it raged with such violence, that few, either officers or soldiers, escaped the infection. Of the whole army, not four thousand men, a number hardly sufficient to defend the camp, were capable of doing duty [s]; and being now besieged in their turn, they suffered all the miseries from which the Imperialists were delivered. Lautrec, after struggling long with so many disappointments and calamities, which preyed on his mind at the same time that the pestilence wasted his body, died, lamenting the negligence of his sovereign, and the infidelity of his allies, to which so many brave men had fallen victims [t]. By his death, and the indisposition of the other

[r] Jovii Hist. lib. xxxvi. p. 31, &c. Sigonii Vita Doriæ, p. 1139. Bellay, 114, &c.
[s] Bellay, 117, &c.
[t] P. Heuter. Rerum Austr. lib. x. c. 2. 231.

generals, the command devolved on the marquis de Saluces, an officer altogether unequal to such a trust. He, with troops no less dispirited than reduced, retreated in disorder to Averla; which town being invested by the prince of Orange, Saluces was under the necessity of consenting, that he himself should remain a prisoner of war, that his troops should lay down their arms and colours, give up their baggage, and march under a guard to the frontiers of France. By this ignominious capitulation, the wretched remains of the French army were saved; and the Emperor, by his own perseverance and the good conduct of his generals, acquired once more the superiority in Italy^u.

The loss of Genoa followed immediately upon the ruin of the army in Naples. To deliver his country from the dominion of foreigners was Doria's highest ambition, and had been his principal inducement to quit the service of France, and enter into that of the Emperor. A most favourable opportunity for executing this honourable enterprise now presented itself. The city of Genoa, afflicted by the pestilence, was almost deserted by its inhabitants; the French garrison being neither regularly paid nor recruited, was reduced to an inconsiderable number; Doria's emissaries found that such of the citizens as remained, being weary alike of the French and

^u Bellay, 117, &c. Jovii Hist. lib. xxv, xxvi.

Imperial yoke, the rigour of which they had alternately felt, were ready to welcome him as their deliverer, and to second all his measures. Things wearing this promising aspect, he sailed towards the coast of Genoa; on his approach the French gallies retired; a small body of men which he landed, surprized one of the gates of Genoa in the night-time; Trivulci, the French governor, with his feeble garrison, shut himself up in the citadel, and Doria took possession of the town without bloodshed or resistance. Want of provisions quickly obliged Trivulci to capitulate; the people, eager to abolish such an odious monument of their servitude, ran together with a tumultuous violence, and levelled the citadel with the ground.

Disinterested conduct of Doria.

It was now in Doria's power to have rendered himself the sovereign of his country, which he had so happily delivered from oppression. The fame of his former actions, the success of his present attempt, the attachment of his friends, the gratitude of his countrymen, together with the support of the Emperor, all conspired to facilitate his attaining the supreme authority, and invited him to lay hold of it. But with a magnanimity of which there are few examples, he sacrificed all thoughts of aggrandizing himself to the virtuous satisfaction of establishing liberty in his country, the highest object at which ambition can aim. Having assembled the whole body of the people in the court before his palace, he assured them, that

that the happiness of seeing them once more in possession of freedom, was to him a full reward for all his services; that, more delighted with the name of citizen than of sovereign, he claimed no preeminence or power above his equals; but remitted entirely to them the right of settling what form of government they would now chuse to be established among them. The people listened to him with tears of admiration and of joy. Twelve persons were elected to new-model the constitution of the republic. The influence of Doria's virtue and example communicated itself to his countrymen; the factions which had long torn and ruined the state, seemed to be forgotten; prudent precautions were taken to prevent their reviving; and the form of government which has subsisted with little variation since that time in Genoa, was established with universal applause. Doria lived to a great age, beloved, respected, and honoured by his countrymen; and adhering uniformly to his professions of moderation, without arrogating any thing unbecoming a private citizen, he preserved a great ascendant over the councils of the republic, which owed its being to his generosity. The authority which he possessed was more flattering, as well as more satisfactory, than that derived from sovereignty; a dominion founded in love and in gratitude; and upheld by veneration for his virtues, not by the dread of his power. His memory is still reverenced by the Genoese, and he is distinguished in their public monuments, and celebrated in in the works of their historians, by the most honourable of all appellations, THE FATHER OF HIS COUNTRY, AND THE RESTORER OF ITS LIBERTY [x].

1529. Operations in the Milanese.

FRANCIS, in order to recover the reputation of his arms, discredited by so many losses, made new efforts in the Milanese. But the count of St. Pol, a rash and unexperienced officer, to whom he gave the command, was no match for Antonio de Leyva, the ablest of the Imperial generals. He, by his superior skill in war, checked, with a handful of men, the brisk, but ill-concerted motions of the French; and though so infirm himself that he was carried constantly in a litter, he surpassed them, when occasion required, no less in activity than in prudence. By an unexpected march, he surprised, defeated, and took prisoner the count of St. Pol, ruining the French army in the Milanese as entirely as the Prince of Orange had ruined that which besieged Naples [y].

Negociations between Charles and Francis.

AMIDST these vigorous operations in the field, each party discovered an impatient desire of peace, and continual negociations were carried on for that purpose. The French King, discouraged, and al-

[x] Guic. l. xix. p. 498. Sigonii Vita Doriæ, p. 1146. Jovii Hist. lib. xxvi. p. 36, &c.
[y] Guic. l. xix. 520. P. Heuter. Rer. Austr. lib. x. c. 3. p. 233. Mem. de Bellay, 121.

most

most exhausted by so many unsuccessful enterprizes, was reduced now to think of obtaining the release of his sons by concessions, not by the terror of his arms. The Pope hoped to recover by a treaty whatever he had lost in the war. The Emperor, notwithstanding the advantages which he had gained, had many reasons to make him wish for an accommodation. Solyman, having over-run Hungary, was ready to break in upon the Austrian territories with the whole force of the East. The Reformation gaining ground daily in Germany, the princes who favoured it had entered into a confederacy which Charles thought dangerous to the tranquillity of the Empire. The Spaniards murmured at a war of such unusual length, the weight of which rested chiefly on them. The variety and extent of the Emperor's operations far exceeded what his revenues could support; his success hitherto had been owing chiefly to his own good fortune and to the abilities of his generals, nor could he flatter himself that they, with troops destitute of every thing necessary, would always triumph over enemies still in a condition to renew their attacks. All parties, however, were at equal pains to conceal or to dissemble their real sentiments. The Emperor, that his inability to carry on the war might not be suspected, insisted on high terms in the tone of a conqueror. The Pope, solicitous not to lose his present allies before he came to any agreement with Charles, continued to make a thousand protestations of fidelity to the former, while he privately negociated

negociated with the latter. Francis, afraid that his confederates might prevent him by treating for themselves with the Emperor, had recourse to many dishonourable artifices, in order to turn their attention from the measures which he was taking to adjust all differences with his rival.

IN this situation of affairs, when all the contending powers wished for peace, but durst not venture too hastily on the steps necessary for attaining it, two ladies undertook to procure this blessing so much desired by all Europe. These were Margaret of Austria, dutchess dowager of Savoy, the Emperor's aunt, and Louise, Francis's mother. They agreed on an interview at Cambray, and being lodged in two adjoining houses, between which a communication was opened, met together without ceremony or observation, and held daily conferences, to which no person whatever was admitted. As both were profoundly skilled in business, thoroughly acquainted with the secrets of their respective courts, and possessed with perfect confidence in each other, they soon made great progress towards a final accommodation; and the ambassadors of all the confederates waited in anxious suspense to know their fate, the determination of which was intirely in the hands of those illustrious negociators [z].

[z] P. Heuter. Rer. Austr. lib. x. c. 3. 133. Mem. de Bellay, p. 122.

BUT

But whatever diligence they used to hasten forward a general peace, the Pope had the address and industry to get the start of his allies, by concluding at Barcelona a particular treaty for himself. The Emperor, impatient to visit Italy in his way to Germany; and desirous of re-establishing tranquillity in the one country, before he attempted to compose the disorders which abounded in the other, found it necessary to secure at least one alliance among the Italian states, on which he might depend. That with Clement, who courted it with unwearied importunity, seemed more proper than any other. Charles being extremely solicitous to make some reparation for the insults which he had offered to the sacred character of the Pope, and to redeem past offences by new merit, granted Clement, notwithstanding all his misfortunes, terms more favourable than he could have expected after a continued series of success. Among other articles, he engaged to restore all the territories belonging to the ecclesiastical state; to re-establish the dominion of the Medici in Florence; to give his natural daughter in marriage to Alexander the head of that family; and to put it in the Pope's power to decide concerning the fate of Sforza, and the possession of the Milanese. In return for these ample concessions, Clement gave the Emperor the investiture of Naples without the reserve of any tribute, but the present of a white steed, in acknowledgment of his sovereignty; absolved all who had been concerned in assaulting and plundering Rome, and permitted Charles and his brother Ferdinand to levy the fourth

1529. Separate treaty between the Pope and Charles. June 20.

of the ecclefiaftical revenues throughout their dominions [a].

1529.

August 5. Peace of Cambray between Charles and Francis.

The account of this tranfaction quickened the negociations at Cambray, and brought Margaret and Louife to an immediate agreement. The treaty of Madrid ferved as the bafis of that which they concluded; the latter being intended to mitigate the rigour of the former. The chief articles were, That the Emperor fhould not, for the prefent, demand the reftitution of Burgundy, referving, however, in full force, his rights and pretenfions to that dutchy; That Francis fhould pay two millions of crowns as the ranfom of his fons, and, before they were fet at liberty, fhould reftore fuch towns as he ftill held in the Milanefe; That he fhould refign his pretenfions to the fovereignty of Flanders and of Artois; That he fhould renounce all his pretenfions to Naples, Milan, Genoa, and every other place beyond the Alps; That he fhould immediately confummate the marriage concluded between him and the Emperor's fifter Eleanora [b].

Advantageous for the Emperor.

Thus Francis, chiefly from his impatience to procure liberty to his fons, facrificed every thing which had at firft prompted him to take arms, or which had induced him, by continuing hoftilities during nine fucceffive campaigns, to

[a] Guic. l. xix. 522.
[b] P. Heuter. Rer. Auftr. lib. x. c. 3. p. 234. Sandov. Hift. dell Emper. Car. V. ii. 28.

protract

protract the war to a length hardly known in Europe before the establishment of standing armies, and the impofition of exorbitant taxes, became univerfal. The Emperor, by this treaty, was rendered fole arbiter of the fate of Italy; he delivered his territories in the Netherlands from an unpleafant badge of fubjection; and after having baffled his rival in the field, he prefcribed to him the conditions of peace. The different conduct and fpirit with which the two monarchs carried on the operations of war, led naturally to fuch an iffue of it. Charles, inclined by temper, as well as obliged by his fituation, concerted all his fchemes with caution, purfued them with perfeverance, and obferving circumftances and events with attention, let none efcape that could be improved to advantage. Francis, more enterprizing than fteady, undertook great defigns with warmth, but often executed them with remiffnefs; and diverted by his pleafures, or deceived by his favourites, he loft on feveral occafions the moft promifing opportunities of fuccefs. Nor had the character of the two rivals themfelves greater influence on the operations of war, than the oppofite qualities of the generals whom they employed. Among the Imperialifts, valour tempered with prudence; fertility of invention aided by experience; difcernment to penetrate the defigns of their enemies; a provident fagacity in conducting their own meafures; in a word, all the talents, which form great commanders and enfure victory, were confpicuous.

Among

BOOK V.
1529.

Among the French, these qualities were either wanting, or the very reverse of them abounded; nor could they boast of one man (unless we except Lautrec, who was always unfortunate) that equalled the merit of Pescara, Leyva, Guasto, the prince of Orange, and other leaders, whom Charles had to set in opposition to them. Bourbon, Moronè, Doria, who by their abilities and conduct might have been capable of balancing the superiority which the Imperialists had acquired, were induced to abandon the service of France, by the carelessness of the King, and the malice or injustice of his counsellors; and the most fatal blows given to France during the progress of the war, proceeded from the despair and resentment of these three persons.

Dishonourable to Francis.

THE hard conditions to which Francis was obliged to submit were not the most afflicting circumstances to him in the treaty of Cambray. He lost his reputation and the confidence of all Europe, by abandoning his allies to his rival. Unwilling to enter into the details necessary for adjusting their interests, or afraid that whatever he claimed for them must have been purchased by farther concessions on his own part, he gave them up in a body; and without the least provision in their behalf, left the Venetians, the Florentines, the duke of Ferrara, together with such of the Neapolitan barons as had joined his army, to the mercy of the Emperor. They exclaimed loudly against this base and perfidious action,

action, of which Francis himself was so much ashamed, that, in order to avoid the pain of hearing from their ambassadors the reproaches which he justly merited, it was some time before he would consent to allow them an audience. Charles, on the other hand, was attentive to the interest of every person who had adhered to him; the rights of some of his Flemish subjects, who had estates or pretensions in France, were secured; one article was inserted, obliging Francis to restore the blood and memory of the Constable Bourbon; and to grant his heirs the possession of his lands which had been forfeited; another, by which indemnification was stipulated for those French gentlemen who had accompanied Bourbon in his exile [c]. This conduct, laudable in itself, and placed in the most striking light by a comparison with that of Francis, gained Charles as much esteem as the success of his arms had acquired him glory.

Francis did not treat the king of England with the same neglect as his other allies. He communicated to him all the steps of his negociation at Cambray, and luckily found that monarch in a situation which left him no choice, but to approve implicitly of his measures, and to concur with them. Henry had been soliciting the Pope for some time, in order to obtain a divorce from Catharine of Ara-

Henry acquiesces in it.

His scheme of being divorced from his Queen.

[c] Guic. l. xix. p. 525. P. Heuter. Rer. Austr. lib. x. c. 4. p. 235.

gon his Queen. Several motives combined in prompting the King to urge his suit. As he was powerfully influenced at some seasons by religious considerations, he entertained many scruples concerning the legitimacy of his marriage with his brother's widow; his affections had long been estranged from the Queen, who was older than himself, and had lost all the charms which she possessed in the earlier part of her life; he was passionately desirous of having male issue: Wolsey artfully fortified his scruples, and encouraged his hopes, that he might widen the breach between him and the Emperor, Catharine's nephew; and, what was more forcible perhaps in its operation than all these united, the King had conceived a violent love for the celebrated Anne Boleyn, a young lady of great beauty, and of greater accomplishments, whom, as he found it impossible to gain her on other terms, he determined to raise to the throne. The Papal authority had often been interposed to grant divorces for reasons less specious than those which Henry produced. When the matter was first proposed to Clement, during his imprisonment in the castle of St. Angelo, as his hopes of recovering liberty depended entirely on the King of England, and his ally of France, he expressed the warmest inclination to gratify him. But no sooner was he set free, than he discovered other sentiments. Charles, who espoused the protection of his aunt with zeal inflamed by resentment, alarmed the Pope on the one hand with threats, which made a deep impression

on

on his timid mind; and allured him on the other with those promises in favour of his family, which he afterwards accomplished. Upon the prospect of these, Clement not only forgot all his obligations to Henry, but ventured to endanger the interest of the Romish religion in England, and to run the risque of alienating that kingdom for ever from the obedience of the Papal see. After amusing Henry during two years, with all the subtleties and chicane which the court of Rome can so dextrously employ to protract or defeat any cause; after displaying the whole extent of his ambiguous and deceitful policy, the intricacies of which the English historians, to whom it properly belongs, have found it no easy matter to trace and unravel; he, at last, recalled the powers of the delegates, whom he had appointed to judge in the point, avocated the cause to Rome, leaving the King no other hope of obtaining a divorce, but from the personal decision of the Pope himself. As Clement was now in strict alliance with the Emperor, who had purchased his friendship by the exorbitant concessions which have been mentioned, Henry despaired of procuring any sentence from the former but what was dictated by the latter. His honour, however, and passions concurred in preventing him from relinquishing his scheme of a divorce, which he determined to accomplish by other means, and at any rate; and the continuance of Francis's friendship being necessary to counterbalance the Emperor's power, he, in order

BOOK V.

order to secure that, not only offered no remonstrances against the total neglect of their allies, in the treaty of Cambray, but made Francis the present of a large sum, as a brotherly contribution towards the payment of the ransom for his sons [d].

Aug. 12.
The Emperor visits Italy.

SOON after the treaty of peace was concluded, the Emperor landed in Italy with a numerous train of the Spanish nobility, and a considerable body of troops. He left the government of Spain during his absence, to the Empress Isabella. By his long residence in that country, he had acquired such thorough knowledge of the character of the people, that he could perfectly accommodate the maxims of his government to their genius. He could even assume, upon some occasions, such popular manners, as gained wonderfully upon the Spaniards. A striking instance of his disposition to gratify them had occurred a few days before he embarked for Italy: He was to make his public entry into the city of Barcelona; and some doubts having arisen among the inhabitants, whether they should receive him as Emperor, or as Count of Barcelona; Charles instantly decided in favour of the latter, declaring that he was more proud of that ancient title, than of his Imperial crown. Soothed with this flattering expression of his regard, the citizens welcomed him with acclamations of joy, and the states of the province swore allegiance to his son

[d] Herbert. Mem. de Bellay, p. 122.

Philip, as heir of the county of Barcelona. A similar oath had been taken in all the kingdoms of Spain, with equal satisfaction.

THE Emperor appeared in Italy with the pomp and power of a conqueror. Ambassadors from all the princes and states of that country attended his court, waiting to receive his decision with regard to their fate. At Genoa, where he first landed, he was received with the acclamations due to the protector of their liberties. Having honoured Doria with many marks of distinction, and bestowed on the republic several new privileges, he proceeded to Bologna, the place fixed upon for his interview with the Pope. He affected to unite in his public entry into that city the state and majesty that suited an Emperor, with the humility becoming an obedient son of the church; and while at the head of twenty thousand veteran soldiers, able to give law to all Italy, he kneeled down to kiss the feet of that very Pope whom he had so lately detained a prisoner. The Italians, after suffering so much from the ferocity and licentiousness of his armies, and after having been long accustomed to form in their imagination a picture of Charles, which bore some resemblance to that of the barbarous monarchs of the Goths or Huns, who had formerly afflicted their country with like calamities, were surprised to see a

*Sandov. ii. p. 50. Ferrer. ix. 116.

prince of a graceful appearance, affable and courteous in his deportment, of regular manners, and of exemplary attention to all the offices of religion [f]. They were still more astonished when he settled all the concerns of the princes and states which now depended on him, with a degree of moderation and equity much beyond what they had expected.

His moderation and the motives of it.

CHARLES himself, when he set out from Spain, far from intending to give any such extraordinary proof of his self-denial, seems to have been resolved to avail himself to the utmost of the superiority which he had acquired in Italy. But various circumstances concurred in pointing out the necessity of pursuing a very different course. The progress of the Turkish Sultan, who, after over-running Hungary, had penetrated into Austria, and laid siege to Vienna with an army of an hundred and fifty thousand men, loudly called upon him to collect his whole force to oppose that torrent; and though the valour of the Germans, the prudent conduct of Ferdinand, together with the treachery of the Vizier, soon obliged Solyman to abandon that enterprize with disgrace and loss, the religious disorders still growing in Germany rendered the presence of the Emperor highly necessary there [g]: The Florentines, instead of giving their consent to

Sept. 13.

Oct. 16.

[f] Sandov. Hist. del Emp. Carl. V. ii. 50. 53, &c.
[g] Sleidan, 121. Guic. l. xx. 550.

the re-establishment of the Medici, which, by the treaty of Barcelona, the Emperor had bound himself to procure, were preparing to defend their liberty by force of arms; the preparations for his journey had involved him in unusual expences; and on this, as well as many other occasions, the multiplicity of his affairs, together with the narrowness of his revenues, obliged him to contract the schemes which his boundless ambition was apt to form, and to forego present and certain advantages, that he might guard against more remote but unavoidable dangers. Charles, from all these considerations, finding it necessary to assume an air of moderation, acted his part with a good grace. He admitted Sforza into his presence, and not only gave him a full pardon of all past offences, but granted him the investiture of the dutchy, together with his niece the King of Denmark's daughter, in marriage. He allowed the duke of Ferrara to keep possession of all his dominions, adjusting the points in dispute between him and the Pope with an impartiality not very agreeable to the latter. He came to a final accommodation with the Venetians, upon the reasonable condition of their restoring whatever they had usurped during the late war, either in the Neapolitan or Papal territories. In return for so many concessions, he exacted considerable sums from each of the powers with whom he treated, which they paid without reluctance, and which afforded him the means of proceeding on his journey

journey towards Germany with a magnificence suitable to his dignity [h].

Re establishes the authority of the Medici in Florence.

THESE treaties, which restored tranquillity to Italy after a tedious war, the calamities of which had chiefly affected that country, were published at Bologna with great solemnity on the first day of the year one thousand five huudred and thirty, amidst the universal acclamations of the people, applauding the Emperor, to whose moderation and generosity they ascribed the blessings of peace which they had so long desired. The Florentines alone did not partake of this general joy. Animated with a zeal for liberty more laudable than prudent, they determined to oppose the restoration of the Medici. The Imperial army had already entered their territories, and formed the siege of their capital. But though deserted by all their allies, and left without any hope of succour, they defended themselves many months with an obstinate valour worthy of better success; and even when they surrendered, they obtained a capitulation which gave them hopes of securing some remains of their liberty. But the Emperor, from his desire to gratify the Pope, frustrated all their expectations, and abolished their ancient form of government, raised Alexander di Medici to the same absolute dominion over that state, which his family have retained to the present times. Philibert de Chalons, prince

[h] Sandov. ii. 55, &c.

of Orange, the Imperial general, was killed during this siege. His estate and titles descended to his sister Claude de Chalons, who was married to René, count of Nassau, and she transmitted to her posterity of the house of Nassau the title of Princes of Orange, which, by their superior talents and valour, they have rendered so illustrious[i].

State of affairs, civil and religious, in Germany. Feb. 22 and 24.

AFTER the publication of the peace at Bologna, and the ceremony of his coronation as King of Lombardy and Emperor of the Romans, which the Pope performed with the accustomed formalities, nothing detained Charles in Italy[k]; and he began to prepare for his journey to Germany. His presence became every day more necessary in that country, and was solicited with equal importunity by the catholics and by the favourers of the new doctrines. During that long interval of tranquillity, which the absence of the Emperor, the contests between him and the Pope, and his attention to the war with France, afforded them, the latter had gained much ground. Most of the princes who had embraced Luther's opinions, had not only established in their territories that form of worship which he approved, but had entirely suppressed the rites of the Romish church. Many of the free cities had imitated their conduct. Almost one half the Germanick body had revolted

[i] Guic. l. xx. p. 341, &c. P. Heuter. Rer. Austr. lib. ii. c. 4. p. 236.

[k] H. Cornel. Agrippa de duplici coronatione Car. V. ap. Scard. ii. 266.

from the Papal see, and its authority, even in those provinces which had not hitherto shaken off the yoke, was considerably weakened, partly by the example of revolt in the neighbouring states, partly by the secret progress of the reformed doctrine even in those countries where it was not openly embraced. Whatever satisfaction the Emperor, while he was at open enmity with the see of Rome, might have felt in those events which tended to mortify and embarrass the Pope, he could not help perceiving now, that the religious divisions in Germany would, in the end, prove extremely hurtful to the Imperial authority. The weakness of former Emperors had suffered the great vassals of the Empire to make such successful encroachments upon their power and prerogative, that during the whole course of a war, which had often required the exertion of his utmost strength, Charles hardly drew any effectual aid from Germany, and found that magnificent titles or obsolete pretensions were almost the only advantages which he had gained by swaying the Imperial sceptre. He became fully sensible, that if he did not recover in some degree the prerogatives which his predecessors had lost, and acquire the authority, as well as possess the name, of head of the Empire, his high dignity would contribute more to obstruct than to promote his ambitious schemes. Nothing, he saw, was more essential towards attaining this, than to suppress opinions which might form new bonds of confederacy among the princes of the Empire, and
unite

unite them by ties stronger and more sacred than any political connection. Nothing seemed to lead more certainly to the accomplishment of his design, than to employ zeal for the established religion, of which he was the natural protector, as the instrument of extending his civil authority.

<small>BOOK V.
1530.</small>

Accordingly, a prospect no sooner opened of coming to an accommodation with the Pope, than, by the Emperor's appointment, a diet of the Empire was held at Spires, in order to take into consideration the state of religion. The decree of the diet assembled there in the year one thousand five hundred and twenty-six, which was almost equivalent to a toleration of Luther's opinions, had given great offence to the rest of Christendom. The greatest delicacy of address, however, was requisite in proceeding to any decision more rigorous. The minds of men, kept in perpetual agitation by a controversy carried on, during twelve years, without intermission of debate, or abatement of zeal, were now inflamed to an high degree. They were accustomed to innovations, and saw the boldest of them successful. Having not only abolished old rites, but substituted new forms in their place, they were influenced as much by attachment to the system which they had embraced, as by aversion to that which they had abandoned. Luther himself, of a spirit not to be worn out by the length and obstinacy of the combat, or to become

<small>Proceedings of the Diet at Spires, March 15. 1529.</small>

come remifs upon fuccefs, continued the attack with as much vigour as he had begun it. His difciples, of whom many equalled him in zeal, and fome furpaffed him in learning, were no lefs capable than their mafter to conduct the controverfy in the propereft manner. Many of the laity, fome even of the princes, trained up amidft thefe inceffant difputations, and in the habit of liftening to the arguments of the contending parties, who alternately appealed to them as judges, came to be profoundly fkilled in all the queftions which were agitated, and, upon occafion, could fhew themfelves not inexpert in any of the arts with which thefe theological encounters were managed. It was obvious from all thefe circumftances, that any violent decifion of the diet muft have immediately precipitated matters into confufion, and have kindled in Germany the flames of a religious war. All, therefore, that the Archduke, and the other commiffioners appointed by the Emperor, demanded of the diet, was, to enjoin thofe ftates of the Empire which had hitherto obeyed the decree iffued againft Luther at Worms in the year one thoufand five hundred and twenty-four, to perfevere in the obfervation of it, and to prohibit the other ftates from attempting any farther innovation in religion, particularly from abolifhing the Mafs, before the meeting of a general council. After much difpute, a decree to that effect was approved of by a majority of voices[1].

[1] Sleid. Hift. 117.

The Elector of Saxony, the marquis of Brandenburgh, the Landgrave of Hesse, the dukes of Lunenburgh, the prince of Anhalt, together with the deputies of fourteen Imperial or free cities [m], entered a solemn protest against this decree, as unjust and impious. On that account they were distinguished by the name of PROTESTANTS [n], an appellation which hath since become better known, and more honourable, by its being applied indiscriminately to all the sects, of whatever denomination, which have revolted from the Roman see. Not satisfied with this declaration of their dissent from the decree of the diet, the Protestants sent ambassadors into Italy, to lay their grievances before the Emperor, from whom they met with the most discouraging reception. Charles was at that time in close union with the Pope, and solicitous to attach him inviolably to his interest. During their long residence at Bologna, they held many consultations concerning the most effectual means of extirpating the heresies which had sprung up in Germany. Clement, whose cautious and timid mind the proposal of a general council filled with horror, even beyond what Popes, the constant enemies of such assemblies, usually feel, employed every argument to dissuade the Emperor from consenting to that measure. He repre-

1530. The followers of Luther protest against them. April 19.

Deliberations of the Pope and Emperor.

---

[m] The fourteen cities were, Strasburgh, Nuremburgh, Ulm, Constance, Reutlingen, Windsheim, Meinengen, Lindaw, Kempten, Hailbron, Isna, Weissemburgh, Nordlingen, and St. Gal.

[n] Sleid. Hist. 119. F. Paul. Hist. p. 45. Seckend. ii. 127.

sented general councils as factious, ungovernable, presumptuous, formidable to civil authority, and too slow in their operations to remedy disorders which required an immediate cure. Experience, he said, had now taught both the Emperor and himself, that forbearance and lenity, instead of soothing the spirit of innovation, had rendered it more enterprizing and presumptuous; it was necessary, therefore, to have recourse to the rigorous methods which such a desperate case required; Leo's sentence of excommunication, together with the decree of the diet at Worms, should be carried into execution, and it was incumbent on the Emperor to employ his whole power, in order to overawe those, on whom the reverence due either to ecclesiastical or civil authority had no longer any influence. Charles, whose views were very different from the Pope's, and who became daily more sensible how obstinate and deep-rooted the evil was, thought of reconciling the Protestants by means less violent, and considered the convocation of a council as no improper expedient for that purpose; but promised, if gentler arts failed of success, that then he would exert himself with rigour to reduce to the obedience of the holy see those stubborn enemies of the Catholic faith °.

Emperor present at the Diet of Augsburg, March 22, 1530.

SUCH were the sentiments with which the Emperor set out for Germany, having already appointed a diet of the Empire to be held at Augs-

° F. Paul, xlvii. Seck. l. ii. 142. Hist. de Confess. d'Auxbourgh, par D. Chytreus, 4to. Antw. 1572, p. 6.

burg. In his journey towards that city, he had many opportunities of obferving the difpofition of the Germans with regard to the points in controverfy, and found their minds every where fo much irritated and inflamed, as convinced him, that nothing tending to feverity or rigour ought to be attempted, until all other meafures proved ineffectual. He made his public entry into Augf- burg with extraordinary pomp; and found there fuch a full affembly of the members of the diet, as was fuitable both to the importance of the affairs which were to come under their confideration, and to the honour of an Emperor, who, after a long abfence, returned to them crowned with reputation and fuccefs. His prefence feems to have communicated to all parties an unufual fpirit of moderation and defire of peace. The Elector of Saxony would not permit Luther to accompany him to the diet, left he fhould offend the Emperor by bringing into his prefence a perfon excommunicated by the Pope, and who had been the author of all thofe diffenfions which it now appeared fo difficult to compofe. At the Emperor's defire, all the Proteftant princes forbad the divines who accompanied them, to preach in public during their refidence at Augfburg. For the fame reafon they employed Melancthon, the man of the greateft learning, as well as of the moft pacific and gentle fpirit among the Reformers, to draw up a confeffion of their faith, expreffed in terms as little offenfive to the Roman Catholics,

Catholics, as a regard for truth would permit. Melancthon, who seldom suffered the rancour of controversy to envenom his style, even in writings purely polemical, executed a task so agreeable to his natural disposition with great moderation and address. The Creed which he composed, known by the name of the *Confession of Augsburg*, from the place where it was presented, was read publicly in the diet. Some Popish divines were appointed to examine it; they brought in their animadversions; a dispute ensued between them and Melancthon, seconded by some of his brethren; but though Melancthon softened some articles, made concessions with regard to others, and put the least exceptionable sense upon all; though the Emperor himself laboured with great earnestness to reconcile the contending parties; so many marks of distinction were now established, and such insuperable barriers placed between the two churches, that all hopes of bringing about a coalition seemed utterly desperate [p].

From the divines, among whom his endeavours had been so unsuccessful, Charles turned to the princes their patrons. Nor did he find them, how desirous soever of accommodation, or willing to oblige the Emperor, more disposed

---

[p] Seckend. lib. ii. 159, &c. Abr. Sculteti Annales Evangelici ap. Herm. Von der Hard. Hist. Liter. Reform. Lipf. 1717. fol. p. 159.

than the former to renounce their opinions. At that time, zeal for religion took poffeffion of the minds of men, to a degree which can fcarcely be conceived by thofe who live in an age when the paffions excited by the firft manifeftation of truth, and the firft recovery of liberty, have in a great meafure ceafed to operate. This zeal was then of fuch ftrength as to overcome attachment to their political intereft, which is commonly the predominant motive among princes. The Elector of Saxony, the Landgrave of Heffe, and other chiefs of the Proteftants, though folicited feparately by the Emperor, and allured by the promife or profpect of thofe advantages which it was known they were moft folicitous to attain, refufed, with a fortitude highly worthy of imitation, to abandon what they deemed the caufe of God, for the fake of any earthly acquifition [q].

EVERY fcheme in order to gain or difunite the Proteftant party proving abortive, nothing now remained for the Emperor but to take fome vigorous meafures towards afferting the doctrines and authority of the eftablifhed church. Thefe, Campeggio, the papal nuncio, had always recommended as the only proper and effectual courfe of dealing with fuch obftinate heretics. In compliance with his opinions and remonftrances, the diet iffued a decree, condemning moft of the peculiar tenets held by the Proteftants;

---

[q] Sleid. 132. Scultet. Annal. 158.

ants; forbidding any person to protect or tolerate such as taught them; enjoining a strict observance of the established rites; and prohibiting any further innovation under severe penalties. All orders of men were required to assist with their persons and fortunes in carrying this decree into execution; and such as refused to obey it, were declared incapable of acting as judges, or of appearing as parties in the Imperial chamber, the supreme court of judicature in the Empire. To all which was subjoined a promise, that an application should be made to the Pope, requiring him to call a general council within six months, in order to terminate all controversies by its sovereign decisions [r].

They enter into a league at Smalkalde.

THE severity of this decree, which was considered as a prelude to the most violent persecution, alarmed the Protestants, and convinced them that the Emperor was resolved on their destruction. The dread of those calamities which were ready to fall on the church, oppressed the feeble spirit of Melancthon; and, as if the cause had already been desperate, he gave himself up to melancholy and lamentation. But Luther, who during the meeting of the diet had endeavoured to confirm and animate his party by several treatises which he addressed to them, was not disconcerted or dismayed at the prospect of this new danger. He comforted Melancthon and his

[r] Sleid. 139.

other

other desponding disciples, and exhorted the princes not to abandon those truths which they had lately asserted with such laudable boldness [s]. His exhortations made the deeper impression upon them, as they were greatly alarmed at that time by the account of a combination among the Popish princes of the Empire for the maintenance of the established religion, to which Charles himself had acceded [t]. This convinced them that it was necessary to stand on their guard; and that their own safety, as well as the success of their cause, depended on union. Filled with this dread of the adverse party, and with these sentiments concerning the conduct proper for themselves, they assembled at Smalkalde. There they concluded a league of mutual defence against all aggressors [u], by which they formed the Protestant states of the Empire into one regular body, and beginning already to consider themselves as such, they resolved to apply to the Kings of France and England, and to implore them to patronize and assist their new confederacy.

BOOK V.
1530.

Decem. 22.

An affair not connected with religion furnished them with a pretence for courting the aid of foreign princes. Charles, whose ambitious views enlarged in proportion to the increase of his power and grandeur, had formed a scheme of continuing the Imperial crown in his family, by procuring

The Emperor proposes to have his brother elected King of the Romans.

---

[s] Seck. ii. 180. Sleid. 140.   [t] Seck. ii. 200. iii. 11.
[u] Sleid. Hist. 142.

E 2   his

his brother Ferdinand to be elected King of the Romans. The present juncture was favourable for the execution of that design. The Emperor's arms had been every where victorious; he had given law to all Europe at the late peace; no rival now remained in a condition to balance or to control him; and the Electors, dazzled with the splendour of his success, or overawed by the greatness of his power, durst scarcely dispute the will of a prince, whose solicitations carried with them the authority of commands. Nor did he want plausible reasons to enforce the measure. The affairs of his other kingdoms, he said, obliged him to be often absent from Germany; the growing disorders occasioned by the controversies about religion, as well as the formidable neighbourhood of the Turks, who continually threatened to break in with their desolating armies into the heart of the Empire, required the constant presence of a prince endowed with prudence capable of composing the former, and with power as well as valour sufficient to repel the latter. His brother Ferdinand possessed these qualities in an eminent degree; by residing long in Germany, he had acquired a thorough knowledge of its constitution and manners; having been present almost from the first rise of the religious dissensions, he knew what remedies were most proper, what the Germans could bear, and how to apply them; as his own dominions lay on the Turkish frontier, he was the natural defender of Germany against the invasions of the Infidels, being

prompted

prompted by interest no less than he would be bound in duty to oppose them.

These arguments made little impression on the Protestants. Experience taught them, that nothing had contributed more to the undisturbed progress of their opinions, than the interregnum after Maximilian's death, the long absence of Charles, and the slackness of the reins of government which these occasioned. Conscious of the advantages which their cause had derived from this relaxation of government, they were unwilling to render it more vigorous, by giving themselves a new and a fixed master. They perceived clearly the extent of Charles's ambition, that he aimed at rendering the Imperial crown hereditary in his family, and would of course establish in the Empire an absolute dominion, to which elective princes could not have aspired with equal facility. They determined therefore to oppose the election of Ferdinand with the utmost vigour, and to rouse their countrymen, by their example and exhortations, to withstand this encroachment on their liberties. The Elector of Saxony, accordingly, not only refused to be present at the electoral college, which the Emperor summoned to meet at Cologne, but instructed his eldest son to appear there, and to protest against the election as informal, illegal, contrary to the articles of the golden bull, and subversive of the liberties of the Empire. But the other Electors, whom Charles had been at great pains to gain, without regarding either his absence or protest, chose **Ferdinand** King of the Romans;

BOOK V.
1531.
Negociations of the Protestants with France;

Feb. 29.

Romans; who a few days after was crowned at Aix-la-Chapelle [x].

WHEN the Protestants, who were assembled a second time at Smalkalde, received an account of this transaction, and heard, at the same time, that prosecutions were commenced, in the Imperial chamber, against some of their number, on account of their religious principles, they thought it necessary, not only to renew their former confederacy, but immediately to dispatch their ambassadors into France and England. Francis had observed, with all the jealousy of a rival, the reputation which the Emperor had acquired by his seeming disinterestedness and moderation in settling the affairs of Italy; and beheld with great concern the successful step which he had taken towards perpetuating and extending his authority in Germany by the election of a King of the Romans. Nothing, however, would have been more impolitic than to precipitate his kingdom into a new war when exhausted by extraordinary efforts, and discouraged by ill success, before it had got time to recruit its strength, or to forget past misfortunes. As no provocation had been given by the Emperor, and hardly a pretext for a rupture had been afforded him, he could not violate a treaty of peace which he himself had so lately solicited, without forfeiting the esteem of all Europe, and being detested as a prince void of probity

[x] Sleid. 142. Seck. iii. 1. P. Heuter. Rer. Austr. lib. x. c. 6. p. 240.

and honour. He obferved, with great joy, powerful factions beginning to form in the Empire; he
liftened with the utmoft eagernefs to the complaints of the Proteftant princes; and without
feeming to countenance their religious opinions,
determined fecretly to cherifh thofe fparks of political difcord which might be afterwards kindled
into a flame. For this purpofe, he sent William
de Bellay, one of the ableft negociators in France,
into Germany, who vifiting the courts of the
malcontent princes, and heightening their ill-
humour by various arts, concluded an alliance
between them and his mafter [y], which though
concealed at that time, and productive of no immediate effects, laid the foundation of an union
fatal on many occafions to Charles's ambitious
projects; and fhewed the difcontented princes of
Germany, where, for the future, they might find
a protector no lefs able than willing to undertake
their defence againft the encroachments of the
Emperor.

THE King of England, highly incenfed againft *with England.*
Charles, in complaifance to whom, the Pope had
long retarded, and now openly oppofed his divorce, was no lefs difpofed than Francis to
ftrengthen a league which might be rendered fo
formidable to the Emperor. But his favourite
project of the divorce led him into fuch a laby-
rinth of fchemes and negociations, and he was,

[y] Bellay, 129, a. 130. b. Seck. iii. 14.

at the same time, so intent on abolishing the papal jurisdiction in England, that he had no leisure for foreign affairs. This obliged him to rest satisfied with giving general promises, together with a small supply in money to the confederates of Smalkalde [z].

Charles courts the Protestants.

MEANWHILE, many circumstances convinced Charles that this was not a juncture when the extirpation of heresy was to be attempted by violence and rigour; that, in compliance with the Pope's inclinations, he had already proceeded with imprudent precipitation; and that it was more his interest to consolidate Germany into one united and vigorous body, than to divide and enfeeble it by a civil war. The Protestants, who were considerable as well by their numbers as by their zeal, had acquired additional weight and importance by their joining in that confederacy into which the rash steps taken at Augsburg had forced them. Having now discovered their own strength, they despised the decisions of the Imperial chamber; and being secure of foreign protection, were ready to set the head of the Empire at defiance. At the same time the peace with France was precarious, the friendship of an irresolute and interested pontiff was not to be relied on; and Solyman, in order to repair the discredit and loss which his arms had sustained in the former campaign, was preparing to enter Austria

[z] Herbert, 152. 154.

with more numerous forces. On all thefe accounts, especially the laft, a fpeedy accommodation with the malcontent princes became neceffary, not only for the accomplifhment of his future fchemes, but for enfuring his prefent fafety. Negociations were, accordingly, carried on by his direction with the Elector of Saxony and his affociates; after many delays, occafioned by their jealoufy of the Emperor, and of each other, after innumerable difficulties arifing from the inflexible nature of religious tenets, which cannot admit of being altered, modified, or relinquifhed in the fame manner as points of political intereft, terms of pacification were agreed upon at Nuremberg, and ratified folemnly in the diet at Ratifbon. In this treaty it was ftipulated, That univerfal peace be eftablifhed in Germany, until the meeting of a general council, the convocation of which within fix months the Emperor fhall endeavour to procure; That no perfon fhall be molefted on account of religion; That a ftop fhall be put to all proceffes begun by the Imperial chamber againft Proteftants, and the fentences already paffed to their detriment fhall be declared void. On their part, the Proteftants engaged to affift the Emperor with all their forces in refifting the invafion of the Turks[a]. Thus, by their firmnefs in adhering to their principles, by the unanimity with which they urged all their claims, and by their dexterity in availing themfelves of the

[a] Du Mont Corps Diplomatique, tom. iv. part ii. 87. 89.

Emperor's situation, the Proteſtants obtained terms which amounted almoſt to a toleration of their religion; all the conceſſions were made by Charles, none by them; even the favourite point of their approving his brother's election was not mentioned; and the Proteſtants of Germany, who had hitherto been viewed only as a religious ſect, came henceforth to be conſidered as a political body of no ſmall conſequence [b].

Campaign in Hungary.

THE intelligence which Charles received of Solyman's having entered Hungary at the head of three hundred thouſand men, brought the deliberations of the diet at Ratiſbon to a period; the contingent both of troops and money, which each prince was to furniſh towards the defence of the Empire, having been already ſettled. The Proteſtants, as a teſtimony of their gratitude to the Emperor, exerted themſelves with extraordinary zeal, and brought into the field forces which exceeded in number the quota impoſed on them; the Catholics imitating their example, one of the greateſt and beſt appointed armies that had ever been levied in Germany, aſſembled near Vienna. Being joined by a body of Spaniſh and Italian veterans under the marquis del Guaſto; by ſome heavy-armed cavalry from the Low-Countries; and by the troops which Ferdinand had raiſed in Bohemia, Auſtria, and his other territories, it amounted in all to ninety thouſand diſciplined

[b] Sleid. 149, &c. Seck. iii. 19.

foot, and thirty thousand horse, besides a prodigious swarm of irregulars. Of this vast army, worthy the first prince in Christendom, the Emperor took the command in person; and mankind waited in suspense the issue of a decisive battle between the two greatest monarchs in the world. But each of them dreading the other's power and good fortune, they both conducted their operations with such excessive caution, that a campaign, for which such immense preparations had been made, ended without any memorable event. Solyman, finding it impossible to gain ground upon an enemy always attentive and on his guard, marched back to Constantinople towards the end of autumn [c]. It is remarkable, that in such a martial age, when every gentleman was a soldier, and every prince a general, this was the first time that Charles, who had already carried on such extensive wars, and gained so many victories, appeared at the head of his troops. In this first essay of his arms, to have opposed such a leader as Solyman, was no small honour; to have obliged him to retreat, merited very considerable praise.

September and October.

About the beginning of this campaign, the Elector of Saxony died, and was succeeded by his son John Frederick. The Reformation rather gained than lost by that event; the new Elector,

August 16.

[c] Jovii Hist. lib. xxx. p. 100, &c. Barre Hist. de l'Empire, i. 8. 347.

no less attached than his predecessors to the opinions of Luther, occupied the station which they had held at the head of the Protestant party, and defended, with the boldness and zeal of youth, that cause which they had fostered and reared with the caution of more advanced age.

The Emperor's interview with the Pope in his way to Spain.

IMMEDIATELY after the retreat of the Turks, Charles, impatient to revisit Spain, set out on his way thither, for Italy. As he was extremely desirous of an interview with the Pope, they met a second time at Bologna, with the same external demonstrations of respect and friendship, but with little of that confidence which had subsisted between them during their late negociations there. Clement was much dissatisfied with the Emperor's proceedings at Augsburg; his concessions with regard to the speedy convocation of a council, having more than cancelled all the merit of the severe decree against the doctrines of the Reformers. The toleration granted to the Protestants at Ratisbon, and the more explicit promise concerning a council, with which it was accompanied, had irritated him still farther. Charles, however, partly from conviction that the meeting of a council would be attended with salutary effects, and partly from his desire to please the Germans, having solicited the Pope by his ambassadors to call that assembly without delay, and now urging the same thing in person, Clement was greatly embarrassed what reply he should make to a request which it was indecent

Negociations concerning a general council;

to refuse, and dangerous to grant. He endeavoured at first to divert Charles from the measure; but, finding him inflexible, he had recourse to artifices, which he knew would delay, if not entirely defeat, the calling of that assembly. Under the plausible pretext of its being previously necessary to settle, with all parties concerned, the place of the council's meeting; the manner of its proceedings; the right of the persons who should be admitted to vote; and the authority of their decisions; he dispatched a nuncio, accompanied by an ambassador from the Emperor, to the Elector of Saxony as head of the Protestants. With regard to each of these articles, inextricable difficulties and contests arose. The Protestants demanded a council to be held in Germany; the Pope insisted that it should meet in Italy: they contended, that all points in dispute should be determined by the words of holy scripture alone; he considered not only the decrees of the church, but the opinions of fathers and doctors, as of equal authority: they required a free council, in which the divines, commissioned by different churches, should be allowed a voice; he aimed at modelling the council in such a manner as would render it entirely dependant on his pleasure. Above all, the Protestants thought it unreasonable, that they should bind themselves to submit to the decrees of a council, before they knew on what principles these decrees were to be founded, by what persons they were to be pronounced, and what forms of proceeding

proceeding they would obferve. The Pope maintained it to be altogether unneceffary to call a council, if thofe who demanded it did not previoufly declare their refolution to acquiefce in its decrees. In order to adjuft fuch a variety of points, many expedients were propofed, and the negociations fpun out to fuch a length, as effectually anfwered Clement's purpofe of putting off the meeting of a council, without drawing on himfelf the whole infamy of obftructing a meafure which all Europe deemed fo effential to the good of the church [d].

and for preferving the tranquillity of Italy.

TOGETHER with this negociation about calling a council, the Emperor carried on another, which he had ftill more at heart, for fecuring the peace eftablifhed in Italy. As Francis had renounced his pretenfions in that country with great reluctance, Charles made no doubt but that he would lay hold on the firft pretext afforded him, or embrace the firft opportunity which prefented itfelf, of recovering what he had loft. It became neceffary on this account, to take meafures for affembling an army able to oppofe him. As his treafury, drained by a long war, could not fupply the fums requifite for keeping fuch a body conftantly on foot, he attempted to throw that burden on his allies, and to provide for the fafety of his own dominions at their expence, by propofing that

[d] F. Paul Hift. 61. Seckend. iii. 73.

the Italian states should enter into a league of defence against all invaders; that, on the first appearance of danger, an army should be raised and maintained at the common charge; and that Antonio de Leyva should be appointed the generalissimo. Nor was the proposal unacceptable to Clement, though for a reason very different from that which induced the Emperor to make it. He hoped, by this expedient, to deliver Italy from the German and Spanish veterans, which had so long filled all the powers in that country with terror, and still kept them in subjection to the Imperial yoke. A league was accordingly concluded; 'all the Italian states, the Venetians excepted, acceded to it; the sum, which each of the contracting parties should furnish towards maintaining the army was fixed; the Emperor agreed to withdraw the troops which gave so much umbrage to his allies, and which he was unable any longer to support. Having disbanded part of them, and removed the rest to Sicily and Spain, he embarked on board Doria's gallies, and arrived at Barcelona[e].

NOTWITHSTANDING all his precautions for securing the peace of Germany, and maintaining that system which he had established in Italy, the Emperor became every day more and more apprehensive that both would be soon disturbed by the intrigues or arms of the French King.

[e] Guic. l. 20. 551. Ferreras, ix. 149.

His apprehensions were well founded, as nothing but the desperate situation of his affairs could have brought Francis to give his consent to a treaty so dishonourable and disadvantageous as that of Cambray: he, at the very time of ratifying it, had formed a resolution to observe it no longer than necessity compelled him, and took a solemn protest, though with the most profound secrecy, against several articles in the treaty, particularly that whereby he renounced all pretensions to the dutchy of Milan, as unjust, injurious to his heirs, and invalid. One of the crown lawyers, by his command, entered a protest to the same purpose, and with the like secrecy, when the ratification of the treaty was registered in the parliament of Paris[f]. Francis seems to have thought that, by employing an artifice unworthy of a King, destructive of public faith, and of the mutual confidence on which all transactions between nations are founded, he was released from any obligation to perform the most solemn promises, or to adhere to the most sacred engagements. From the moment he concluded the peace of Cambray, he wished and watched for an opportunity of violating it with safety. He endeavoured for that reason to strengthen his alliance with the King of England, whose friendship he cultivated with the greatest assiduity. He put the military force of his own kingdom on a better and more respectable footing than ever.

[f] Du Mont Corps Diplom. tom. iv. part 2. p. 52.

He artfully fomented the jealousy and discontent of the German princes.

But above all, Francis laboured to break the strict confederacy which subsisted between Charles and Clement; and he had soon the satisfaction to observe appearances of disgust and alienation arising in the mind of that suspicious and interested Pontiff, which gave him hopes that their union would not be lasting. As the Emperor's decision in favour of the duke of Ferrara had greatly irritated the Pope, Francis aggravated the injustice of that proceeding, and flattered Clement that the papal see would find in him a more impartial and no less powerful protector. As the importunity with which Charles demanded a council was extremely offensive to the Pope, Francis artfully created obstacles to prevent it, and attempted to divert the German princes, his allies, from insisting so obstinately on that point[t]. As the Emperor had gained such an ascendant over Clement by contributing to aggrandize his family, Francis endeavoured to allure him by the same irresistible bait, proposing a marriage between his second son, Henry duke of Orleans, and Catharine, the daughter of the Pope's cousin Laurence di Medici. On the first overture of this match, the Emperor could not persuade himself that Francis really intended to debase the royal blood of France, by an

particularly with the Pope.

---

[t] Bellay, 141, &c. Seck. iii. 48. F. Paul, 63.

alliance with Catharine, whose ancestors had been so lately private citizens and merchants in Florence, and believed that he meant only to flatter or amuse the ambitious Pontiff. He thought it necessary, however, to efface the impression which such a dazzling offer might have made, by promising to break off the marriage which had been agreed on between his own niece the King of Denmark's daughter, and the Duke of Milan, and to substitute Catharine in her place. But the French ambassador producing unexpectedly full powers to conclude the marriage treaty with the duke of Orleans, this expedient had no effect. Clement was so highly pleased with an honour which added such lustre and dignity to the house of Medici, that he offered to grant Catharine the investiture of considerable territories in Italy, by way of portion; he seemed ready to support Francis in prosecuting his ancient claims in that country, and consented to a personal interview with that Monarch [s].

Interview between the Pope and Francis.

CHARLES was at the utmost pains to prevent a meeting, in which nothing was likely to pass but what would be of detriment to him; nor could he bear, after he had twice condescended to visit the Pope in his own territories, that Clement should bestow such a mark of distinction on his rival, as to venture on a voyage by sea, at an un-

---

[s] Guic. l. xx. 551. 553. Bellay, 138.

favour-

favourable season, in order to pay court to Francis in the French dominions. But the Pope's eagerness to accomplish the match overcame all the scruples of pride, or fear, or jealousy, which would probably have influenced him on any other occasion. The interview, notwithstanding several artifices of the Emperor to prevent it, took place at Marseilles with extraordinary pomp, and demonstrations of confidence on both sides; and the marriage, which the ambition and abilities of Catharine rendered in the sequel as pernicious to France, as it was then thought dishonourable, was consummated. But whatever schemes may have been secretly concerted by the Pope and Francis in favour of the duke of Orleans, to whom his father proposed to make over all his rights in Italy, so careful were they to avoid giving any cause of offence to the Emperor, that no treaty was concluded between them [h]; and even in the marriage-articles, Catharine renounced all claims and pretensions in Italy, except to the dutchy of Urbino [i].

But at the very time when he was carrying on these negociations, and forming this connection with Francis, which gave so great umbrage to the Emperor, such was the artifice and duplicity of Clement's character, that he suffered the latter to direct all his proceedings with regard to the King of England, and was no less attentive to gratify

[h] Guic. l. xx. 555.
[i] Du Mont. Corps Diplom. iv. p. ii. 101.

him

him in that particular, than if the most cordial union had still subsisted between them. Henry's suit for a divorce had now continued near six years; during all which period the Pope negociated, promised, retracted, and concluded nothing. After bearing repeated delays and disappointments longer than could have been expected from a prince of such a choleric and impetuous temper, the patience of Henry was at last so much exhausted, that he applied to another tribunal for that decree which he had solicited in vain at Rome. Cranmer, archbishop of Canterbury, by a sentence founded on the authority of Universities, Doctors, and Rabbies, who had been consulted with respect to the point, annulled the King's marriage with Catharine; her daughter was declared illegitimate; and Anne Boleyne acknowledged as Queen of England. At the same time Henry began not only to neglect and to threaten the Pope, whom he had hitherto courted, but to make innovations in the church, of which he had formerly been such a zealous defender. Clement, who had already seen so many provinces and kingdoms revolt from the Holy See, became apprehensive at last that England might imitate their example, and partly from his solicitude to prevent that fatal blow, partly in compliance with the French King's solicitations, determined to give Henry such satisfaction as might still retain him within the bosom of the church. But the violence of the Cardinals, devoted to the Emperor, did not allow the Pope leisure for executing

ing this prudent resolution, and hurried him, with a precipitation fatal to the Roman See, to issue a bull rescinding Cranmer's sentence, confirming Henry's marriage with Catharine, and declaring him excommunicated, if, within a time specified, he did not abandon the wife he had taken, and return to her whom he had deserted. Enraged at this unexpected decree, Henry kept no longer any measures with the court of Rome; his subjects seconded his resentment and indignation; an act of Parliament was passed, abolishing the papal power and jurisdiction in England; by another, the King was declared supreme head of the church, and all the authority of which the Popes were deprived was vested in him. That vast fabric of ecclesiastical dominion which had been raised with such art, and of which the foundations seemed to have been laid so deep, being no longer supported by the veneration of the people, was overturned in a moment. Henry himself, with the caprice peculiar to his character, continued to defend the doctrines of the Romish church as fiercely as he attacked its jurisdiction. He alternately persecuted the Protestants for rejecting the former, and the Catholics for acknowledging the latter. But his subjects, being once permitted to enter into new paths, did not chuse to stop short at the precise point prescribed by him. Having been encouraged by his example to break some of their fetters, they were so impatient to shake off what still remained[k], that, in the following reign, with the ap-

[k] Herbert. Burn. Hist. of Reform.

plause of the greater part of the nation, a total separation was made from the church of Rome in articles of doctrine, as well as in matters of discipline and jurisdiction.

Death of Clement VII.

A SHORT delay might have saved the See of Rome from all the unhappy consequences of Clement's rashness. Soon after his sentence against Henry, he fell into a languishing distemper, which gradually wasting his constitution, put an end to his Pontificate, the most unfortunate, both during its continuance, and by its effects, that the church had known for many ages. The very day on which the cardinals entered the conclave, they raised to the papal throne Alexander Farnese, dean of the sacred college, and the oldest member of that body, who assumed the name of Paul III. The account of his promotion was received with extraordinary acclamations of joy by the people of Rome, highly pleased, after an interval of more than an hundred years, to see the crown of St. Peter placed on the head of a Roman citizen. Persons more capable of judging, formed a favourable presage of his administration, from the experience which he had acquired under four Pontificates, as well as the character of prudence and moderation which he had uniformly maintained in a station of great eminence, and during an active period that required both talents and address [1].

Sept. 25.

Election of Paul III. Oct. 13.

EUROPE, it is probable, owed the continuance of its peace to the death of Clement; for although

[1] Guic. l. xx. 556. F. Paul, 64.

no traces remain in hiftory of any league concluded between him and Francis, it is fcarcely to be doubted but that he would have feconded the operations of the French arms in Italy, that he might have gratified his ambition by feeing one of his family poffeffed of the fupreme power in Florence, and another in Milan. But upon the election of Paul III. who had hitherto adhered uniformly to the Imperial intereft, Francis found it neceffary to fufpend his operations for fome time, and to put off the commencement of hoftilities againft the Emperor, on which, before the death of Clement, he had been fully determined.

Infurrection of the Anabaptifts in Germany.

WHILE Francis waited for an opportunity to renew a war which had hitherto proved fo fatal to himfelf and his fubjects, a tranfaction of a very fingular nature was carried on in Germany. Among many beneficial and falutary effects of which the Reformation was the immediate caufe, it was attended, as muft be the cafe in all actions and events wherein men are concerned, with fome confequences of an oppofite nature. When the human mind is roufed by grand objects, and agitated by ftrong paffions, its operations acquire fuch force, that they are apt to become irregular and extravagant. Upon any great revolution in religion, fuch irregularities abound moft, at that particular period, when men, having thrown off the authority of their ancient principles, do not yet fully comprehend the nature, or feel the obligation of those new tenets which they have embraced. The mind, in that situation, pushing forward with the boldness which prompted it to reject established opinions, and not guided by a clear knowledge of the system substituted in their place, disdains all restraint, and runs into wild notions, which often lead to scandalous or immoral conduct. Thus, in the first ages of the christian church, many of the new converts, having renounced their ancient systems of religious faith, and being but imperfectly acquainted with the doctrines and precepts of Christianity, broached the most extravagant opinions, equally subversive of piety and virtue; all which errors disappeared or were exploded when the knowledge of religion increased, and came to be more generally diffused. In like manner, soon after Luther's appearance, the rashness or ignorance of some of his disciples led them to publish tenets no less absurd than pernicious, which being proposed to men extremely illiterate, but fond of novelty, and at a time when their minds were occupied chiefly with religious speculations, gained too easy credit and authority among them. To these causes must be imputed the extravagances of Muncer, in the year one thousand five hundred and twenty-five, as well as the rapid progress which his opinions made among the peasants; but though the insurrection excited by that fanatic was soon suppressed, several of his followers lurked in different places, and endeavoured privately to propagate his opinions.

In those provinces of Upper Germany, which had already been so cruelly wasted by their enthusiastic rage, the magistrates watched their motions with such severe attention, that many of them found it necessary to retire into other countries, some were punished, others driven into exile, and their errors were entirely rooted out. But in the Netherlands and Westphalia, where the pernicious tendency of their opinions was more unknown, and guarded against with less care, they got admittance into several towns, and spread the infection of their principles. The most remarkable of their religious tenets related to the Sacrament of Baptism, which, as they contended, ought to be administered only to persons grown up to years of understanding, and should be performed, not by sprinkling them with water, but by dipping them in it: for this reason they condemned the baptism of infants, and rebaptising all whom they admitted into their society, the sect came to be distinguished by the name of Anabaptists. To this peculiar notion concerning baptism, which has the appearance of being founded on the practice of the church in the apostolic age, and contains nothing inconsistent with the peace and order of human society, they added other principles of a most enthusiastic as well as dangerous nature. They maintained that, among Christians who had the precepts of the gospel to direct, and the spirit of God to guide them, the office of magistracy was not only unnecessary, but an unlawful encroachment on their spiritual

spiritual liberty; that the distinctions occasioned by birth, or rank, or wealth, being contrary to the spirit of the gospel, which considers all men as equal, should be entirely abolished; that all Christians, throwing their possessions into one common stock, should live together in that state of equality which becomes members of the same family; that as neither the laws of nature, nor the precepts of the New Testament, had imposed any restraints upon men with regard to the number of wives which they might marry, they should use that liberty which God himself had granted to the patriarchs.

Settle in Munster.

SUCH opinions, propagated and maintained with enthusiastic zeal and boldness, were not long without producing the violent effects natural to them. Two Anabaptist prophets, John Matthias, a baker of Haerlem, and John Boccold, or Beükels, a journeyman taylor of Leyden, possessed with the rage of making proselytes, fixed their residence at Munster, an Imperial city in Westphalia, of the first rank, under the sovereignty of its bishop, but governed by its own senate and consuls. As neither of these fanatics wanted the talents requisite in desperate enterprises, great resolution, the appearance of sanctity, bold pretensions to inspiration, and a confident and plausible manner of discoursing, they soon gained many converts. Among these were Rothman, who had first preached the Protestant doctrine in Munster, and Cnipperdoling, a citizen of good birth and considerable eminence,

eminence. Emboldened by the countenance of such disciples, they openly taught their opinions; and not satisfied with that liberty, they made several attempts, though without success, to become masters of the town, in order to get their tenets established by public authority. At last, having secretly called in their associates from the neighbouring country, they suddenly took possession of the arsenal and senate-house in the night-time, and running through the streets with drawn swords, and horrible howlings, cried out alternately, "Repent, and be baptised," and "Depart ye ungodly." The senators, the canons, the nobility, together with the more sober citizens, whether Papists or Protestants, terrified at their threats and outcries, fled in confusion, and left the city under the dominion of a frantic multitude, consisting chiefly of strangers. Nothing now remaining to overawe or control them, they set about modelling the government according to their own wild ideas; and though at first they showed so much reverence for the ancient constitution, as to elect senators of their own sect, and to appoint Cnipperdoling and another proselyte consuls, this was nothing more than form; for all their proceedings were directed by Matthias, who, in the style, and with the authority of a prophet, uttered his commands, which it was instant death to disobey. Having begun with enouraging the multitude to pillage the churches, and deface their ornaments; he enjoined them to destroy all books except the Bible, as useless or impious; he ordered

Become masters of that city.

February.

Establish a new form of government.

the estates of such as fled, to be confiscated, and sold to the inhabitants of the adjacent country; he commanded every man to bring forth his gold, silver, and other precious effects, and to lay them at his feet; the wealth amassed by these means, he deposited in a public treasury, and named deacons to dispense it for the common use of all. The members of this commonwealth being thus brought to a perfect equality, he commanded all of them to eat at tables prepared in public, and even prescribed the dishes which were to be served up each day. Having finished his plan of reformation, his next care was to provide for the defence of the city; and he took measures for that purpose with a prudence which favoured nothing of fanaticism. He collected large magazines of every kind; he repaired and extended the fortifications, obliging every person without distinction to work in his turn; he formed such as were capable of bearing arms into regular bodies, and endeavoured to add the stability of discipline to the impetuosity of enthusiasm. He sent emissaries to the Anabaptists in the Low-Countries, inviting them to assemble at Munster, which he dignified with the name of Mount-Sion, that from thence they might set out to reduce all the nations of the earth under their dominion. He himself was unwearied in attending to every thing necessary for the security or increase of the sect; animating his disciples by his own example to decline no labour, as well as to submit to every hardship; and their enthusiastic passions being kept from subsiding

by

by a perpetual succession of exhortations, revelations, and prophecies, they seemed ready to undertake or to suffer any thing in maintenance of their opinions.

The bishop of Munster takes arms against them.

While they were thus employed, the bishop of Munster having assembled a considerable army, advanced to besiege the town. On his approach, Matthias sallied out at the head of some chosen troops, attacked one quarter of his camp, forced it, and after great slaughter returned to the city loaded with glory and spoil. Intoxicated with this success, he appeared next day brandishing a spear, and declared, that, in imitation of Gideon, he would go forth with a handful of men and smite the host of the ungodly. Thirty persons, whom he named, followed him without hesitation in this wild enterprize, and, rushing on the enemy with a frantic courage, were cut off to a man. The death of their prophet occasioned at first great consternation among his disciples; but Boccold, by the same gifts and pretensions which had gained Matthias credit, soon revived their spirits and hopes to such a degree, that he succeeded the deceased prophet in the same absolute direction of all their affairs. As he did not possess that enterprizing courage which distinguished his predecessor, he satisfied himself with carrying on a defensive war; and, without attempting to annoy the enemy by sallies, he waited for the succours he expected from the Low-Countries, the arrival of which was often foretold and promised by their prophets.

May.

John of Leyden acquires great authority among the Anabaptists.

BOOK V.
1534.

prophets. But though less daring in action than Matthias, he was a wilder enthusiast, and of more unbounded ambition. Soon after the death of his predecessor, having, by obscure visions and prophecies, prepared the multitude for some extraordinary event, he stripped himself naked, and, marching through the streets, proclaimed with a loud voice, " That the kingdom of Sion was at hand; that whatever was highest on earth should be brought low, and whatever was lowest should be exalted." In order to fulfil this, he commanded the churches, as the most lofty buildings in the city, to be levelled with the ground; he degraded the senators chosen by Matthias, and depriving Cnipperdoling of the consulship, the highest office in the commonwealth, appointed him to execute the lowest and most infamous, that of common hangman, to which strange transition the other agreed, not only without murmuring, but with the utmost joy; and such was the despotic rigour of Boccold's administration, that he was called almost every day to perform some duty or other of his wretched function. In place of the deposed senators, he named twelve judges, according to the number of tribes in Israel, to preside in all affairs; retaining to himself the same authority which Moses anciently possessed as legislator of that people.

Elected King.

NOT satisfied, however, with power or titles, which were not supreme, a prophet, whom he had

had gained and tutored, having called the mul- BOOK V.
titude together, declared it to be the will of
God, that John Boccold fhould be King of Sion, 1535.
and fit on the throne of David. John kneeling June 24.
down, accepted of the heavenly call, which he
folemnly protefted had been revealed likewife to
himfelf, and was immediately acknowledged as
Monarch by the deluded multitude. From that
moment he affumed all the ftate and pomp of
royalty. He wore a crown of gold, and was
clad in the richeft and moft fumptuous garments.
A Bible was carried on his one hand, a naked
fword on the other. A great body of guards
accompanied him when he appeared in public.
He coined money ftamped with his own image,
and appointed the great officers of his houfehold
and kingdom, among whom Cnipperdoling was
nominated governor of the city, as a reward for his
former fubmiffion.

HAVING now attained the height of power, His licen-
Boccold began to difcover paffions, which he tious tenets
had hitherto reftrained, or indulged only in fe- andconduct.
cret. As the exceffes of enthufiafm have been
obferved in every age to lead to fenfual gratifi-
cations, the fame conftitution that is fufceptible
of the former, being remarkably prone to the
latter, he inftructed the prophets and teachers to
harangue the people for feveral days concerning the lawfulnefs, and even neceffity of taking
more wives than one, which they afferted to be
one of the privileges granted by God to the
faints.

saints. When their ears were once accustomed to this licentious doctrine, and their passions inflamed with the prospect of such unbounded indulgence, he himself set them an example of using what he called their Christian liberty, by marrying at once three wives, among which the widow of Matthias, a woman of singular beauty, was one. As he was allured by beauty, or the love of variety, he gradually added to the number of his wives, until they amounted to fourteen, though the widow of Matthias was the only one dignified with the title of Queen, or who shared with him the splendour and ornaments of royalty. After the example of their prophet, the multitude gave themselves up to the most licentious and uncontrolled gratification of their desires. No man remained satisfied with a single wife. Not to use their Christian liberty was deemed a crime. Persons were appointed to search the houses for young women grown up to maturity, whom they instantly compelled to marry. Together with polygamy, freedom of divorce, its inseparable attendant, was introduced, and became a new source of corruption. Every excess was committed, of which the passions of men are capable, when restrained neither by the authority of laws nor the sense of decency [m]; and by a monstrous

[m] Prophetæ & concionatorum autoritate juxta et exemplo, totâ urbe ad rapiendas pulcherrimas quasque fæminas discurſum eſt. Nec intra paucos dies, in tanta hominum turbâ fere ulla reperta eſt ſupra annum decimum quartum quæ ſtuprum paſſa non fuerit. Lamb. Hortenſ. p. 303. Vulgò

EMPEROR CHARLES V.

monstrous and almost incredible conjunction, voluptuousness was engrafted on religion, and dissolute riot accompanied the austerities of fanatical devotion.

BOOK V.
1534.

MEANWHILE the German princes were highly offended at the insult offered to their dignity by Boccold's presumptuous usurpation of royal honours; and the profligate manners of his followers, which were a reproach to the Christian name, filled men of all professions with horror. Luther, who had testified against this fanatical spirit on its first appearance, now deeply lamented its progress, and having exposed the delusion with great strength of argument, as well as acrimony of style, called loudly on all the states of Germany to put a stop to a phrenfy no less pernicious to society, than fatal to religion. The Emperor, occupied with other cares and projects, had not leisure to attend to such a distant object; but the princes of the Empire, assembled by the King of the Romans, voted a supply of men and money to the bishop of Munster, who being unable to keep a sufficient army on foot, had converted the

A confederacy against the Anabaptists.

Vulgò viris quinas esse uxores; pluribus senas, nonnullis septenas & octonas. Puellas supra duodecimum ætatis annum statim amare. Id. 305. Nemo unâ contentus fuit, neque cuiquam extra effœtas & viris immaturas continenti esse licuit. Id. 307. Tacebo hìc, ut sit suus honor auribus, quantâ barbariê et malitiâ usi sunt in puellis vitiandis nondum aptis matrimonio, id quod mihi neque ex vano, neque ex vulgi sermonibus haustum est, sed ex eâ vetulâ, cui cura sit vitiatarum demandata fuit, auditum. Joh. Corvinus, 316.

VOL. III.   G   siege

siege of the town into a blockade. The forces raised in consequence of this resolution, were put under the command of an officer of experience, who approaching the town towards the end of spring, in the year one thousand five hundred and thirty-five, pressed it more closely than formerly; but found the fortifications so strong, and so diligently guarded, that he durst not attempt an assault. It was now about fifteen months since the Anabaptists had established their dominion in Munster; they had during that time undergone prodigious fatigue in working on the fortifications, and performing military duty. Notwithstanding the prudent attention of their King to provide for their subsistence, and his frugal as well as regular œconomy in their public meals, they began to feel the approach of famine. Several small bodies of their brethren, who were advancing to their assistance from the Low-Countries, had been intercepted and cut to pieces; and while all Germany was ready to combine against them, they had no prospect of succour. But such was the ascendant which Boccold had acquired over the multitude, and so powerful the fascination of enthusiasm, that their hopes were as sanguine as ever, and they hearkened with implicit credulity to the visions and predictions of their prophets, who assured them that the Almighty would speedily interpose, in order to deliver the city. The faith, however, of some few, shaken by the violence and length of their sufferings, began to fail; but being suspected

pected of an inclination to surrender to the enemy, they were punished with immediate death, as guilty of impiety in distrusting the power of God. One of the King's wives, having uttered certain words which implied some doubt concerning his divine mission, he instantly called the whole number together, and commanding the blasphemer, as he called her, to kneel down, cut off her head with his own hands; and so far were the rest from expressing any horror at this cruel deed, that they joined him in dancing with a frantic joy around the bleeding body of their companion.

By this time, the besieged endured the utmost rigour of famine; but they chose rather to suffer hardships, the recital of which is shocking to humanity, than to listen to the terms of capitulation offered them by the bishop. At last, a deserter, whom they had taken into their service, being either less intoxicated with the fumes of enthusiasm, or unable any longer to bear such distress, made his escape to the enemy. He informed their general of a weak part in the fortifications which he had observed, and assuring him that the besieged, exhausted with hunger and fatigue, kept watch there with little care, he offered to lead a party thither in the night. The proposal was accepted, and a chosen body of troops appointed for the service; who, scaling the walls unperceived, seized one of the gates, and admitted the rest of the army. The Ana-

BOOK V.

1535.
June 24.

Punishment of the King and his associates.

Anabaptists, though surprised, defended themselves in the market-place with valour, heightened by despair; but being overpowered by numbers, and surrounded on every hand, most of them were slain, and the remainder taken prisoners. Among the last were the King and Cnipperdoling. The King, loaded with chains, was carried from city to city as a spectacle to gratify the curiosity of the people, and was exposed to all their insults. His spirit, however, was not broken or humbled by this sad reverse of his condition; and he adhered with unshaken firmness to the distinguishing tenets of his sect. After this, he was brought back to Munster, the scene of his royalty and crimes, and put to death with the most exquisite as well as lingering tortures, all which he bore with astonishing fortitude. This extraordinary man, who had been able to acquire such amazing dominion over the minds of his followers, and to excite commotions so dangerous to society, was only twenty-six years of age [n].

Character of the sect since that period.

TOGETHER with its Monarch, the kingdom of the Anabaptists came to an end. Their principles having taken deep root in the Low-Coun-

[n] Sleid. 190, &c. Tumultuum Anabaptistarum Liber unus. Ant. Lamberto Hortensio auctore ap. Scardium, vol. ii. p. 298, &c. De Miserabili Monasteriensium Obsidione, &c. libellus Antonii Corvini ap. Scar. 313. Annales Anabaptistici a Joh. Henrico Ottio, 4to. Basileæ, 1672. Cor. Heersbachius Hist. Anab. edit. 1637, p. 140.

tries,

ties, the party still subsists there, under the name of Mennonites; but by a very singular revolution, this sect, so mutinous and sanguinary at its first origin, hath become altogether innocent and pacific. Holding it unlawful to wage war, or to accept of civil offices, they devote themselves entirely to the duties of private citizens, and by their industry and charity endeavour to make reparation to human society for the violence committed by their founders[o]. A small number of this sect which is settled in England, retain its peculiar tenets concerning baptism, but without any dangerous mixture of enthusiasm.

Proceedings and authority of the league of Smalkalde.

THE mutiny of the Anabaptists, though it drew general attention, did not so entirely engross the princes of Germany, as not to allow leisure for other transactions. The alliance between the French King and the confederates at Smalkalde, began about this time to produce great effects. Ulric, Duke of Wurtemberg, having been expelled his dominions in the year one thousand five hundred and nineteen, on account of his violent and oppressive administration, the house of Austria had got possession of his dutchy. That prince having now by a long exile atoned for the errors in his conduct, which were the effect rather of inexperience than of a tyrannical disposition, was become the object of general compassion. The Landgrave of Hesse, in parti-

[o] Bayle Diction. art. *Anabaptistes.*

cular,

cular, his near relation, warmly espoused his interest, and used many efforts to recover for him his ancient inheritance. But the King of the Romans obstinately refused to relinquish a valuable acquisition which his family had made with so much ease. The Landgrave, unable to compel him, applied to the King of France his new ally. Francis, eager to embrace any opportunity of distressing the house of Austria, and desirous of wresting from it a territory, which gave it footing and influence in a part of Germany at a distance from its other dominions, encouraged the Landgrave to take arms, and secretly supplied him with a large sum of money. This he employed to raise troops; and marching with great expedition towards Wurtemberg, attacked, defeated, and dispersed a considerable body of Austrians, entrusted with the defence of the country. All the Duke's subjects hastened, with emulation, to receive their native Prince, and re-invested him with that authority which is still enjoyed by his descendants. At the same time the exercise of the Protestant religion was established in his dominions [p].

The King of the Romans courts them.

FERDINAND, how sensible soever of this unexpected blow, not daring to attack a Prince whom all the Protestant powers in Germany were ready to support, judged it expedient to conclude a treaty with him, by which, in the most ample

[p] Sleid. 172. Bellay, 159, &c.

form, he recognifed his title to the dutchy. The fuccefs of the Landgrave's operations, in behalf of the Duke of Wurtemberg, having convinced Ferdinand that a rupture with a league, fo formidable as that of Smalkalde, was to be avoided with the utmoft care, he entered likewife into a negociation with the Elector of Saxony, the head of that union, and by fome conceffions in favour of the Proteftant religion, and others of advantage to the Elector himfelf, he prevailed on him, together with his confederates, to acknowledge his title as King of the Romans. At the fame time, in order to prevent any fuch precipitate or irregular election in times to come, it was agreed that no perfon fhould hereafter be promoted to that dignity without the unanimous confent of the Electors; and the Emperor foon after confirmed this ftipulation [q].

Paul III. calls a general council to meet at Mantua.

THESE acts of indulgence towards the Proteftants, and the clofe union into which the King of the Romans feemed to be entering with the Princes of that party, gave great offence at Rome. Paul III., though he had departed from a refolution of his predeceffor, never to confent to the calling of a general council, and had promifed, in the firft confiftory held after his election, that he would convoke that affembly fo much defired by all Chriftendom, was no lefs enraged than Clement at the innovations in Germany,

[q] Sleid. 173. Corps Diplom. tom. iv. p. 2. 119.

and no less averse to any scheme for reforming either the doctrines of the church, or the abuses in the court of Rome: But having been a witness of the universal censure which Clement had incurred by his obstinacy with regard to these points, he hoped to avoid the same reproach by the seeming alacrity with which he proposed a council; flattering himself, however, that such difficulties would arise concerning the time and place of meeting, the persons who had a right to be present, and the order of their proceedings, as would effectually defeat the intention of those who demanded that assembly, without exposing himself to any imputation for refusing to call it. With this view he dispatched nuncios to the several courts, in order to make known his intention, and that he had fixed on Mantua as a proper place in which to hold the council. Such difficulties as the Pope had foreseen, immediately presented themselves in great number. The French King did not approve of the place which Paul had chosen, as the Papal and Imperial influence would necessarily be too great in a town situated in that part of Italy. The King of England not only concurred with Francis in urging that objection, but refused, besides, to acknowledge any council called in the name and by the authority of the Pope. The German Protestants having met together at Smalkalde, insisted on their original demand of a council to be held in Germany, and pleading the Emperor's promise, as well as the agreement at Ratisbon to that effect, declared that they would

not

not confider an affembly held at Mantua as a legal or free reprefentative of the church. By this diverfity of fentiments and views, fuch a field for intrigue and negociation opened, as made it eafy for the Pope to affume the merit of being eager to affemble a council, while at the same time he could put off its meeting at pleafure. The Proteftants, on the other hand, fufpecting his defigns, and fenfible of the importance which they derived from their union, renewed for ten years the league of Smalkalde, which now became ftronger and more formidable by the acceffion of feveral new members[r].

During thefe tranfactions in Germany, the Emperor undertook his famous enterprife againft the piratical ftates in Africa. That part of the African continent lying along the coaft of the Mediterranean fea, which anciently formed the kingdoms of Mauritania and Maffylia, together

The Emperor's expedition to Africa, and ftate of that country.

---

[r] This league was concluded December, one thoufand five hundred and thirty-five, but not extended or figned in form till September in the following year. The Princes who acceded to it were, John Elector of Saxony, Erneft Duke of Brunfwick, Philip Landgrave of Heffe, Ulric Duke of Wurtemberg, Barnim and Philip Dukes of Pomerania, John, George, and Joachim, Princes of Anhalt, Gebhard and Albert Counts of Mansfield, William Count of Naffau. The cities, Strafburg, Nuremburg, Conftance, Ulm, Magdeburg, Bremen, Reutlingen, Hailbron, Memmengen, Lindaw, Campen, Ifna, Bibrac, Windfheim, Augfburg, Francfort, Efling, Brunfwick, Goflar, Hanover, Gottingen, Eimbeck, Hamburg, Minden.

with

with the republic of Carthage, and which is now known by the general name of Barbary, had undergone many revolutions. Subdued by the Romans, it became a province of their empire. When it was conquered afterwards by the Vandals, they erected a kingdom there. That being overturned by Belisarius, the country became subject to the Greek Emperors, and continued to be so until it was over-run, towards the end of the seventh century, by the rapid and irresistible arms of the Arabians. It remained for some time a part of that vast empire which the Caliphs governed with absolute authority. Its immense distance, however, from the seat of government, encouraged the descendants of those leaders, who had subdued the country, or the chiefs of the Moors, its ancient inhabitants, to throw off the yoke, and to assert their independence. The Caliphs, who derived their authority from a spirit of enthusiasm, more fitted for making conquests than for preserving them, were obliged to connive at acts of rebellion which they could not prevent; and Barbary was divided into several kingdoms, of which Morocco, Algiers, and Tunis were the most considerable. The inhabitants of these kingdoms were a mixed race, Arabs, Negroes from the southern provinces, and Moors, either natives of Africa, or who had been expelled out of Spain; all zealous professors of the Mahometan religion, and inflamed against Christianity with a bigoted hatred proportional to their ignorance and barbarous manners.

Among these people, no less daring, inconstant, and treacherous, than the ancient inhabitants of the same country described by the Roman historians, frequent seditions broke out, and many changes in government took place. These, as they affected only the internal state of a country extremely barbarous, are but little known, and deserve to be so: But about the beginning of the sixteenth century a sudden revolution happened, which, by rendering the states of Barbary formidable to the Europeans, hath made their history worthy of more attention. This revolution was brought about by persons born in a rank of life which entitled them to act no such illustrious part. Horuc and Hayradin, the sons of a potter in the Isle of Lesbos, prompted by a restless and enterprizing spirit, forsook their father's trade, ran to sea, and joined a crew of pirates. They soon distinguished themselves by their valour and activity, and becoming masters of a small brigantine, carried on their infamous trade with such conduct and success, that they assembled a fleet of twelve galleys, besides many vessels of smaller force. Of this fleet Horuc, the elder brother, called Barbarossa from the red colour of his beard, was admiral, and Hayradin second in command, but with almost equal authority. They called themselves the friends of the sea, and the enemies of all who sail upon it; and their names soon became terrible from the Straits of the Dardanels to those of Gibraltar. Together with their fame and power, their ambitious views extended, and while acting

BOOK V.

1535. Rise of the piratical states,

and of the Barbarossas.

as

as Corsairs, they adopted the ideas, and acquired the talents of conquerors. They often carried the prizes which they took on the coasts of Spain and Italy into the ports of Barbary, and enriching the inhabitants by the sale of their booty, and the thoughtless prodigality of their crews, were welcome guests in every place at which they touched. The convenient situation of these harbours, lying so near the greatest commercial states at that time in Christendom, made the brothers wish for an establishment in that country. An opportunity of accomplishing this quickly presented itself, which they did not suffer to pass unimproved. Eutemi, King of Algiers, having attempted several times, without success, to take a fort which the Spanish governors of Oran had built not far from his capital, was so ill advised as to apply for aid to Barbarossa, whose valour the Africans considered as irresistible. The active Corsair gladly accepted of the invitation, and leaving his brother Hayradin with the fleet, marched at the head of five thousand men to Algiers, where he was received as their deliverer. Such a force gave him the command of the town; and as he perceived that the Moors neither suspected him of any bad intentions, nor were capable with their light-armed troops of opposing his diciplined veterans, he secretly murdered the Monarch whom he had come to assist, and proclaimed himself King of Algiers in his stead. The authority which he had thus boldly usurped, he endeavoured to establish by arts suited to the genius

genius of the people whom he had to govern; by liberality without bounds to those who favoured his promotion, and by cruelty no less unbounded towards all whom he had any reason to distrust. Not satisfied with the throne which he had acquired, he attacked the neighbouring King of Tremecen, and having vanquished him in battle, added his dominions to those of Algiers. At the same time, he continued to infest the coast of Spain and Italy with fleets which resembled the armaments of a great monarch, rather than the light squadrons of a Corsair. Their frequent and cruel devastations obliged Charles, about the beginning of his reign, to furnish the marquis de Comares, governor of Oran, with troops sufficient to attack him. That officer, assisted by the dethroned King of Tremecen, executed the commission with such spirit, that Barbarossa's troops being beat in several encounters, he himself was shut up in Tremecen. After defending it to the last extremity, he was overtaken in attempting to make his escape, and slain while he fought with an obstinate valour, worthy of his former fame and exploits.

His brother Hayradin, known likewise by the name of Barbarossa, assumed the sceptre of Algiers with the same ambition and abilities, but with better fortune. His reign being undisturbed by the arms of the Spaniards, which had full occupation in the wars among the European powers, he regulated with admirable prudence the interior police of his

his kingdom, carried on his naval operations with great vigour, and extended his conquests on the continent of Africa. But perceiving that the Moors and Arabs submitted to his government with the utmost reluctance, and being afraid that his continual depredations would, one day, draw upon him the arms of the Christians, he put his dominions under the protection of the Grand Seignior, and received from him a body of Turkish soldiers sufficient for his security against his domestic as well as his foreign enemies. At last, the fame of his exploits daily increasing, Solyman offered him the command of the Turkish fleet, as the only person whose valour and skill in naval affairs entitled him to command against Andrew Doria, the greatest sea-officer of that age. Proud of this distinction, Barbarossa repaired to Constantinople, and with a wonderful versatility of mind, mingling the arts of a courtier with the boldness of a Corsair, gained the entire confidence both of the Sultan and his Vizier. To them he communicated a scheme which he had formed of making himself master of Tunis, the most flourishing kingdom, at that time, on the coast of Africa; and this being approved of by them, he obtained whatever he demanded for carrying it into execution.

His hopes of success in this undertaking were founded on the intestine divisions in the kingdom of Tunis. Mahmed, the last King of that country, having thirty-four sons by different wives, appointed

appointed Muley-Hafcen, one of the youngeft among them, to be his fucceffor. That weak Prince, who owed this preference, not to his own merit, but to the afcendant which his mother had acquired over a monarch doating with age, firft poifoned Mahmed his father in order to prevent him from altering his deftination with refpect to the fucceffion; and then, with the barbarous policy which prevails wherever polygamy is permitted, and the right of fucceffion is not precifely fixed, he put to death all his brothers whom he could get into his power. Alrafchid, one of the eldeft, was fo fortunate as to efcape his rage; and finding a retreat among the wandering Arabs, made feveral attempts, by the affiftance of fome of their chiefs, to recover the throne, which of right belonged to him. But thefe proving unfuccefsful, and the Arabs, from their natural levity, being ready to deliver him up to his mercilefs brother, he fled to Algiers, the only place of refuge remaining, and implored the protection of Barbaroffa, who, difcerning at once all the advantages which might be gained by fupporting his title, received him with every poffible demonftration of friendfhip and refpect. Being ready, at that time, to fet fail for Conftantinople, he eafily perfuaded Alrafchid, whofe eagernefs to obtain a crown difpofed him to believe or undertake any thing, to accompany him thither, promifing him effectual affiftance from Solyman, whom he reprefented to be the moft generous, as well as moft powerful Monarch in the world. But no fooner were they arrived at Conftantinople, than the

BOOK V.
1535.

the treacherous Corsair, regardless of all his promises to him, opened to the Sultan a plan for conquering Tunis, and annexing it to the Turkish empire, by making use of the name of this exiled Prince, and co-operating with the party in the kingdom which was ready to declare in his favour. Solyman approved, with too much facility, of this perfidious proposal, extremely suitable to the character of its author, but altogether unworthy of a great Prince. A powerful fleet and numerous army were soon assembled; at the sight of which the credulous Alraschid flattered himself that he should soon enter his capital in triumph.

Its success.

But just as this unhappy Prince was going to embark, he was arrested by order of the Sultan, shut up in the seraglio, and was never heard of more. Barbarossa sailed with a fleet of two hundred and fifty vessels towards Africa. After ravaging the coasts of Italy, and spreading terror through every part of that country, he appeared before Tunis; and landing his men, gave out that he came to assert the right of Alraschid, whom he pretended to have left sick aboard the admiral galley. The fort of Goletta, which commands the bay, soon fell into his hands, partly by his own address, partly by the treachery of its commander; and the inhabitants of Tunis, weary of Muley-Hascen's government, took arms, and declared for Alraschid with such zeal and unanimity, as obliged the former to fly so precipitately, that he left all his treasures behind him. The gates,

gates were immediately set open to Barbarossa, as the restorer of their lawful sovereign. But when Alraschid himself did not appear, and when instead of his name, that of Solyman alone was heard among the acclamations of the Turkish soldiers marching into the town, the people of Tunis began to suspect the Corsair's treachery. Their suspicions being soon converted into certainty, they ran to arms with the utmost fury, and surrounded the citadel, into which Barbarossa had led his troops. But having foreseen such a revolution, he was not unprepared for it: he immediately turned against them the artillery on the ramparts, and by one brisk discharge, dispersed the numerous but undirected assailants, and forced them to acknowledge Solyman as their sovereign, and to submit to himself as his viceroy.

His first care was to put the kingdom, of which he had thus got possession, in a proper posture of defence. He strengthened the citadel which commands the town; and fortifying the Goletta in a regular manner, at vast expence, made it the principal station for his fleet, and his great arsenal for military as well as naval stores. Being now possessed of such extensive territories, he carried on his depredations against the Christian States to a greater extent, and with more destructive violence than ever. Daily complaints of the outrages committed by his cruizers were brought to the Emperor by his subjects, both in Spain

Barbarossa's formidable power.

Spain and Italy. All Christendom seemed to expect from him, as its greatest and most fortunate Prince, that he would put an end to this new and odious species of oppression. At the same time Muley-Hascen, the exiled King of Tunis, finding none of the Mahometan Princes in Africa willing or able to assist him in recovering his throne, applied to Charles as the only person who could assert his rights in opposition to such a formidable usurper. The Emperor, equally desirous of delivering his dominions from the dangerous neighbourhood of Barbarossa; of appearing as the protector of an unfortunate Prince; and of acquiring the glory annexed in that age to every expedition against the Mahometans, readily concluded a treaty with Muley-Hascen, and began to prepare for invading Tunis. Having made trial of his own abilities for war in the late campaign in Hungary, he was now become so fond of the military character, that he determined to command on this occasion in person. The united strength of his dominions was called out upon an enterprize in which the Emperor was about to hazard his glory, and which drew the attention of all Europe. A Flemish fleet carried from the ports of the Low-Country a body of German infantry^s; the gallies of Naples and Sicily took on board the veteran bands of Italians and Spaniards, which had distinguished themselves by so many victories over the French; the Emperor

---

^s Heræi Annales Brabant. i. 599.

himself embarked at Barcelona with the flower of the Spanish nobility, and was joined by a considerable squadron from Portugal, under the command of the Infant Don Lewis, the Empress's brother; Andrew Doria conducted his own gallies, the best appointed at that time in Europe, and commanded by the most skilful officers; the Pope furnished all the assistance in his power towards such a pious enterprize; and the order of Malta, the perpetual enemies of the Infidels, equipped a squadron, which, though small, was formidable by the valour of the knights who served on board it. The port of Cagliari in Sardinia was the general place of rendezvous. Doria was appointed High-Admiral of the fleet; the command of the land-forces under the Emperor was given to the marquis de Guasto.

Lands in Africa. On the sixteenth of July, the fleet, consisting of near five hundred vessels, having on board above thirty thousand regular troops, set sail from Cagliari, and after a prosperous navigation landed within sight of Tunis. Barbarossa having received early intelligence of the Emperor's immense armament, and suspecting its destination, prepared with equal prudence and vigour for the defence of his new conquest. He called in all his corsairs from their different stations; he drew from Algiers what forces could be spared; he dispatched messengers to all the African Princes, Moors as well as Arabs, and by representing Muley-Hascen as an infamous apostate, prompted by ambition and

and revenge, not only to become the vassal of a Christian Prince, but to conspire with him to extirpate the Mahommedan faith, he inflamed those ignorant and bigoted chiefs to such a degree, that they took arms as in a common cause. Twenty thousand horse, together with a great body of foot, soon assembled at Tunis; and by a proper distribution of presents among them from time to time, Barbarossa kept the ardour which had brought them together from subsiding. But as he was too well acquainted with the enemy whom he had to oppose, to think that these light troops could resist the heavy-armed cavalry and veteran infantry which composed the Imperial army, his chief confidence was in the strength of the Goletta, and in his body of Turkish soldiers, who were armed and disciplined after the European fashion. Six thousand of these, under the command of Sinan, a renegado Jew, the bravest and most experienced of all his corsairs, he threw into that fort, which the Emperor immediately invested. As Charles had the command of the sea, his camp was so plentifully supplied not only with the necessaries, but with all the luxuries of life, that Muley-Hascen, who had not been accustomed to see war carried on with such order and magnificence, was filled with admiration of the Emperor's power. His troops, animated by his presence, and considering it as meritorious to shed their blood in such a pious cause, contended with each other for the posts of honour and danger. Three separate attacks were concerted, and the Germans,

Lays siege to Goletta.

Germans, Spaniards, and Italians, having one of these committed to each of them, pushed them forward with the eager courage which national emulation inspires. Sinan displayed resolution and skill becoming the confidence which his master had put in him; the garrison performed the hard service on which they were ordered with great fortitude. But though he interrupted the besiegers by frequent sallies, though the Moors and Arabs alarmed the camp with their continual incursions; the breaches soon became so considerable towards the land, while the fleet battered those parts of the fortifications which it could approach with no less fury and success, that an assault being given on all sides at once, the place was taken by storm. Sinan, with the remains of his garrison, retired, after an obstinate resistance, over a shallow part of the bay towards the city. By the reduction of the Goletta, the Emperor became master of Barbarossa's fleet, consisting of eighty-seven gallies and galliots, together with his arsenal, and three hundred cannon, mostly brass, which were planted on the ramparts; a prodigious number in that age, and a remarkable proof of the strength of the fort, as well as of the greatness of the corsair's power. The Emperor marched into the Goletta through the breach, and turning to Muley-Hascen who attended him, "Here," says he, "is a gate open to you, by which you shall return to take possession of your dominions."

Takes it by storm, July 25.

BARBAROSSA, though he felt the full weight of the blow which he had received, did not, however, lose courage, or abandon the defence of Tunis. But as the walls were of great extent, and extremely weak; as he could not depend on the fidelity of the inhabitants, nor hope that the Moors and Arabs would sustain the hardships of a siege, he boldly determined to advance with his army, which amounted to fifty thousand men [t], towards the Imperial camp, and to decide the fate of his kingdom by the issue of a battle. This resolution he communicated to his principal officers, and representing to them the fatal consequences which might follow, if ten thousand Christian slaves, whom he had shut up in the citadel, should attempt to mutiny during the absence of the army, he proposed, as a necessary precaution for the public security, to massacre them without mercy before he began his march. They all approved warmly of his intention to fight; but inured as they were, in their piratical depredations, to scenes of bloodshed and cruelty, the barbarity of his proposal concerning the slaves filled them with horror; and Barbarossa, rather from the dread of irritating them, than swayed by motives of humanity, consented to spare the lives of the slaves.

Defeats Barbarossa's army.

BY this time the Emperor had begun to advance towards Tunis; and though his troops suf-

[t] Epistres des Princes, par Ruscelli, p. 119, &c.

fered

fered inconceivable hardships in their march, over burning sands, destitute of water, and exposed to the intolerable heat of the sun, they soon came up with the enemy. The Moors and Arabs, emboldened by their vast superiority in number, immediately rushed on to the attack with loud shouts, but their undisciplined courage could not long stand the shock of regular battalions; and though Barbarossa, with admirable presence of mind, and by exposing his own person to the greatest dangers, endeavoured to rally them, the rout became so general, that he himself was hurried along with them in their flight back to the city. There he found every thing in the utmost confusion; some of the inhabitants flying with their families and effects; others, ready to set open their gates to the conqueror; the Turkish soldiers preparing to retreat; and the citadel, which in such circumstances might have afforded him some refuge, already in the possession of the Christian captives. These unhappy men, rendered desperate by their situation, had laid hold on the opportunity which Barbarossa dreaded. As soon as his army was at some distance from the town, they gained two of their keepers, by whose assistance, knocking off their fetters, and bursting open their prisons, they overpowered the Turkish garrison, and turned the artillery of the fort against their former masters. Barbarossa, disappointed and enraged, exclaiming sometimes against the false compassion of his officers, and sometimes condemning his own imprudent

BOOK V.
1535.

prudent compliance with their opinion, fled precipitately to Bona.

Tunis surrenders.

MEANWHILE Charles, satisfied with the easy and almost bloodless victory which he had gained, and advancing slowly with the precaution necessary in an enemy's country, did not yet know the whole extent of his own good fortune. But at last, a messenger dispatched by the slaves acquainted him with the success of their noble effort for the recovery of their liberty; and at the same time deputies arrived from the town, in order to present him the keys of their gates, and to implore his protection from military violence. While he was deliberating concerning the proper measures for this purpose, the soldiers, fearing that they should be deprived of the booty which they had expected, rushed suddenly, and without orders, into the town, and began to kill and plunder without distinction. It was then too late to restrain their cruelty, their avarice, or licentiousness. All the outrages of which soldiers are capable in the fury of a storm, all the excesses of which men can be guilty when their passions are heightened by the contempt and hatred which difference in manners and religion inspire, were committed. Above thirty thousand of the innocent inhabitants perished on that unhappy day, and ten thousand were carried away as slaves. Muley-Hascen took possession of a throne surrounded with carnage, abhorred by his subjects on whom he had brought such calamities, and pitied

pitied even by those whose rashness had been the occasion of them. The Emperor lamented the fatal accident which had stained the lustre of this victory; and amidst such a scene of horror there was but one spectacle that afforded him any satisfaction. Ten thousand Christian slaves, among whom were several persons of distinction, met him as he entered the town; and falling on their knees, thanked and blessed him as their deliverer.

At the same time that Charles accomplished his promise to the Moorish King, of re-establishing him in his dominions, he did not neglect what was necessary for bridling the power of the African corsairs, for the security of his own subjects, and for the interest of the Spanish crown: In order to gain these ends, he concluded a treaty with Muley-Hascen on the following conditions: that he should hold the kingdom of Tunis in fee of the crown of Spain, and do homage to the Emperor as his liege lord; that all the Christian slaves now within his dominions, of whatever nation, should be set at liberty without ransom; that no subject of the Emperor's should for the future be detained in servitude; that no Turkish corsair should be admitted into the ports of his dominions; that free trade, together with the public exercise of the Christian religion, should be allowed to all the Emperor's subjects; that the Emperor should not only retain the Goletta, but that all the other sea-ports in the kingdom which were fortified should be put into his hands; that Muley-Hascen should pay annually

Restores the exiled King to his throne.

BOOK V.
1535.

ally twelve thousand crowns for the subsistence of the Spanish garrison in the Goletta; that he should enter into no alliance with any of the Emperor's enemies, and should present to him every year, as an acknowledgment of his vassalage, six Moorish horses, and as many hawks [u]. Having thus settled the affairs of Africa; chastised the insolence of the corsairs; secured a safe retreat for the ships of his subjects, and a proper station to his own fleets, on that coast from which he was most

August 17. infested by piratical depredations; Charles embarked again for Europe, the tempestuous weather, and sickness among his troops, not permitting him to pursue Barbarossa [x].

The glory which the Emperor acquired.

BY this expedition, the merit of which seems to have been estimated in that age, rather by the apparent generosity of the undertaking, the magnificence wherewith it was conducted, and the success which crowned it, than by the importance of the consequences that attended it, the Emperor attained a greater height of glory, than at any other period of his reign. Twenty thousand slaves whom he freed from bondage, either by his arms, or by

[u] Du Mont Corps Diplomat. ii. 128. Summonte Hist. di Napoli, iv. 89.

[x] Joh. Etropii Diarium Expedition. Tunetanæ, ap. Scard. v. ii. p. 320, &c. Jovii Histor. lib. xxxiv. 153, &c. Sandov. ii. 154, &c. Vertot Hist. de Cheval de Malthe. Epistres des Princes, par Ruscelli, traduites par Belleforest, p. 119, 120, &c. Anton. Pontii Consentini Hist. Belli adv. Barbar. ap. Matthæi Analecta.

his

his treaty with Muley-Hafcen[y], each of whom he
clothed and furnished with the means of returning
to their respective countries, spread over all Europe
the fame of their benefactor's munificence, extolling his power and abilities with the exaggeration
flowing from gratitude and admiration. In comparison with him, the other monarchs of Europe
made an inconsiderable figure. They seemed to
be solicitous about nothing but their private and
particular interests; while Charles, with an elevation of sentiment which became the first Prince in
Christendom, appeared to be concerned for the
honour of the Christian name, and attentive to the
public security and welfare.

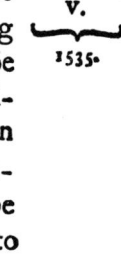

[y] Summonte Hist. de Nap. vol. iv. p. 103.

THE HISTORY OF THE REIGN OF THE EMPEROR CHARLES V.

BOOK VI.

1535. The causes of a new war between the Emperor and Francis.

UNFORTUNATELY for the reputation of Francis I. among his contemporaries, his conduct, at this juncture, appeared a perfect contrast to that of his rival, as he laid hold on the opportunity afforded him, by the Emperor's having turned his whole force against the common enemy of Christendom, to revive his pretensions in Italy, and to plunge Europe into a new war. The treaty of Cambray, as has been observed, did not remove the causes of enmity between the two contending Princes; it covered up, but did not extinguish the flames of discord. Francis in particular, who waited with impatience for a proper occasion of recovering the reputation as well as the territories which he had lost, continued to carry on his negociations in different

ferent courts againſt the Emperor, taking the ut-moſt pains to heighten the jealouſy which many Princes entertained of his power or deſigns, and to inſpire the reſt with the ſame ſuſpicion and fear: among others, he applied to Francis Sforza, who, though indebted to Charles for the poſſeſſion of the dutchy of Milan, had received it on ſuch hard conditions, as rendered him not only a vaſſal of the Empire, but a tributary dependant upon the Emperor. The honour of having married the Emperor's niece, did not reconcile him to this ignominious ſtate of ſubjection, which became ſo intolerable even to Sforza, though a weak and poor-ſpirited Prince, that he liſtened with eagerneſs to the firſt propoſals Francis made of reſcuing him from the yoke. Theſe propoſals were conveyed to him by Maraviglia, or Merveille, as he is called by the French hiſtorians, a Milaneſe gentleman reſiding at Paris; and ſoon after, in order to carry on the negociation with greater advantage, Merveille was ſent to Milan, on pretence of viſiting his relations, but with ſecret credentials from Francis as his envoy. In this character he was received by Sforza. But notwithſtanding his care to keep that circumſtance concealed, Charles ſuſpecting, or having received information of it, remonſtrated and threatened in ſuch an high tone, that the Duke and his miniſters, equally intimidated, gave the world immediately a moſt infamous proof of their ſervile fear of offending the Emperor. As Merveille had neither the prudence nor the temper which the function wherein he was employed required, they art-

BOOK VI.

1535.
Dec. 1533.

fully decoyed him into a quarrel, in which he happened to kill his antagonist, one of the Duke's domestics, and having instantly seized him, they ordered him to be tried for that crime, and to be beheaded. Francis, no less astonished at this violation of a character held sacred among the most uncivilized nations, than enraged at the insult offered to the dignity of his crown, threatened Sforza with the effects of his indignation, and complained to the Emperor, whom he considered as the real author of that unexampled outrage. But receiving no satisfaction from either, he appealed to all the Princes of Europe, and thought himself now entitled to take vengeance for an injury, which it would have been indecent and pusillanimous to let pass with impunity.

Francis destitute of allies.

BEING thus furnished with a pretext for beginning a war, on which he had already resolved, he multiplied his efforts in order to draw in other Princes to take part in the quarrel. But all his measures for this purpose were disconcerted by unforeseen events. After having sacrificed the honour of the royal family of France by the marriage of his son with Catharine of Medici, in order to gain Clement, the death of that Pontiff had deprived him of all the advantages which he expected to derive from his friendship. Paul, his successor, though attached by inclination to the Imperial interest, seemed determined to maintain the neutrality suitable to his character as the common father of the contending Princes. The King of England,

occupied

occupied with domestic cares and projects, declined, for once, engaging in the affairs of the continent, and refused to assist Francis, unless he would imitate his example, in throwing off the Papal supremacy. These disappointments led him to solicit, with greater earnestness, the aid of the Protestant Princes associated by the league of Smalkalde. That he might the more easily acquire their confidence, he endeavoured to accommodate himself to their predominant passion, zeal for their religious tenets. He affected a wonderful moderation with regard to the points in dispute; he permitted Bellay, his envoy in Germany, to explain his sentiments concerning some of the most important articles, in terms not far different from those used by the Protestants [a]; he even condescended to invite Melancthon, whose gentle manners and pacific spirit distinguished him among the Reformers, to visit Paris, that by his assistance he might concert the most proper measures for reconciling the contending sects which so unhappily divided the church [b]. These concessions must be considered rather as arts of policy, than the result of conviction; for whatever impression the new opinions in religion had made on his sisters, the Queen of Navarre and Dutchess of Ferrara, the gaiety of Francis's own temper, and his love of pleasure, allowed

[a] Freheri Script. Rer. German. iii. 354, &c. Sleid. Hist. 178. 183. Seckend. lib. iii. 103.
[b] Camerarii Vita Ph. Melancthonis, 12º. Hag. 1655. p. 12.

him little leisure to examine theological controversies.

Irritates them.

But soon after he lost all the fruits of this disingenuous artifice, by a step very inconsistent with his declarations to the German Princes. This step, however, the prejudices of the age, and the religious sentiments of his own subjects, rendered it necessary for him to take. His close union with the King of England, an excommunicated heretic; his frequent negociations with the German Protestants; but above all, his giving public audience to an envoy from Sultan Solyman, had excited violent suspicions concerning the sincerity of his attachment to religion. To have attacked the Emperor, who, on all occasions, made high pretensions to zeal in defence of the Catholic faith, and at the very juncture when he was preparing for his expedition against Barbarossa, which was then considered as a pious enterprise, could not have failed to confirm such unfavourable sentiments with regard to Francis, and called on him to vindicate himself by some extraordinary demonstration of his reverence for the established doctrines of the church. The indiscreet zeal of some of his subjects, who had imbibed the Protestant opinions, furnished him with such an occasion as he desired. They had affixed to the gates of the Louvre, and other public places, papers containing indecent reflections on the doctrines and rites of the Popish church. Six of the persons concerned in this rash action were discovered

vered and seized. The King, in order to avert the judgments which it was supposed their blasphemies might draw down upon the nation, appointed a solemn procession. The holy sacrament was carried through the city in great pomp; Francis walked uncovered before it, bearing a torch in his hand; the princes of the blood supported the canopy over it; the nobles marched in order behind. In the presence of this numerous assembly, the King, accustomed to express himself on every subject in strong and animated language, declared, that if one of his hands were infected with heresy, he would cut it off with the other, and would not spare even his own children, if found guilty of that crime. As a dreadful proof of his being in earnest, the six unhappy persons were publicly burnt before the procession was finished, with circumstances of the most shocking barbarity attending their execution [c].

THE Princes of the league of Smalkalde, filled with resentment and indignation at the cruelty with which their brethren were treated, could not conceive Francis to be sincere, when he offered to protect in Germany those very tenets, which he persecuted with such rigour in his own dominions; so that all Bellay's art and eloquence in vindicating his master, or apologising for his conduct, made but little impression upon them. They considered

They refuse to join him.

[c] Belcarii Comment. Rer. Gallic. 646. Sleid. Hist. 175. &c.

likewise, that the Emperor, who hitherto had never employed violence against the doctrines of the Reformers, nor even given them much molestation in their progress, was now bound by the agreement at Ratisbon, not to disturb such as had embraced the new opinions; and the Protestants wisely regarded this as a more certain and immediate security, than the precarious and distant hopes with which Francis endeavoured to allure them. Besides, the manner in which he had behaved to his allies at the peace of Cambray, was too recent to be forgotten, and did not encourage others to rely much on his friendship or generosity. Upon all these accounts, the Protestant Princes refused to assist the French King in any hostile attempt against the Emperor. The Elector of Saxony, the most zealous among them, in order to avoid giving any umbrage to Charles, would not permit Melancthon to visit the court of France, although that Reformer, flattered perhaps by the invitation of so great a Monarch, or hoping that his presence there might be of signal advantage to the Protestant cause, discovered a strong inclination to undertake the journey [d].

The French army advances towards Italy.

But though none of the many Princes who envied or dreaded the power of Charles, would second Franc efforts in order to reduce and

[d] Camerarii Vita Melan. 142, &c. 415. Seckend. lib. iii. 107.

circumscribe it, he, nevertheless, commanded his
army to advance towards the frontiers of Italy. As
his sole pretext for taking arms was that he might
chastise the Duke of Milan for his insolent and cruel
breach of the law of nations, it might have been
expected that the whole weight of his vengeance was
to have fallen on his territories. But on a sudden,
and at their very commencement, the operations of
war took another direction. Charles Duke of Savoy, one of the least active and able Princes of the
line from which he descended, had married Beatrix
of Portugal, the sister of the Empress. By her
great talents, she soon acquired an absolute ascendant over her husband; and proud of her affinity to
the Emperor, or allured by the magnificent promises with which he flattered her ambition, she
formed an union between the Duke and the Imperial court, extremely inconsistent with that neutrality, which wise policy as well as the situation of his
dominions had hitherto induced him to observe in
all the quarrels between the contending Monarchs.
Francis was abundantly sensible of the distress to
which he might be exposed, if, when he entered
Italy, he should leave behind him the territories of
a Prince, devoted so obsequiously to the Emperor,
that he had sent his eldest son to be educated in the
court of Spain, as a kind of hostage for his fidelity.
Clement the Seventh, who had represented this
danger in a strong light during his interview with
Francis at Marseilles, suggested to him, at the
same time, the proper method of guarding against it,

it, having advised him to begin his operations against the Milanese, by taking possession of Savoy and Piedmont, as the only certain way of securing a communication with his own dominions. Francis, highly irritated at the Duke on many accounts, particularly for having supplied the Constable Bourbon with the money that enabled him to levy the body of troops which ruined the French army in the fatal battle of Pavia, was not unwilling to let him now feel both how deeply he resented, and how severely he could punish these injuries. Nor did he want several pretexts which gave some colour of equity to the violence that he intended. The territories of France and Savoy lying contiguous to each other, and intermingled in many places, various disputes, unavoidable in such a situation, subsisted between the two sovereigns concerning the limits of their respective property; and besides, Francis, in right of his mother Louise of Savoy, had large claims upon the Duke her brother, for her share in their father's succession. Being unwilling, however, to begin hostilities without some cause of quarrel more specious than these pretensions, many of which were obsolete, and others dubious, he demanded permission to march through Piedmont in his way to the Milanese, hoping that the Duke, from an excess of attachment to the Imperial interest, might refuse this request, and thus give a greater appearance of justice to all his operations against him. But, if we may believe the historians of Savoy, who appear to be better informed with regard to this particular than those of of France, the Duke readily, and with a good grace, granted what it was not in his power to deny, promising free passage to the French troops as was desired; so that Francis, as the only method now left of justifying the measures which he determined to take, was obliged to insist for full satisfaction with regard to every thing that either the crown of France or his mother Louise could demand of the house of Savoy[e]. Such an evasive answer, as might have been expected, being made to this requisition, the French army under the admiral Biron poured at once into the Duke's territories at different places. The countries of Bresse and Bugey, united at that time to Savoy, were over-run in a moment. Most of the towns in the dutchy of Savoy opened their gates at the approach of the enemy; a few which attempted to make resistance were easily taken; and before the end of the campaign, the Duke saw himself stripped of all his dominions, but the province of Piedmont, in which there were not many places in a condition to be defended.

The city of Geneva recovers its liberty. To complete the Duke's misfortunes, the city of Geneva, the sovereignty of which he claimed, and in some degree possessed, threw off his yoke, and its revolt drew along with it the loss of the adjacent territories. Geneva was, at that time, an

[e] Histoire Genealogique de Savoye, par Guichenon, 2 tom. fol. Lyon. 1660. i. 639; &c.

Imperial city, and though under the direct dominion of its own bishops, and the remote sovereignty of the Dukes of Savoy, the form of its internal constitution was purely republican, being governed by syndics and a council chosen by the citizens. From these distinct and often clashing jurisdictions, two opposite parties took their rise, and had long subsisted in the state; the one, composed of the advocates for the privileges of the community, assumed the name of *Eignotz*, or confederates in defence of liberty; and branded the other, which supported the episcopal or ducal prerogatives, with the name of *Mammelukes*, or slaves. At length, the Protestant opinions beginning to spread among the citizens, inspired such as embraced them with that bold enterprising spirit which always accompanied or was naturally produced by them in their first operations. As both the Duke and Bishop were from interest, from prejudice, and from political considerations, violent enemies of the Reformation, all the new converts joined with warmth the party of the Eignotz; and zeal for religion, mingling with the love of liberty, added strength to that generous passion. The rage and animosity of two factions, shut up within the same walls, occasioned frequent insurrections, which terminating mostly to the advantage of the friends of liberty, they daily became more powerful.

The Duke and Bishop, forgetting their ancient contests about jurisdiction, had united against their common

common enemies, and each attacked them with his proper weapons. The Bishop excommunicated the people of Geneva as guilty of a double crime; of impiety, in apostatising from the established religion; and of sacrilege, in invading the rights of his see. The Duke attacked them as rebels against their lawful Prince, and attempted to render himself master of the city, first by surprise, and then by open force. The citizens, despising the thunder of the Bishop's censures, boldly asserted their independence against the Duke; and partly by their own valour, partly by the powerful assistance which they received from the canton of Berne, together with some small supplies both of men and money, secretly furnished by the King of France, they defeated all his attempts. Not satisfied with having repulsed him, or with remaining always upon the defensive themselves, they now took advantage of the Duke's inability to resist them, while overwhelmed by the armies of France, and seized several castles and places of strength which he possessed in the neighbourhood of Geneva; thus delivering the city from those odious monuments of its former subjection, and rendering the public liberty more secure for the future. At the same time the canton of Berne invaded and conquered the Pays de Vaud, to which it had some pretensions. The canton of Friburgh, though zealously attached to the Catholic religion, and having no subject of contest with the Duke, laid hold on part of the spoils of that unfortunate Prince. A great portion

portion of these conquests or usurpations being still retained by the two cantons, add considerably to their power, and have become the most valuable part of their territories. Geneva, notwithstanding many schemes and enterprizes of the Dukes of Savoy to re-establish their dominion over it, still keeps possession of its independence; and in consequence of that blessing, has attained a degree of consideration, wealth, and elegance, which it could not otherwise have reached [f].

The Emperor unable to assist the Duke of Savoy.

AMIDST such a succession of disastrous events, the Duke of Savoy had no other resource but the Emperor's protection, which, upon his return from Tunis, he demanded with the most earnest importunity; and as his misfortunes were occasioned chiefly by his attachment to the Imperial interest, he had a just title to immediate assistance. Charles, however, was not in a condition to support him with that vigour and dispatch which the exigency of his affairs called for. Most of the troops employed in the African expedition, having been raised for that service alone, were disbanded as soon as it was finished; the veteran forces under Antonio de Leyva were hardly sufficient for the defence of the Milanese; and the

[f] Hist. de la Ville de Geneve, par Spon, 12°, Utr. 1685, p. 99. Hist. de la Reformation de Suisse, par Rouchat. Gen. 1728, tom. iv. p. 294, &c. tom. v. p. 216, &c. Mem. de Bellay, 181.

Emperor's treasury was entirely drained by his extraordinary efforts against the Infidels.

BOOK VI.

1535.

But the death of Francis Sforza, occasioned, according to some historians, by the terror of a French invasion, which had twice been fatal to his family, afforded the Emperor full leisure to prepare for action. By this unexpected event, the nature of the war, and the causes of discord, were totally changed. Francis's first pretext for taking arms, in order to chastise Sforza for the insult offered to the dignity of his crown, was at once cut off; but as that Prince died without issue, all Francis's rights to the dutchy of Milan, which he had yielded only to Sforza and his posterity, returned back to him in full force. As the recovery of the Milanese was the favourite object of that Monarch, he instantly renewed his claim to it; and if he had supported his pretensions by ordering the powerful army quartered in Savoy to advance without losing a moment towards Milan, he could hardly have failed to secure the important point of possession. But Francis, who became less enterprising as he advanced in years, and who was overawed at some times into an excess of caution by the remembrance of his past misfortunes, endeavoured to establish his rights by negociation, not by arms; and from a timid moderation, fatal in all great affairs, neglected to improve the favourable opportunity which presented itself. Charles was more decisive in his operations, and in quality of sovereign, took possession

Oct. 24. Death of Sforza Duke of Milan.

Francis's pretensions to that dutchy.

possession of the dutchy, as a vacant fief of the Empire. While Francis endeavoured to explain and assert his title to it, by arguments and memorials, or employed various arts in order to reconcile the Italian powers to the thoughts of his regaining footing in Italy, his rival was silently taking effectual steps to prevent it. The Emperor, however, was very careful not to discover too early an intention of this kind; but seeming to admit the equity of Francis's claim, he appeared solicitous only about giving him possession in such a manner as might not disturb the peace of Europe, or overturn the balance of power in Italy, which the politicians of that country were so desirous of preserving. By this artifice he deceived Francis, and gained so much confidence with the rest of Europe, that, almost without incurring any suspicion, he involved the affair in new difficulties, and protracted the negociation at pleasure. Sometimes he proposed to grant the investiture of Milan to the Duke of Orleans, Francis's second son, sometimes to the Duke of Angouleme, his third son; as the views and inclinations of the French court varied, he transferred his choice alternately from the one to the other, with such profound and well-conducted dissimulation, that neither Francis nor his ministers seem to have penetrated his real intention; and all military operations were entirely suspended, as if nothing had remained but to enter quietly into possession of what they demanded.

DURING

DURING the interval of leisure gained in this manner, Charles, on his return from Tunis, assembled the states both of Sicily and Naples, and as they thought themselves greatly honoured by the presence of their sovereign, and were no less pleased with the apparent disinterestedness of his expedition into Africa, than dazzled by the success which had attended his arms, he prevailed on them to vote him such liberal subsidies as were seldom granted in that age. This enabled him to recruit his veteran troops, to levy a body of Germans, and to take every other proper precaution for executing or supporting the measures on which he had determined. Bellay, the French envoy in Germany, having discovered the intention of raising troops in that country, notwithstanding all the pretexts employed in order to conceal it, first alarmed his master, with this evident proof of the Emperor's insincerity [g]. But Francis was so possessed at that time with the rage of negociation, in all the artifices and refinements of which his rival far surpassed him, that instead of beginning his military operations, and pushing them with vigour, or seizing the Milanese before the Imperial army was assembled, he satisfied himself with making new offers to the Emperor, in order to procure the investiture by his voluntary deed. His offers were, indeed, so liberal and advantageous, that if ever Charles had intended to grant his demand, he could not have rejected them with decency. He dexterously

[g] Mem. de Bellay, 192.

eluded

eluded them by declaring that until he consulted the Pope in person, he could not take his final resolution with regard to a point which so nearly concerned the peace of Italy. By this evasion he gained some farther time for ripening the schemes which he had in view.

The Emperor enters Rome. April 6.

THE Emperor at last advanced towards Rome, and made his public entry into that city with extraordinary pomp; but it being found necessary to remove the ruins of an ancient temple of Peace, in order to widen one of the streets, through which the cavalcade had to pass, all the historians take notice of this trivial circumstance, and they are fond to interpret it as an omen of the bloody war that followed. Charles, it is certain, had by this time banished all thoughts of peace; and at last threw off the mask, with which he had so long covered his designs from the court of France, by a declaration of his sentiments no less singular than explicit. The French ambassadors having in their master's name demanded a definitive reply to his propositions concerning the investiture of Milan, Charles promised to give it next day in presence of the Pope and Cardinals assembled in full consistory. These being accordingly met, and all the foreign ambassadors invited to attend, the Emperor stood up, and addressing himself to the Pope, expatiated for some time on the sincerity of his own wishes for the peace of Christendom, as well as his abhorrence of war, the miseries of which he enumerated at

His public invective against Francis.

great

great length, with studied and elaborate oratory; he complained that all his endeavours to preserve the tranquillity of Europe had hitherto been defeated by the restless and unjust ambition of the French King; that even during his minority he had proofs of the unfriendly and hostile intentions of that Monarch; that, afterwards, he had openly attempted to wrest from him the Imperial crown which belonged to him by a title no less just than natural; that he had next invaded his kingdom of Navarre; that not satisfied with this, he had attacked his territories as well as those of his allies both in Italy and the Low-Countries; that when the valour of the Imperial troops, rendered irresistible by the protection of the Almighty, had checked his progress, ruined his armies, and seized his person, he continued to pursue by deceit what he had undertaken with injustice; that he had violated every article in the treaty of Madrid to which he owed his liberty, and as soon as he returned to his dominions took measures for rekindling the war which that pacification had happily extinguished; that when new misfortunes compelled him to sue again for peace at Cambray, he concluded and observed it with equal insincerity; that soon after he had formed dangerous connexions with the heretical Princes in Germany, and incited them to disturb the tranquillity of the Empire; that now he had driven the Duke of Savoy, a Prince married to a sister of the Empress, and joined in close alliance with Spain, out of the greater part of his territories; that after injuries so often repeated,

BOOK VI.
1536.

Challenges him to single combat.

repeated, and amidst so many sources of discord, all hope of amity or concord became desperate; and though he himself was still willing to grant the investiture of Milan to one of the Princes of France, there was little probability of that event taking place, as Francis, on the one hand, would not consent to what was necessary for securing the tranquillity of Europe; nor on the other, could he think it reasonable or safe to give a rival the unconditional possession of all that he demanded. "Let us not, however, added he, continue wantonly to shed the blood of our innocent subjects; let us decide the quarrel man to man, with what arms he pleases to chuse, in our shirts, on an island, a bridge, or aboard a galley moored in a river; let the dutchy of Burgundy be put in deposit on his part, and that of Milan on mine; these shall be the prize of the conqueror; and after that, let the united forces of Germany, Spain, and France, be employed to humble the power of the Turk, and to extirpate heresy out of Christendom. But if he, by declining this method of terminating our differences, renders war inevitable, nothing shall divert me from prosecuting it to such extremity, as shall reduce one of us to be the poorest gentleman in his own dominions. Nor do I fear that it will be on me this misfortune shall fall; I enter upon action with the fairest prospect of success; the justice of my cause, the union of my subjects, the number and valour of my troops, the experience and fidelity of my generals, all combine to ensure it. Of all these advantages, the

the King of France is deftitute; and were my re-
fources no more certain, and my hopes of victory
no better founded than his, I would inftantly throw
myfelf at his feet, and with folded hands, and a
rope about my neck, implore his mercy [h]."

THIS long harangue the Emperor delivered
with an elevated voice, a haughty tone, and the
greateft vehemence of expreffion and gefture. The
French ambaffadors, who did not fully comprehend his meaning, as he fpake in the Spanifh
tongue, were totally difconcerted, and at a lofs how
they fhould anfwer fuch an unexpected invective;
when one of them began to vindicate his mafter's
conduct, Charles interpofed abruptly, and would
not permit him to proceed. The Pope, without
entering into any particular detail, fatisfied himfelf
with a fhort but pathetic recommendation of peace,
together with an offer of employing his fincere
endeavours in order to procure that bleffing to
Chriftendom; and the affembly broke up in the
greateft aftonifhment at the extraordinary fcene
which had been exhibited. In no part of his
conduct, indeed, did Charles ever deviate fo
widely from his general character. Inftead of *The motives*
that prudent recollection, that compofed and re- *of this rafh*
gular deportment fo ftrictly attentive to decorum, *meafure.*
and fo admirably adapted to conceal his own paffions, for which he was at all other times confpicuous, he appears on this occafion before one of the

[h] Bellay, 199. Sandov. Hiftor. del' Emper. ii. 226.

most august assemblies in Europe, boasting of his own power and exploits with insolence; inveighing against his enemy with indecency; and challenging him to combat with an ostentatious valour, more becoming a champion in romance, than the first Monarch in Christendom. But the well-known and powerful operation of continued prosperity, as well as of exaggerated praise, even upon the firmest minds, sufficiently account for this seeming inconsistency. After having compelled Solyman to retreat, and having stripped Barbarossa of a kingdom, Charles began to consider his arms as invincible. He had been entertained, ever since his return from Africa, with repeated scenes of triumphs and public rejoicings; the orators and poets of Italy, the most elegant at that time in Europe, had exhausted their genius in panegyric on his conduct and merit, to which the astrologers added magnificent promises of a more splendid fortune still in store. Intoxicated with all these, he forgot his usual reserve and moderation, and was unable to restrain this extravagant sally of vanity, which became the more remarkable, by being both so uncommon and so public.

He himself seems to have been immediately sensible of the impropriety of his behaviour; and when the French ambassadors demanded next day a more clear explanation of what he had said concerning the combat, he told them that they were not to consider his proposal as a formal challenge to their master, but as an expedient for preventing bloodshed;

bloodshed; he endeavoured to soften several expres-   BOOK VI.
sions in his discourse; and spoke in terms full of
respect towards Francis. But though this slight   1536.
apology was far from being sufficient to remove the
offence which had been given, Francis, by an un-
accountable infatuation, continued to negociate, as
if it had still been possible to bring their differences
to a period by an amicable composition. Charles,
finding him so eager to run into the snare, favoured
the deception, and, by seeming to listen to his proposals, gained farther time to prepare for the execution of his own designs[1].

AT last, the Imperial army assembled on the   Charles invades France.
frontiers of the Milanese, to the amount of forty
thousand foot and ten thousand horse, while that
of France encamped near Vercelli in Piedmont,
being greatly inferior in number, and weakened
by the departure of a body of Swifs, whom Charles
artfully persuaded the popish cantons to recal, that
they might not serve against the Duke of Savoy,
their ancient ally. The French general not daring to risque a battle, retired as soon as the Imperialists advanced. The Emperor put himself at the   May 6.
head of his forces, which the Marquis del Guasto,
the Duke of Alva, and Ferdinand de Gonzaga
commanded under him, though the supreme direction of the whole was committed to Antonio de
Leyva, whose abilities and experience justly entitled him to that distinction. Charles soon disco-

[1] Mem. de Bellay, 205, &c.

vered his intention not to confine his operations to the recovery of Piedmont and Savoy, but to push forward and invade the southern provinces of France. This scheme he had long meditated, and had long been taking measures for executing it with such vigour as might ensure success. He had remitted large sums to his sister, the governess of the Low-Countries, and to his brother, the King of the Romans, instructing them to levy all the forces in their power, in order to form two separate bodies, the one to enter France on the side of Picardy, the other on the side of Champagne; while he, with the main army, fell upon the opposite frontier of the kingdom. Trusting to these vast preparations, he thought it impossible that Francis could resist so many unexpected attacks on such different quarters; and began his enterprise with such confidence of its happy issue, that he desired Jovius the historian, to make a large provision of paper sufficient to record the victories which he was going to obtain.

His ministers and generals, instead of entertaining the same sanguine hopes, represented to him in the strongest terms the danger of leading his troops so far from his own territories, to such a distance from his magazines, and into provinces which did not yield sufficient subsistence for their own inhabitants. They entreated him to consider the inexhaustible resources of France in maintaining a defensive war, and the active zeal with which a gallant a gallant nobility would ferve a Prince whom they loved, in repelling the enemies of their country; they recalled to his remembrance the fatal mifcarriage of Bourbon and Pefcara, when they ventured upon the fame enterprife under circumftances which feemed as certainly to promife fuccefs; the Marquis del Guafto, in particular, fell on his knees, and conjured him to abandon the undertaking as defperate. But many circumftances combined in leading Charles to difregard all their remonftrances. He could feldom be brought, on any occafion, to depart from a refolution which he had once taken; he was too apt to under-rate and defpife the talents of his rival the King of France, becaufe they differed fo widely from his own; he was blinded by the prefumption which accompanies profperity; and relied, perhaps, in fome degree, on the prophecies which predicted the increafe of his own grandeur. He not only adhered obftinately to his own plan, but determined to advance towards France without waiting for the reduction of any part of Piedmont, except fuch towns as were abfolutely neceffary for preferving his communication with the Milanefe.

THE Marquis de Saluces, to whom Francis had entrufted the command of a fmall body of troops left for the defence of Piedmont, rendered this more eafy than Charles had any reafon to expect. That nobleman, educated in the court of France, diftinguifhed by continual marks of the King's favour,

Recovers part of the Duke of Savoy's dominions.

vour, and honoured so lately with a charge of such importance, suddenly, and without any provocation or pretext of disgust, revolted from his benefactor. His motives to this treacherous action were as childish as the deed itself was base. Being strongly possessed with a superstitious faith in divination and astrology, he believed with full assurance, that the fatal period of the French nation was at hand; that on its ruins the Emperor would establish an universal monarchy; that therefore he ought to follow the dictates of prudence, in attaching himself to his rising fortune, and could incur no blame for deserting a Prince whom Heaven had devoted to destruction [k]. His treason became still more odious, by his employing that very authority with which Francis had invested him, in order to open the kingdom to his enemies. Whatever measures were proposed or undertaken by the officers under his command for the defence of their conquests, he rejected or defeated. Whatever properly belonged to himself, as commander in chief, to provide or perform for that purpose, he totally neglected. In this manner, he rendered towns even of the greatest consequence untenable, by leaving them destitute either of provisions, or ammunition, or artillery, or a sufficient garrison; and the Imperialists must have reduced Piedmont in as short a time as was necessary to march through it, if Montpezat, the governor of Fossano, had not, by

[k] Bellay, 222, a. 246, b.

an extraordinary effort of courage and military conduct, detained them almost a month before that inconsiderable place.

Francis's plan for the defence of his kingdom.

By this meritorious and seasonable service, he gained his master sufficient time for assembling his forces, and for concerting a system of defence against a danger which he now saw to be inevitable. Francis fixed upon the only proper and effectual plan for defeating the invasion of a powerful enemy; and his prudence in chusing this plan, as well as his perseverance in executing it, deserve the greater praise, as it was equally contrary to his own natural temper, and to the genius of the French nation. He determined to remain altogether upon the defensive; never to hazard a battle, or even a great skirmish, without certainty of success; to fortify his camps in a regular manner; to throw garrisons only into towns of great strength; to deprive the enemy of subsistence, by laying waste the country before them; and to save the whole kingdom, by sacrificing one of its provinces. The execution of this plan he committed entirely to the marechal Montmorency, who was the author of it; a man wonderfully fitted by nature for such a trust. Haughty, severe, confident in his own abilities, and despising those of other men; incapable of being diverted from any resolution by remonstrances or entreaties; and, in prosecuting any scheme, regardless alike of love or of pity.

Entrusts Montmorency with the execution of it.

Montmorency made choice of a ftrong camp under the walls of Avignon, at the confluence of the Rhone and the Durance, one of which plentifully fupplied his troops with all neceffaries from the inland provinces, and the other covered his camp on that fide where it was moft probable the enemy would approach. He laboured with unwearied induftry to render the fortifications of this camp impregnable, and affembled there a confiderable army, though greatly inferior to that of the enemy; while the King with another body of troops encamped at Valence higher up the Rhone. Marfeilles and Arles were the only towns he thought it neceffary to defend; the former, in order to retain the command of the fea; the latter, as the barrier of the province of Languedoc; and each of thefe he furnifhed with numerous garrifons of his beft troops, commanded by officers on whofe fidelity and valour he could rely. The inhabitants of the other towns, as well as of the open country, were compelled to abandon their houfes, and were conducted to the mountains, to the camp at Avignon, or to the inland provinces. The fortifications of fuch places as might have afforded fhelter or defence to the enemy, were thrown down. Corn, forage, and provifions of every kind, were carried away or deftroyed; all the mills and ovens were ruined, and the wells filled up or rendered ufelefs. The devaftation extended from the Alps to Marfeilles, and from the fea to the confines of Dauphiné;

phiné; nor does history afford any instance among civilized nations, in which this cruel expedient for the public safety was employed with the same rigour.

At length, the Emperor arrived with the van of his army on the frontiers of Provence, and was still so possessed with confidence of success, that, during a few days when he was obliged to halt until the rest of his troops came up, he began to divide his future conquests among his officers; and as a new incitement to serve him with zeal, gave them liberal promises of offices, lands, and honours in France [1]. The face of desolation, however, which presented itself to him, when he entered the country, began to damp his hopes, and convinced him that a Monarch, who, in order to distress an enemy, had voluntarily ruined one of his richest provinces, would defend the rest with desperate obstinacy. Nor was it long before he became sensible that Francis's plan of defence was as prudent as it appeared to be extraordinary. His fleet, on which Charles chiefly depended for subsistence, was prevented for some time by contrary winds, and other accidents to which naval operations are subject, from approaching the French coast; even after his arrival, it afforded at best a precarious and scanty supply to such a numerous body of troops [m]; nothing was to be found in the country itself for their support; nor

[1] Bellay, 266, a. [m] Sandov. ii. 231.

could they draw any confiderable aid from the dominions of the Duke of Savoy, exhaufted already by maintaining two great armies. The Emperor was no lefs embarraffed how to employ, than how to fubfift his forces; for though he was now in poffeffion of almoft an entire province, he could not be faid to have the command of it, while he held only defencelefs towns; and while the French, befides their camp at Avignon, continued mafters of Marfeilles and Arles. At firft he thought of attacking the camp, and of terminating the war by one decifive blow; but fkilful officers, who were appointed to view it, declared the attempt to be utterly impracticable. He then gave orders to inveft Marfeilles and Arles, hoping that the French would quit their advantageous poft in order to relieve them; but Montmorency adhering firmly to his plan, remained immoveable at Avignon, and the Imperialifts met with fuch a warm reception from the garrifons of both towns, that they relinquifhed their enterprifes with lofs and difgrace. As a laft effort, the Emperor advanced once more towards Avignon, though with an army haraffed by the perpetual incurfions of fmall parties of the French light troops, weakened by difeafes, and difpirited by difafters, which feemed the more intolerable, becaufe they were unexpected.

During thefe operations, Montmorency found himfelf expofed to greater danger from his own troops than from the enemy; and their inconfiderate

derate valour went near to have precipitated the kingdom into those calamities which he with such industry and caution had endeavoured to avoid. Unaccustomed to behold an enemy ravaging their country almost without controul; impatient of such long inaction; unacquainted with the flow and remote, but certain effects of Montmorency's system of defence; the French wished for a battle with no less ardour than the Imperialists. They considered the conduct of their general as a disgrace to their country. His caution they imputed to timidity; his circumspection to want of spirit; and the constancy with which he pursued his plan, to obstinacy or pride. These reflections, whispered at first among the soldiers and subalterns, were adopted, by degrees, by officers of higher rank; and as many of them envied Montmorency's favour with the King, and more were dissatisfied with his harsh disgusting manner, the discontent soon became great in his camp, which was filled with general murmurings, and almost open complaints against his measures. Montmorency, on whom the sentiments of his own troops made as little impression as the insults of the enemy, adhered steadily to his system; though, in order to reconcile the army to his maxims, no less contrary to the genius of the nation, than to the ideas of war among undisciplined troops, he assumed an unusual affability in his deportment, and often explained, with great condescension, the motives of his conduct, the advantages which had already resulted from it, and the

certain

certain succefs which which it would be attended. At last, Francis joined his army at Avignon, which, having received several reinforcements, he now considered as of strength sufficient to face the enemy. As he had put no small constraint upon himself, in consenting that his troops should remain so long upon the defensive, it can hardly be doubted but that his fondness for what was daring and splendid, added to the impatience both of officers and soldiers, would at last have over-ruled Montmorency's salutary caution [n].

The retreat and wretched condition of the Imperial army.

HAPPILY the retreat of the enemy delivered the kingdom from the danger which any rash resolution might have occasioned. The Emperor, after spending two inglorious months in Provence, without having performed any thing suitable to his vast preparations, or that could justify the confidence with which he had boasted of his own power, found that, besides Antonio de Leyva, and other officers of distinction, he had lost one half of his troops by diseases or by famine; and that the rest were in no condition to struggle any longer with calamities, by which so many of their companions had perished. Necessity, therefore, extorted from him orders to retire; and though he was some time in motion before the French suspected his intention, a body of light troops, assisted by crowds of peasants, eager to be revenged on those who had brought such desolation

[n] Mem. de Bellay, 269, &c. 312, &c.

on their country, hung upon the rear of the Imperialists, and by seizing every favourable opportunity of attacking them, threw them often into confusion. The road by which they fled, for they pursued their march with such disorder and precipitation that it scarcely deserves the name of a retreat, was strewed with arms or baggage, which in their hurry and trepidation they had abandoned, and covered with the sick, the wounded, and the dead; insomuch that Martin Bellay, an eye-witness of their calamities, endeavours to give his readers some idea of them, by comparing their miseries to those which the Jews suffered from the victorious and destructive arms of the Romans[o]. If Montmorency, at this critical moment, had advanced with all his forces, nothing could have saved the whole Imperial army from utter ruin. But that general, by standing so long and so obstinately on the defensive, had become cautious to excess; his mind, tenacious of any bent it had once taken, could not assume a contrary one as suddenly as the change of circumstances required; and he still continued to repeat his favourite maxims, that it was more prudent to allow the lion to escape, than to drive him to despair, and that a bridge of gold should be made for a retreating enemy.

The Emperor having conducted the shattered remains of his troops to the frontiers of Milan,

---

[o] Mem. de Bellay, 316. Sandov. Hist. del Emper. ii. 232.

and appointed the marquis del Guasto to succeed Leyva in the government of that dutchy, set out for Genoa. As he could not bear to expose himself to the scorn of the Italians, after such a sad reverse of fortune; and did not chuse, under his present circumstances, to revisit those cities through which he had so lately passed in triumph for one conquest, and in certain expectation of another, he embarked directly for Spain [p].

Nor was the progress of his arms on the opposite frontier of France such as to alleviate, in any degree, the losses which he had sustained in Provence. Bellay, by his address and intrigues, had prevailed on so many of the German Princes to withdraw the contingent of troops which they had furnished to the King of the Romans, that he was obliged to lay aside all thoughts of his intended irruption into Champagne. Though a powerful army levied in the Low-Countries entered Picardy, which they found but feebly guarded, while the strength of the kingdom was drawn towards the south; yet the nobility, taking arms with their usual alacrity, supplied by their spirit the defects of the king's preparations, and defended Peronne, and other towns which were attacked with such vigour, as obliged the enemy to retire, without making any conquest of importance [q].

[p] Jovii Histor. lib. xxxv. p. 174, &c.
[q] Mem. de Bellay, 318, &c.

THUS

THUS Francis, by the prudence of his own measures, and by the union and valour of his subjects, rendered abortive those vast efforts in which his rival had almost exhausted his whole force. As this humbled the Emperor's arrogance no less than it checked his power, he was mortified more sensibly on this occasion than on any other, during the course of the long contests between him and the French Monarch.

ONE circumstance alone embittered the joy with which the success of the campaign inspired Francis. That was the death of the Dauphin, his eldest son, a Prince of great hopes, and extremely beloved by the people on account of his resemblance to his father. This happening suddenly, was imputed to poison, not only by the vulgar, fond of ascribing the death of illustrious personages to extraordinary causes, but by the King and his ministers. The count de Montecuculi, an Italian nobleman, cupbearer to the Dauphin, being seized on suspicion and put to the torture, openly charged the Imperial generals, Gonzaga and Leyva, with having instigated him to the commission of that crime; he even threw out some indirect and obscure accusations against the Emperor himself. At a time when all France was exasperated to the utmost against Charles, this uncertain and extorted charge was considered as an incontestible proof of guilt; while the confidence with which both he and his officers asserted their own innocence, together with

Death of the Dauphin.

Imputed to poison.

with the indignation, as well as horror, which they expressed on their being supposed capable of such a detestable action, were little attended to, and less regarded [r]. It is evident, however, that the Emperor could have no inducement to perpetrate such a crime, as Francis was still in the vigour of life himself, and had two sons, beside the Dauphin, grown up almost to the age of manhood. That single consideration, without mentioning the Emperor's general character, unblemished by the imputation of any deed resembling this in atrocity, is more than sufficient to counterbalance the weight of a dubious testimony uttered during the anguish of torture [s]. According to the most unprejudiced historians, the Dauphin's death was occasioned by his having drunk too freely of cold water after over-heating himself at tennis; and this account, as it is the most simple, is likewise the most credible. But if his days were cut short by poison, it is not improbable that the Emperor conjectured rightly, when he affirmed that it had been administered by the direction of Catherine of Medici, in order to secure the crown to the duke of Orleans, her husband [t]. The advantages resulting to her by the Dauphin's death, were obvious as well as great; nor did her boundless and daring ambition ever recoil from any action necessary towards attaining the objects which she had in view.

[r] Mem. de Bellay, 289.
[s] Sandov. Hist. del Emper. ii. 231.
[t] Vera y Zuniga Vida de Carlo V. p. 75.

NEXT

NEXT year opened with a transaction very uncommon, but so incapable of producing any effect, that it would not deserve to be mentioned, if it were not a striking proof of the personal animosity which mingled itself in all the hostilities between Charles and Francis, and which often betrayed them into such indecencies towards each other, as lessened the dignity of both. Francis, accompanied by the peers and princes of the blood, having taken his seat in the parliament of Paris with the usual solemnities, the advocate-general appeared; and after accusing Charles of Austria (for so he affected to call the Emperor) of having violated the treaty of Cambray, by which he was absolved from the homage due to the crown of France for the counties of Artois and Flanders; insisted that this treaty being now void, he was still to be considered as a vassal of the crown, and by consequence had been guilty of rebellion in taking arms against his sovereign; and therefore he demanded that Charles should be summoned to appear in person, or by his counsel, before the parliament of Paris, his legal judges, to answer for this crime. The request was granted; a herald repaired to the frontiers of Picardy, and summoned him with the accustomed formalities to appear against a day prefixed. That term being expired, and no person appearing in his name, the parliament gave judgment, " That Charles of Austria had forfeited by rebellion and contumacy those fiefs; declared Flanders and Artois to be re-united to the crown of France;"

1537. Decree of the parliament of Paris against the Emperor.

and

and ordered their decree for this purpose to be published by sound of trumpet on the frontiers of these provinces [u].

Campaign opens in the Low-Countries.

March.

SOON after this vain display of his resentment, rather than of his power, Francis marched towards the Low-Countries, as if he had intended to execute the sentence which his parliament had pronounced, and to seize those territories which it had awarded to him. As the Queen of Hungary, to whom her brother the Emperor had committed the government of that part of his dominions, was not prepared for so early a campaign, he at first made some progress, and took several towns of importance. But being obliged soon to leave his army, in order to superintend the other operations of war, the Flemings, having assembled a numerous army, not only recovered most of the places which they had lost, but began to make conquests in their turn. At last they invested Terouenne, and the Duke of Orleans, now Dauphin, by the death of his brother, and Montmorency, whom Francis had honoured with the constable's sword, as the reward of his great services during the former campaign, determined to hazard a battle in order to relieve it. While they were advancing for this purpose, and within a few miles of the enemy, they were stopt short by the arrival of an herald from the Queen of

A suspension of arms there;

[u] Lettres et Memoires d'Etat, par Ribier, 2 tom. Blois, 1666. tom. i. p. 1.

Hungary,

Hungary, acquainting him that a suspension of arms was now agreed upon.

BOOK VI.
1537.

THIS unexpected event was owing to the zealous endeavours of the two sisters, the Queens of France and of Hungary, who had long laboured to reconcile the contending Monarchs. The war in the Netherlands had laid waste the frontier provinces of both countries, without any real advantage to either. The French and Flemings equally regretted the interruption of their commerce, which was beneficial to both. Charles as well as Francis, who had each strained to the utmost, in order to support the vast operations of the former campaign, found that they could not now keep armies on foot in this quarter, without weakening their operations in Piedmont, where both wished to push the war with the greatest vigour. All these circumstances facilitated the negociations of the two Queens; a truce was concluded, to continue in force for ten months, but it extended no farther than the Low-Countries [x].

July 30.

IN Piedmont the war was still prosecuted with great animosity; and though neither Charles nor Francis could make the powerful efforts to which this animosity prompted them, they continued to exert themselves like combatants, whose rancour remains after their strength is exhausted. Towns were alternately lost and retaken; skirmishes were

and in Piedmont.

[x] Memoires de Ribier, 56.

VOL. III.   L   fought

fought every day; and much blood was shed, without any action that gave a decided superiority to either side. At last the two Queens determining not to leave unfinished the good work which they had begun, prevailed, by their importunate solicitations, the one on her brother, the other on her husband, to consent also to a truce in Piedmont for three months. The conditions of it were, that each should keep possession of what was in his hands, and after leaving garrisons in the towns, should withdraw his army out of the province; and that plenipotentiaries should be appointed to adjust all matters in dispute by a final treaty [y].

Motives of it.

THE powerful motives which inclined both Princes to this accommodation, have been often mentioned. The expences of the war had far exceeded the sums which their revenues were capable of supplying; nor durst they venture upon any great addition to the impositions then established, as subjects had not yet learnt to bear with patience the immense burdens to which they have become accustomed in modern times. The Emperor in particular, though he had contracted debts which in that age appeared prodigious [z], had it not in his power to pay the large arrears long due to his army. At the same time he had no prospect of deriving any aid in money, or men either from the Pope or Venetians, though

[y] Memoires de Ribier, 62.   [z] Ribier, i. 294.

he

he had employed promises and threats, alternately, in order to procure it. But he found the former not only fixed in his resolution of adhering steadily to the neutrality which he had always declared to be suitable to his character, but passionately desirous of bringing about a peace. He perceived that the latter were still intent on their ancient object of holding the balance even between the rivals, and solicitous not to throw too great a weight into either scale.

WHAT made a deeper impression on Charles than all these, was the dread of the Turkish arms, which, by his league with Solyman, Francis had drawn upon him. Though Francis, without the assistance of a single ally, had a war to maintain against an enemy greatly superior in power to himself, yet so great was the horror of Christians, in that age, at any union with Infidels, which they considered not only as dishonourable but profane, that it was long before he could be brought to avail himself of the obvious advantages resulting from such a confederacy. Necessity at last surmounted his delicacy and scruples. Towards the close of the preceding year, La Forest, a secret agent at the Ottoman Porte, had concluded a treaty with the Sultan, whereby Solyman engaged to invade the kingdom of Naples, during the next campaign, and to attack the King of the Romans in Hungary with a powerful army, while Francis undertook to enter the Milanese at the same time with a proper force. Solyman had punctually

Of which Francis's alliance with the Turkish Emperor the most considerable.

punctually performed what was incumbent on him. Barbaroffa with a great fleet appeared on the coaft of Naples, filled that kingdom, from which all the troops had been drawn towards Piedmont, with confternation, landed without refiftance near Taranto, obliged Caftro, a place of fome ftrength, to furrender, plundered the adjacent country, and was taking meafures for fecuring and extending his conquefts, when the unexpected arrival of Doria, together with the Pope's gallies, and a fquadron of the Venetian fleet, made it prudent for him to retire. In Hungary the progrefs of the Turks was more formidable. Mahmet, their general, after gaining feveral fmall advantages, defeated the Germans in a great battle at Effek on the Drave [a]. Happily for Chriftendom, it was not in Francis's power to execute with equal exactnefs what he had ftipulated; nor could he affemble at this juncture an army ftrong enough to penetrate into the Milanefe. By this he failed in recovering poffeffion of that dutchy; and Italy was not only faved from the calamities of a new war, but from feeling the defolating rage of the Turkifh arms, as an addition to all that it had fuffered [b]. As the Emperor knew that he could not long refift the efforts of two fuch powerful confederates, nor could expect that the fame fortunate accidents would concur a fecond time to deliver Naples,

[a] Iftuanheffi Hift. Hung. lib. xiii. p. 139.
[b] Jovii Hift. lib. xxxv. p. 183.

and

and to preferve the Milanese: as he forefaw that the Italian states would not only tax him loudly with infatiable ambition, but might even turn their arms againſt him, if he ſhould be ſo regardleſs of their danger as obſtinately to protract the war, he thought it neceſſary, both for his ſafety and reputation, to give his conſent to a truce. Nor was Francis willing to ſuſtain all the blame of obſtructing the re-eſtabliſhment of tranquillity, or to expoſe himſelf on that account to the danger of being deſerted by the Swiſs and other foreigners in his ſervice. He even began to apprehend that his own ſubjects would ſerve him coldly, if by contributing to aggrandize the power of the Infidels, which it was his duty, and had been the ambition of his anceſtors to depreſs, he continued to act in direct oppoſition to all the principles which ought to influence a Monarch diſtinguiſhed by the title of Moſt Chriſtian King. He choſe for all theſe reaſons, rather to run the riſk of diſobliging his new ally the Sultan, than, by an unſeaſonable adherence to the treaty with him, to forfeit what was of greater conſequence.

BOOK VI.

1537.

BUT though both parties conſented to a truce, the plenipotentiaries found inſuperable difficulties in ſettling the articles of a definitive treaty. Each of the Monarchs, with the arrogance of a conqueror, aimed at giving law to the other; and neither would ſo far acknowledge his inferiority, as to ſacrifice any point of honour, or to relinquiſh any matter of right; ſo that the plenipotentiaries

Negociations of a peace between Charles and Francis.

L 3 ſpent

spent the time in long and fruitless negociations, and separated after agreeing to prolong the truce for a few months.

The Pope conducts these in person.

THE Pope, however, did not despair of accomplishing a point in which the plenipotentiaries had failed, and took upon himself the sole burden of negociating a peace. To form a confederacy capable of defending Christendom from the formidable inroads of the Turkish arms, and to concert effectual measures for the extirpation of the Lutheran heresy, were two great objects which Paul had much at heart, and he considered the union of the Emperor with the King of France as an essential preliminary to both. To be the instrument of reconciling these contending Monarchs, whom his predecessors by their interested and indecent intrigues had so often embroiled, was a circumstance which could not fail of throwing a distinguished lustre on his character and administration. Nor was he without hopes that, while he pursued this laudable end, he might secure advantages to his own family, the aggrandizing of which he did not neglect, though he aimed at it with a less audacious ambition than was common among the Popes of that century. Influenced by these considerations, he proposed an interview between the two Monarchs at Nice, and offered to repair thither in person, that he might act as mediator in composing all their differences. When a Pontiff of a venerable character, and of a very advanced age, was willing,
from

from his zeal for peace, to undergo the fatigues of so long a journey, neither Charles nor Francis could with decency decline the interview. But though both came to the place of rendezvous, so great was the difficulty of adjusting the ceremonial, or such the remains of distrust and rancour on each side, that they refused to see one another, and every thing was transacted by the intervention of the Pope, who visited them alternately. With all his zeal and ingenuity he could not find out a method of removing the obstacles which prevented a final accommodation, particularly those arising from the possession of the Milanese; nor was all the weight of his authority sufficient to overcome the obstinate perseverance of either Monarch in asserting his own claims. At last, that he might not seem to have laboured altogether without effect, he prevailed on them to sign a truce for ten years, upon the same condition with the former, that each should retain what was now in his possession, and in the mean time should send ambassadors to Rome, to discuss their pretensions at leisure [e].

A truce for ten years concluded at Nice, June 18.

Thus ended a war of no long continuance, but very extensive in its operations, and in which both parties exerted their utmost strength. Though Francis failed in the object which he had prin-

[e] Recueil des Traitez, ii. 219. Relatione del Nicolo Tiepolo de l'Abocamento di Nizza, chez Du Mont Corps Diplomat. par. ii. p. 174.

pally in view, the recovery of the Milanese, he acquired, nevertheless, great reputation by the wisdom of his measures as well as the success of his arms in repelling a formidable invasion; and by keeping possession of one half of the Duke of Savoy's dominions, he added no inconsiderable accession of strength to his kingdom. Whereas Charles, repulsed and baffled, after having boasted so arrogantly of victory, purchased an inglorious truce, by sacrificing an ally who had rashly confided too much in his friendship and power. The unfortunate Duke murmured, complained, and remonstrated against a treaty so much to his disadvantage, but in vain; he had no means of redress, and was obliged to submit. Of all his dominions, Nice, with its dependencies, was the only corner of which he himself kept possession. He saw the rest divided between a powerful invader and the ally to whose protection he had trusted, while he remained a sad monument of the imprudence of weak princes, who, by taking part in the quarrel of mighty neighbours, between whom they happen to be situated, are crushed and overwhelmed in the shock.

Interview between Charles and Francis at Aiguesmortes.

A FEW days after signing the treaty of truce, the Emperor set sail for Barcelona, but was driven by contrary winds to the island St. Margaret on the coast of Provence. When Francis, who happened to be not far distant, heard of this, he considered it as an office of civility to invite him to take shelter in his dominions, and proposed a personal

personal interview with him at Aigues-mortes. The Emperor, who would not be outdone by his rival in complaisance, instantly repaired thither. As soon as he cast anchor in the road, Francis, without waiting to settle any point of ceremony, but relying implicitly on the Emperor's honour for his security, visited him on board his galley, and was received and entertained with the warmest demonstrations of esteem and affection. Next day the Emperor repaid the confidence which the King had placed in him. He landed at Aigues-mortes with as little precaution, and met with a reception equally cordial. He remained on shore during the night, and in both visits the two Monarchs vied with each other in expressions of respect and friendship [d]. After twenty years of open hostilities, or of secret enmity; after so many injuries reciprocally inflicted or endured; after having formally given the lie, and challenged one another to single combat; after the Emperor had inveighed so publicly against Francis as a Prince void of honour or integrity; and after Francis had accused him of being accessary to the murder of his eldest son; such an interview appears altogether singular and even unnatural. But the history of these Monarchs abounds with such surprising transitions. From implacable hatred they appeared to pass, in a moment, to the most cordial reconcilement; from

---

[d] Sandov. Hist. vol. ii. 238. Relation de l'Entrevue de Charl. V. & Fran. I. par M. de la Rivoire. Hist. de Langued. par D. D. De Vic. & Vaisette, tom. v. Preuves, p. 93.

suspicion and distrust, to perfect confidence; and from practising all the dark arts of a deceitful policy, they could assume, of a sudden, the liberal and open manners of two gallant gentlemen.

THE Pope, besides the glory of having restored peace to Europe, gained, according to his expectation, a point of great consequence to his family, by prevailing on the Emperor to betroth Margaret of Austria, his natural daughter, formerly the wife of Alexander di Medici, to his grandson Octavio Farnese, and in consideration of this marriage, to bestow several honours and territories upon his future son-in-law. A very tragical event, which happened about the beginning of the year one thousand five hundred and thirty-seven, had deprived Margaret of her first husband. That young Prince, whom the Emperor's partiality had raised to the supreme power in Florence, upon the ruins of the public liberty, neglected entirely the cares of government, and abandoned himself to the most dissolute debauchery. Lorenzo di Medici his nearest kinsman was not only the companion but director of his pleasures, and employing all the powers of a cultivated and inventive genius in this dishonourable ministry, added such elegance as well as variety to vice, as gained him an absolute ascendant over the mind of Alexander. But while Lorenzo seemed to be sunk in luxury, and affected such an appearance of indolence and effeminacy, that he would not wear a sword, and trembled at the sight

The assassination of Alexander di Medici.

of blood, he concealed under that difguife, a dark, defigning, audacious fpirit. Prompted either by the love of liberty, or allured by the hope of attaining the fupreme power, he determined to affaſſinate Alexander his benefactor and friend. Though he long revolved this defign in his mind, his referved and fufpicious temper prevented him from communicating it to any perfon whatever; and continuing to live with Alexander in their ufual familiarity, he, one night, under pretence of having fecured him an affignation with a lady of high rank whom he had often folicited, drew that unwary Prince into a fecret apartment of his houfe, and there ftabbed him, while he lay carelefsly on a couch expecting the arrival of the lady whofe company he had been promifed. But no fooner was the deed done, than ftanding aftonifhed, and ftruck with horror at its atrocity, he forgot, in a moment, all the motives which had induced him to commit it. Inftead of roufing the people to recover their liberty by publifhing the death of the tyrant, inftead of taking any ftep towards opening his own way to the dignity now vacant, he locked the door of the apartment, and, like a man bereaved of reafon and prefence of mind, fled with the utmoft precipitation out of the Florentine territories. It was late next morning before the fate of the unfortunate Prince was known, as his attendants, accuftomed to his irregularities, never entered his apartment early. Immediately the chief perfons in the ftate affembled. Being induced partly by the zeal of cardinal Cibo

for

for the house of Medici, to which he was nearly related, partly by the authority of Francis Guicciardini, who recalled to their memory, and represented in striking colours the caprice as well as turbulence of their ancient popular government, they agreed to place Cosmo di Medici, a youth of eighteen, the only male heir of that illustrious house, at the head of the government; though at the same time such was their love of liberty, that they established several regulations in order to circumscribe and moderate his power.

MEANWHILE, Lorenzo having reached a place of safety, made known what he had done, to Philip Strozzi and the other Florentines who had been driven into exile, or who had voluntarily retired, when the republican form of government was abolished, in order to make way for the dominion of the Medici. By them, the deed was extolled with extravagant praises, and the virtue of Lorenzo was compared with that of the elder Brutus, who disregarded the ties of blood, or with that of the younger, who forgot the friendship and favours of the tyrant, that they might preserve or recover the liberty of their country [e]. Nor did they rest satisfied with empty panegyrics; they immediately quitted their different places of retreat, assembled forces, animated their vassals and partizans to take arms, and to seize this opportunity of re-establishing the public liberty on its an-

[e] Lettere di Principi, tom. iii. p. 52.

cient foundation. Being openly assisted by the French ambassador at Rome, and secretly encouraged by the Pope, who bore no good-will to the house of Medici, they entered the Florentine dominions with a considerable body of men. But the persons who had elected Cosmo possessed not only the means of supporting his government, but abilities to employ them in the most proper manner. They levied, with the greatest expedition, a good number of troops; they endeavoured by every art to gain the citizens of greatest authority, and to render the administration of the young Prince agreeable to the people. Above all, they courted the Emperor's protection, as the only firm foundation of Cosmo's dignity and power. Charles, knowing the propensity of the Florentines to the friendship of France, and how much all the partizans of a republican government detested him as the oppressor of their liberties, saw it to be greatly for his interest to prevent the re-establishment of the ancient constitution in Florence. For this reason, he not only acknowledged Cosmo as head of the Florentine state, and conferred on him all the titles of honour with which Alexander had been dignified, but engaged to defend him to the utmost; and as a pledge of this, ordered the commanders of such of his troops as were stationed on the frontiers of Tuscany, to support him against all aggressors. By their aid, Cosmo obtained an easy victory over the exiles, whose troops he surprised in the night-time, and took most of the

chiefs

BOOK V.
1538.

chiefs prisoners: an event which broke all their measures, and fully established his own authority. But though he was extremely desirous of the additional honour of marrying the Emperor's daughter, the widow of his predecessor, Charles, secure already of his attachment, chose rather to gratify the Pope, by bestowing her on his nephew [f]

The friendship between Francis and Henry VIII. begins to abate.

DURING the war between the Emperor and Francis, an event had happened which abated in some degree the warmth and cordiality of friendship which had long subsisted between the latter and the King of England. James the Fifth of Scotland, an enterprising young Prince, having heard of the Emperor's intention to invade Provence, was so fond of shewing that he did not yield to any of his ancestors in the sincerity of his attachment to the French crown, and so eager to distinguish himself by some military exploit, that he levied a body of troops with an intention of leading them in person to the assistance of the King of France. Though some unfortunate accidents prevented his carrying any troops into France, nothing could divert him from going thither in person. Immediately upon his landing, he hastened to Provence, but had been detained so long in his voyage, that he came too late to have any share in the military operations, and met the King on his return

[f] Jovii Hist. c. xcviii. p. 218, &c. Belcarii Comment. l. xxii. p. 696. Istoria de sui Tempi di Giov. Bat. Adriani. Ven. 1587. p. 10.

after

after the retreat of the Imperialists. But Francis was so greatly pleased with his zeal, and no less with his manners and conversation, that he could not refuse him his daughter Magdalen, whom he demanded in marriage. It mortified Henry extremely to see a Prince of whom he was immoderately jealous, form an alliance, from which he derived such an accession of reputation as well as security [g]. He could not, however, with decency, oppose Francis's bestowing his daughter upon a Monarch descended from a race of Princes, the most ancient and faithful allies of the French crown. But when James, upon the sudden death of Magdalen, demanded as his second wife Mary of Guise, he warmly solicited Francis to deny his suit, and in order to disappoint him, asked that lady in marriage for himself. When Francis preferred the Scottish King's sincere courtship to his artful and malevolent proposal, he discovered much dissatisfaction. The pacification agreed upon at Nice, and the familiar interview of the two rivals at Aigues-mortes, filled Henry's mind with new suspicions, as if Francis had altogether renounced his friendship for the sake of new connections with the Emperor. Charles, thoroughly acquainted with the temper of the English King, and watchful to observe all the shiftings and caprices of his passions, thought this a favourable opportunity of renewing his negociations with

BOOK VI.

1538.
Jan. 1, 1537.

The Emperor courts Henry.

[g] Hist. of Scotland, vol. i. p. 77.

him,

BOOK VI.
1538.

him, which had been long broken off. By the death of Queen Catharine, whose interest the Emperor could not with decency have abandoned, the chief cause of their discord was removed; so that without touching upon the delicate question of her divorce, he might now take what measures he thought most effectual for regaining Henry's good-will. For this purpose, he began with proposing several marriage-treaties to the King. He offered his niece, a daughter of the King of Denmark, to Henry himself; he demanded the princess Mary for one of the Princes of Portugal, and was even willing to receive her as the King's illegitimate daughter [h]. Though none of these projected alliances ever took place, or perhaps were ever seriously intended, they occasioned such frequent intercourse between the courts, and so many reciprocal professions of civility and esteem, as considerably abated the edge of Henry's rancour against the Emperor, and paved the way for that union between them which afterwards proved so disadvantageous to the French King.

Progress of the Reformation.

THE ambitious schemes in which the Emperor had been engaged, and the wars he had been carrying on for some years, proved, as usual, extremely favourable to the progress of the Reformation in Germany. While Charles was absent upon his African expedition, or intent on his projects against France, his chief object in Ger-

[h] Mem. de Ribier, t. i. 496.

many

many was to prevent the diffenfions about religion from difturbing the public tranquillity, by granting fuch indulgence to the Proteftant Princes as might induce them to concur with his meafures, or at leaft hinder them from taking part with his rival. For this reafon, he was careful to fecure to the Proteftants the poffeffion of all the advantages which they had gained by the articles of pacification at Nuremberg, in the year one thoufand five hundred and thirty-two[1]; and except fome flight trouble from the proceedings of the Imperial chamber, they met with nothing to difturb them in the exercife of their religion, or to interrupt the fuccefsful zeal with which they propagated their opinions. Meanwhile the Pope continued his negociations for convoking a general council; and though the Proteftants had expreffed great diffatisfaction with his intention to fix upon Mantua as the place of meeting, he adhered obftinately to his choice, iffued a bull on the fecond of June, one thoufand five hundred and thirty-fix, appointing it to affemble in that city on the twenty-third of May the year following: he nominated three cardinals to prefide in his name; enjoined all Chriftian Princes to countenance it by their authority, and invited the Prelates of every nation to attend in perfon. This fummons of a council, an affembly which from its nature and intention demanded quiet times, as well as pacific difpofitions, at the very juncture when the Emperor was

Negociations and intrigues with refpect to a general council.

---

[1] Du Mont Corps Diplom. tom. iv. part 2. p. 138.

on his march towards France, and ready to involve a great part of Europe in the confusions of war, appeared to every person extremely unseasonable. It was intimated, however, to all the different courts by nuncios dispatched of purpose [k]. With an intention to gratify the Germans, the Emperor, during his residence in Rome, had warmly solicited the Pope to call a council; but being at the same time willing to try every art in order to persuade Paul to depart from the neutrality which he preserved between him and Francis, he sent Heldo his vice-chancellor into Germany, along with a nuncio dispatched thither, instructing him to second all the nuncio's representations, and to enforce them with the whole weight of the Imperial authority. The Protestants gave them audience at Smalkalde, where they had assembled in a body in order to receive them. But after weighing all their arguments they unanimously refused to acknowledge a council summoned in the name and by the authority of the Pope alone; in which he assumed the sole right of presiding; which was to be held in a city not only far distant from Germany, but subject to a Prince, who was a stranger to them, and closely connected with the court of Rome; and to which their divines could not repair with safety, especially after their doctrines had been stigmatized in the very bull of convocation with the name of heresy. These and many other ob-

[k] Pallavic. Hist. Conc. Trid. 1-13.

jections

jections against the council, which appeared to them unanswerable, they enumerated in a large manifests, which they published in vindication of their conduct[1].

AGAINST this the court of Rome exclaimed as a flagrant proof of their obstinacy and presumption, and the Pope still persisted in his resolution to hold the council at the time and in the place appointed. But some unexpected difficulties being started by the Duke of Mantua, both about the right of jurisdiction over the persons who reforted to the council, and the security of his capital amidst such a concourse of strangers, the Pope, after fruitless endeavours to adjust these, first prorogued the council for some months, and afterwards, transferring the place of meeting to Vicenza in the Venetian territories, appointed it to assemble on the first of May in the following year. As neither the Emperor nor the French King, who had not then come to any accommodation, would permit their subjects to repair thither, not a single prelate appeared on the day prefixed, and the Pope, that his authority might not become altogether contemptible by so many ineffectual efforts to convoke that assembly, put off the meeting by an indefinite prorogation [m].

[1] Sleidan, l. xii. 123, &c. Seckend. Com. lib. iii. p. 143, &c.
[m] F. Paul, 117. Pallavic. 117.

1538.
A partial reformation of abuses by the Pope.

But, that he might not seem to have turned his whole attention towards a reformation which he was not able to accomplish, while he neglected that which was in his own power, he deputed a certain number of cardinals and bishops, with full authority to inquire into the abuses and corruptions of the Roman court; and to propose the most effectual method of removing them. This scrutiny, undertaken with reluctance, was carried on slowly and with remissness. All defects were touched with a gentle hand, afraid of probing too deep, or of discovering too much. But even by this partial examination, many irregularities were detected, and many enormities exposed to light, while the remedies which they suggested as most proper, were either inadequate, or were never applied. The report and resolution of these deputies, though intended to be kept secret, were transmitted by some accident into Germany, and being immediately made public, afforded ample matter for reflection, and triumph to the Protestants[n]. On the one hand they demonstrated the necessity of a reformation in the head as well as the members of the church, and even pointed out many of the corruptions against which Luther and his followers had remonstrated with the greatest vehemence. They shewed, on the other hand, that it was vain to expect this reformation from ecclesiastics themselves, who, as Luther strongly

[n] Sleidan, 233.

expressed

expressed it, piddled at curing warts, while they overlooked or confirmed ulcers [o].

A league formed in opposition to that of Smalkalde.

THE earnestness with which the Emperor seemed, at first, to press their acquiescing in the Pope's scheme of holding a council in Italy, alarmed the Protestant Princes so much, that they thought it prudent to strengthen their confederacy, by admitting several new members who solicited that privilege, particularly the King of Denmark. Heldo, who, during his residence in Germany, had observed all the advantages which they derived from that union, endeavoured to counterbalance its effects by an alliance among the Catholic powers of the Empire. This league, distinguished by the name of *Holy*, was merely defensive; and though concluded by Heldo in the Emperor's name, was afterwards disowned by him, and subscribed by very few Princes [p].

Alarms the Protestants.

THE Protestants soon got intelligence of this association, notwithstanding all the endeavours of the contracting parties to conceal it; and their zeal, always apt to suspect and to dread, even to excess, every thing that seemed to threaten religion, instantly took the alarm, as if the Emperor had been just ready to enter upon the execution of some formidable plan for the extirpation of their opinions. In order to disappoint this, they

[o] Seck. l. iii. 164.   [p] Seck. l. iii. 171. Recueil des Traitez.

held frequent consultations, they courted the Kings of France and England with great assiduity, and even began to think of raising the respective contingents both in men and money which they were obliged to furnish by the treaty of Smalkalde. But it was not long before they were convinced that these apprehensions were without foundation, and that the Emperor, to whom repose was absolutely necessary after efforts so much beyond his strength in the war with France, had no thoughts of disturbing the tranquillity of Germany. As a proof of this, at an interview with the Protestant Princes in Francfort, his ambassadors agreed that all concessions in their favour, particularly those contained in the pacification of Nuremberg, should continue in force for fifteen months; that during this period all proceedings of the Imperial chamber against them should be suspended; that a conference should be held by a few divines of each party, in order to discuss the points in controversy, and to propose articles of accommodation which should be laid before the next Diet. Though the Emperor, that he might not irritate the Pope, who remonstrated against the first part of this agreement as impolitic, and against the latter as an impious encroachment upon his prerogative, never formally ratified this convention, it was observed with considerable exactness, and greatly strengthened the basis of that ecclesiastical liberty, for which the Protestants contended [q].

[q] F. Paul, 82. Sleid. 247. Seck. l. iii. 200.

A few days after the convention at Francfort, George Duke of Saxony died, and his death was an event of great advantage to the Reformation. That Prince, the head of the Albertine, or younger branch of the Saxon family, poſſeſſed, as marquis of Miſnia and Thuringia, extenſive territories, comprehending Dreſden, Leipſic, and other cities now the moſt conſiderable in the electorate. From the firſt dawn of the Reformation, he had been its enemy as avowedly as the electoral Princes were its protectors, and had carried on his oppoſition not only with all the zeal flowing from religious prejudices, but with a virulence inſpired by perſonal antipathy to Luther, and imbittered by the domeſtic animoſity ſubſiſting between him and the other branch of his family. By his death without iſſue, his ſucceſſion fell to his brother Henry, whoſe attachment to the Proteſtant religion ſurpaſſed, if poſſible, that of his predeceſſor to popery. Henry no ſooner took poſſeſſion of his new dominions, than, diſregarding a clauſe in George's will, dictated by his bigotry, whereby he bequeathed all his territories to the Emperor and King of the Romans, if his brother ſhould attempt to make any innovation in religion, he invited ſome Proteſtant divines, and among them Luther himſelf, to Leipſic. By their advice and aſſiſtance, he overturned in a few weeks the whole ſyſtem of ancient rites, eſtabliſhing the full exerciſe of the reformed religion, with the univerſal applauſe of his ſubjects, who had long wiſhed for this change, which the authority

thority of their Duke alone had hitherto prevented[r]. This revolution delivered the Protestants from the danger to which they were exposed by having an inveterate enemy situated in the middle of their territories; and they had now the satisfaction of seeing that the possessions of the princes and cities attached to their cause, extended now in one great and almost unbroken line from the shore of the Baltic to the banks of the Rhine.

A mutiny of the Imperial troops.

Soon after the conclusion of the truce at Nice, an event happened, which satisfied all Europe that Charles had prosecuted the war to the utmost extremity that the state of his affairs would permit. Vast arrears were due to his troops, whom he had long amused with vain hopes and promises. As they now foresaw what little attention would be paid to their demands, when by the re-establishment of peace their services became of less importance, they lost all patience, broke out into an open mutiny, and declared that they thought themselves entitled to seize by violence what was detained from them contrary to all justice. Nor was this spirit of sedition confined to one part of the Emperor's dominions; the mutiny was almost as general as the grievance which gave rise to it. The soldiers in the Milanese plundered the open country without controul, and filled the capital itself with consternation. Those in garrison at Goletta threatened to give up that important fortress to Barbarossa. In Sicily, the troops pro-

[r] Sleidan, 249.

ceeded

ceeded to still greater excesses; having driven away their officers, they elected others in their stead, defeated a body of men whom the viceroy sent against them, took and pillaged several cities, conducting themselves all the while in such a manner, that their operations resembled rather the regular proceedings of a concerted rebellion, than the rashness and violence of a military mutiny. But by the address and prudence of the generals, who partly by borrowing money in their own name, or in that of their master, partly by extorting large sums from the cities in their respective provinces, raised what was sufficient to discharge the arrears of the soldiers, these insurrections were quelled. The greater part of the troops were disbanded, such a number only being kept in pay as was necessary for garrisoning the principal towns, and protecting the sea-coasts from the insults of the Turks[t].

Cortes of Castile held at Toledo.

It was happy for the Emperor that the abilities of his generals extricated him out of these difficulties, which it exceeded his own power to have removed. He had depended, as his chief resource for discharging the arrears due to his soldiers, upon the subsidies which he expected from his Castilian subjects. For this purpose, he assembled the Cortes of Castile at Toledo, and having represented to them the extraordinary expence of his military operations, together with the

[t] Jovii Histor. l. xxxvii. 203. c. Sandov. Ferreras, ix. 209.

great

BOOK VI.

1539.

The complaints and dissatisfaction of that assembly.

great debts in which these had necessarily involved him, he proposed to levy such supplies as the present exigency of his affairs demanded, by a general excise on commodities. But the Spaniards already felt themselves oppressed with a load of taxes unknown to their ancestors. They had often complained that their country was drained not only of its wealth but of its inhabitants, in order to prosecute quarrels in which it was not interested, and to fight battles from which it could reap no benefit, and they determined not to add voluntarily to their own burdens, or to furnish the Emperor with the means of engaging in new enterprizes no less ruinous to the kingdom than most of those which he had hitherto carried on. The nobles, in particular, inveighed with great vehemence against the imposition proposed, as an encroachment upon the valuable and distinguishing privilege of their order, that of being exempted from the payment of any tax. They demanded a conference with the representatives of the cities concerning the state of the nation. They contended that if Charles would imitate the example of his predecessors, who had resided constantly in Spain, and would avoid entangling himself in a multiplicity of transactions foreign to the concerns of his Spanish dominions, the stated revenues of the crown would be fully sufficient to defray the necessary expences of government. They represented to him, that it would be unjust to lay new burdens upon the people, while this prudent and effectual method of re-establishing public credit, and

and securing national opulence, was totally neglected[t]. Charles, after employing arguments, entreaties, and promises, but without success, in order to overcome their obstinacy, dismissed the assembly with great indignation. From that period neither the nobles nor the prelates have been called to these assemblies, on pretence that such as pay no part of the public taxes, should not claim any vote in laying them on. None have been admitted to the Cortes but the procurators or representatives of eighteen cities. These, to the number of thirty-six, being two from each community, form an assembly which bears no resemblance either in power or dignity or independence to the ancient Cortes, and are absolutely at the devotion of the court in all their determinations[u]. Thus the imprudent zeal with which the Castilian nobles had supported the regal prerogative, in opposition to the claims of the commons during the commotions in the year one thousand five hundred and twenty-one, proved at last fatal to their own body. By enabling Charles to depress one of the orders in the state, they destroyed that balance to which the constitution owed its security, and put it in his power, or in that of his successors, to humble the other, and to strip it gradually of its most valuable privileges.

The ancient constitution of the Cortes subverted.

[t] Sandov. Hist. vol. ii. 269.

[u] Sandov. ibid. Le Science du Gouvernement, par M. de Real, tom. ii. p. 102.

1539.
The Spanish grandees still possessed high privileges.

At that time, however, the Spanish grandees still possessed extraordinary power as well as privileges, which they exercised and defended with an haughtiness peculiar to themselves. Of this the Emperor himself had a mortifying proof during the meeting of the Cortes at Toledo. As he was returning one day from a tournament accompanied by most of the nobility, one of the serjeants of the court, out of officious zeal to clear the way for the Emperor, struck the Duke of Infantado's horse with his batton, which that haughty grandee resenting, drew his sword, beat and wounded the officer. Charles, provoked at such an insolent deed in his presence, immediately ordered Ronquillo the judge of the court to arrest the Duke; Ronquillo advanced to execute his charge, when the constable of Castile interposing, checked him, claimed the right of jurisdiction over a grandee as a privilege of his office, and conducted Infantado to his own apartment. All the nobles present were so pleased with the boldness of the constable in asserting the rights of their order, that, deserting the Emperor, they attended him to his house with infinite applauses, and Charles returned to the palace unaccompanied by any person but the cardinal Tavera. The Emperor, how sensible soever of the affront, saw the danger of irritating a jealous and high-spirited order of men, whom the slightest appearance of offence might drive to the most unwarrantable extremities. For that reason, instead of straining

at

at any ill-timed exertion of his prerogative, he prudently connived at the arrogance of a body too potent for him to controul, and sent next morning to the Duke of Infantado, offering to inflict what punishment he pleased on the person who had affronted him. The Duke considering this as a full reparation to his honour, instantly forgave the officer; bestowing on him, besides, a considerable present as a compensation for his wound. Thus the affair was entirely forgotten[x]; nor would it have deserved to be mentioned, if it were not a striking example of the high and independent spirit of the Spanish nobles in that age, as well as an instance of the Emperor's dexterity in accommodating his conduct to the circumstances in which he was placed.

Charles was far from discovering the same condescension or lenity towards the citizens of Ghent, who not long after broke out into open rebellion against his government. An event which happened in the year one thousand five hundred and thirty-six, gave occasion to this rash insurrection so fatal to that flourishing city. At that time the Queen-dowager of Hungary, governess of the Netherlands, having received orders from her brother to invade France with all the forces which she could raise, she assembled the States of the United Provinces, and obtained from them a subsidy of twelve hundred thousand

[x] Sandov. ii. 274. Ferreras, ix. 212. Miniana, 113.

florins,

BOOK VI.
1539.
Pretensions of the citizens.

florins, to defray the expence of that undertaking. Of this sum, the county of Flanders was obliged to pay a third part as its proportion. But the citizens of Ghent, the most considerable city in that country, averse to a war with France, with which they carried on an extensive and gainful commerce, refused to pay their quota, and contended, that in consequence of stipulations between them and the ancestors of their present sovereign the Emperor, no tax could be levied upon them, unless they had given their express consent to the imposition of it. The governess, on the other hand, maintained, that as the subsidy of twelve hundred thousand florins had been granted by the States of Flanders, of which their representatives were members, they were bound, of course, to conform to what was enacted by them, as it is the first principle in society, on which the tranquillity and order of government depend, that the inclinations of the minority must be overruled by the judgment and decision of the superior number.

Proceedings against them.

THE citizens of Ghent, however, were not willing to relinquish a privilege of such high importance as that which they claimed. Having been accustomed, under the government of the house of Burgundy, to enjoy extensive immunities, and to be treated with much indulgence, they disdained to sacrifice to the delegated power of a regent, those rights and liberties which they had often and successfully asserted against their greatest Princes.

Princes. The Queen, though she endeavoured at first to sooth them, and to reconcile them to their duty by various conceffions, was at last so much irritated by the obstinacy with which they adhered to their claim, that she ordered all the citizens of Ghent, on whom she could lay hold in any part of the Netherlands, to be arrested. But this rash action made an impreffion very different from what she expected, on men, whose minds were agitated with all the violent paffions which indignation at oppreffion and zeal for liberty inspire. Less affected with the danger of their friends and companions, than irritated at the governess, they openly despised her authority, and sent deputies to the other towns of Flanders, conjuring them not to abandon their country at such a juncture, but to concur with them in vindicating its rights against the encroachments of a woman, who either did not know or did not regard their immunities. All but a few inconfiderable towns declined entering into any confederacy against the governess: they joined, however, in petitioning her to put off the term for payment of the tax so long, that they might have it in their power to send some of their number into Spain, in order to lay their title to exemption before their sovereign. This she granted with some difficulty. But Charles received their commiffioners with an haughtiness to which they were not accustomed from their ancient Princes, and enjoining them to yield the same respectful obedience to his fifter, which they owed to him in perfon, son, remitted the examination of their claim to the council of Malines. This court, which is properly a standing committee of the parliament or states of the country, and which possesses the supreme jurisdiction in all matters civil as well as criminal [y], pronounced the claim of the citizens of Ghent to be ill-founded, and appointed them forthwith to pay their proportion of the tax.

They take arms, and offer to submit to France.

ENRAGED at this decision, which they considered as notoriously unjust, and rendered desperate on seeing their rights betrayed by that very court which was bound to protect them, the people of Ghent ran to arms in a tumultuary manner; drove such of the nobility as resided among them out of the city; secured several of the Emperor's officers; put one of them to the torture, whom they accused of having stolen or destroyed the record that contained a ratification of the privileges of exemption from taxes which they pleaded; chose a council to which they committed the direction of their affairs; gave orders for repairing and adding to their fortifications; and openly erected the standard of rebellion against their sovereign [z]. Sensible, however, of their inability to support what their zeal had prompted them to undertake, and desirous of securing a protector against the for-

[y] Descrittione di tutti Paesi Bassi di Lud. Guicciardini. Ant. 1571. fol. p. 53.

[z] Memoires sur la Revolte de Gantois en 1539, par Jean d'Hollander, ecrit en 1547. A la Haye, 1747. P. Heuter. Rer. Austr. lib. xi. p. 262. Sandov. Histor. tom. ii. p. 282.

midable

midable forces by which they might expect soon to be attacked, they sent some of their number to Francis, offering not only to acknowledge him as their sovereign, and to put him in immediate possession of Ghent, but to assist him with all their forces in recovering those provinces in the Netherlands, which had anciently belonged to the crown of France, and had been so lately re-united to it by the decree of the parliament of Paris. This unexpected proposition coming from persons who had it in their power to have performed instantly one part of what they undertook, and who could contribute so effectually towards the execution of the whole, opened great as well as alluring prospects to Francis's ambition. The counties of Flanders and Artois were of greater value than the dutchy of Milan, which he had so long laboured to acquire with passionate but fruitless desire; their situation with respect to France rendered it more easy to conquer or to defend them; and they might be formed into a separate principality for the Duke of Orleans, no less suitable to his dignity than that which his father aimed at obtaining. To this, the Flemings, who were acquainted with the French manners and government, would not have been averse; and his own subjects, weary of their destructive expeditions into Italy, would have turned their arms towards this quarter with more goodwill, and with greater vigour. Several considerations, nevertheless, prevented Francis from laying hold of this opportunity, the most favourable in

BOOK VI.

1539.

Francis declines their offer.

appearance which had ever presented itself, of extending his own dominions, or distressing the Emperor. From the time of their interview at Aiguesmortes, Charles had continued to court the King of France with wonderful attention; and often flattered him with hopes of gratifying at last his wishes concerning the Milanese, by granting the investiture of it either to him or to one of his sons. But though these hopes and promises were thrown out with no other intention than to detach him from his confederacy with the Grand Seignior, or to raise suspicions in Solyman's mind by the appearance of a cordial and familiar intercourse subsisting between the courts of Paris and Madrid, Francis was weak enough to catch at the shadow by which he had been so often amused, and from eagerness to seize it, relinquished what must have proved a more substantial acquisition. Besides this, the Dauphin, jealous to excess of his brother, and unwilling that a Prince who seemed to be of a restless and enterprizing nature should obtain an establishment, which from its situation might be considered almost as a domestic one, made use of Montmorency, who, by a singular piece of good fortune, was at the same time the favourite of the father and of the son, to defeat the application of the Flemings, and to divert the King from espousing their cause. Montmorency, accordingly, represented, in strong terms, the reputation and power which Francis would acquire by recovering that footing which he had formerly in Italy, and that nothing could be so efficacious to over-

overcome the Emperor's averſion to this as a ſacred adherence to the truce, and refuſing, on an occaſion ſo inviting, to countenance the rebellious ſubjects of his rival. Francis, apt of himſelf to over-rate the value of the Milaneſe, becauſe he eſtimated it from the length of time as well as from the great efforts which he had employed in order to reconquer it, and fond of every action which had the appearance of generoſity, aſſented without difficulty to ſentiments ſo agreeable to his own, rejected the propoſitions of the citizens of Ghent, and diſmiſſed their deputies with an harſh anſwer [a].

Not ſatisfied with this, by a farther refinement in generoſity, he communicated to the Emperor his whole negociation with the malecontents, and all that he knew of their ſchemes and intentions [b]. This convincing proof of Francis's diſintereſtedneſs relieved Charles from the moſt diſquieting apprehenſions, and opened a way to extricate himſelf out of all his difficulties. He had already received full information of all the tranſactions in the Netherlands, and of the rage with which the people of Ghent had taken arms againſt his government. He was thoroughly acquainted with the genius and qualities of his ſubjects in that country; with their love of liberty; their attachment to their ancient privileges and cuſtoms; as well as the invincible

[a] Mem. de Bellay, p. 263. P. Heuter. Rer. Auſtr. lib. xi. 263.   [b] Sandov. Hiſtor. tom. ii. 284.

obstinacy with which their minds, slow but firm and persevering, adhered to any measure on which they had deliberately resolved. He easily saw what encouragement and support they might have derived from the assistance of France; and though now free from any danger on that quarter, he was still sensible that some immediate as well as vigorous interposition was necessary, in order to prevent the spirit of disaffection from spreading in a country where the number of cities, the multitude of people, together with the great wealth diffused among them by commerce, rendered it peculiarly formidable, and would supply it with inexhaustible resources. No expedient, after long deliberation, appeared to him so effectual as his going in person to the Netherlands; and the governess his sister being of the same opinion, warmly solicited him to undertake the journey. There were only two routes which he could take; one by land through Italy and Germany, the other entirely by sea, from some port in Spain to one in the Low-Countries. But the former was more tedious than suited the present exigency of his affairs; nor could he in consistency with his dignity, or even his safety, pass through Germany without such a train both of attendants and of troops, as would have added greatly to the time that he must have consumed in his journey; the latter was dangerous at this season, and while he remained uncertain with respect to the friendship of the King of England, was not to be ventured upon, unless under the convoy

voy of a powerful fleet. This perplexing situation, in which he was under the necessity of chusing, and did not know what to chuse, inspired him at last with the singular and seemingly extravagant thought of passing through France, as the most expeditious way of reaching the Netherlands. He proposed in his council to demand Francis's permission for that purpose. All his counsellors joined with one voice in condemning the measure as no less rash than unprecedented, and which must infallibly expose him to disgrace or to danger; to disgrace, if the demand were rejected in the manner that he had reason to expect; to danger, if he put his person in the power of an enemy whom he had often offended, who had ancient injuries to revenge, as well as subjects of present contest still remaining undecided. But Charles, who had studied the character of his rival with greater care and more profound discernment than any of his ministers, persisted in his plan, and flattered himself that it might be accomplished not only without danger to his own person, but even without the expence of any concession detrimental to his crown.

Proposes to pass through France.

WITH this view he communicated the matter to the French ambassador at his court, and sent Granvelle his chief minister to Paris, in order to obtain from Francis permission to pass through his dominions, and to promise that he would soon settle the affair of the Milanese to his satisfaction. But at the same time he entreated that Francis

To which Francis consents.

would not exact any new promise, or even insist on former engagements, at this juncture, lest whatever he should grant, under his present circumstances, might seem rather to be extorted by necessity, than to flow from friendship or the love of justice. Francis, instead of attending to the snare which such a slight artifice scarcely concealed, was so dazzled with the splendour of overcoming an enemy by acts of generosity, and so pleased with the air of superiority which the rectitude and disinterestedness of his proceedings gave him on this occasion, that he at once assented to all that was demanded. Judging of the Emperor's heart by his own, he imagined that the sentiments of gratitude, arising from the remembrance of good offices and liberal treatment, would determine him more forcibly to fulfil what he had so often promised, than the most precise stipulations that could be inserted in any treaty.

His reception in that kingdom.

Upon this, Charles, to whom every moment was precious, set out, notwithstanding the fears and suspicions of his Spanish subjects, with a small but splendid train of about an hundred persons. At Bayonne, on the frontiers of France, he was received by the Dauphin and the Duke of Orleans, attended by the constable Montmorency. The two Princes offered to go into Spain, and to remain there as hostages for the Emperor's safety; but this he rejected, declaring, that he relied with implicit confidence on the King's honour, and had never demanded, nor would accept of any other pledge

pledge for his security. In all the towns through which he passed, the greatest possible magnificence was displayed; the magistrates presented him the keys of the gates; the prison doors were set open; and, by the royal honours paid to him, he appeared more like the sovereign of the country than a foreign prince. The King advanced as far as Chatelherault to meet him; their interview was distinguished by the warmest expressions of friendship and regard. They proceeded together towards Paris, and presented to the inhabitants of that city, the extraordinary spectacle of two rival Monarchs, whose enmity had disturbed and laid waste Europe during twenty years, making their solemn entry together with all the symptoms of a confidential harmony, as if they had forgotten for ever past injuries, and would not revive hostilities for the future^e.

The Emperor's solicitude.

CHARLES remained six days at Paris; but amidst the perpetual caresses of the French court, and the various entertainments contrived to amuse or to do him honour, he discovered an extreme impatience to continue his journey, arising as much from an apprehension of danger which constantly haunted him, as from the necessity of his presence in the Low-Countries. Conscious of the disingenuity of his own intentions, he trembled when he reflected that some fatal accident might betray them to his rival, or lead him to suspect

^e Thuan. Hist. lib. i. c. 14. Mem. de Bellay, 264.

BOOK VI.
1549.

them; and though his artifices to conceal them should be succefsful, he could not help fearing that motives of interest might at last triumph over the scruples of honour, and tempt Francis to avail himself of the advantage now in his hands. Nor were there wanting persons among the French ministers, who advised the King to turn his own arts against the Emperor, and as the retribution due for so many instances of fraud or falsehood, to seize and detain his person until he granted him full satisfaction with regard to all the just claims of the French crown. But no consideration could induce Francis to violate the faith which he had pledged, nor could any argument convince him that Charles, after all the promises that he had given, and all the favours which he had received, might still be capable of deceiving him. Full of this false confidence, he accompanied him to St. Quintin; and the two Princes, who had met him on the borders of Spain, did not take leave of him until he entered his dominions in the Low-Countries.

and difingenuity.
January 24.

As soon as the Emperor reached his own territories, the French ambassadors demanded the accomplishment of what he had promised concerning the investiture of Milan; but Charles, under the plausible pretext that his whole attention was then engrossed by the consultations necessary towards suppressing the rebellion in Ghent, put off the matter for some time. But in order to prevent Francis from suspecting his sincerity,

he

he still continued to talk of his resolutions with respect to that matter in the same strain as when he entered France, and even wrote to the King much to the same purpose, though in general terms, and with equivocal expressions, which he might afterwards explain away or interpret at pleasure [a].

Reduction of Ghent;

MEANWHILE, the unfortunate citizens of Ghent, destitute of leaders capable either of directing their councils, or conducting their troops; abandoned by the French King, and unsupported by their countrymen; were unable to resist their offended sovereign, who was ready to advance against them with one body of troops which he had raised in the Netherlands, with another drawn out of Germany, and a third which had arrived from Spain by sea. The near approach of danger made them, at last, so sensible of their own folly, that they sent ambassadors to the Emperor, imploring his mercy, and offering to set open their gates at his approach. Charles, without vouchsafing them any other answer, than that he would appear among them as their sovereign, with the sceptre and the sword in his hand, began his march at the head of his troops. Though he chose to enter the city on the twenty-fourth of February, his birth-day, he was touched with nothing of that tenderness or indulgence which was natural to-

[a] Memoires de Ribier, i. 504.

wards

wards the place of his nativity. Twenty-six of the principal citizens were put to death; a greater number was sent into banishment; the city was declared to have forfeited all its privileges and immunities; the revenues belonging to it were confiscated; its ancient form of government was abolished; the nomination of its magistrates was vested for the future in the Emperor and his successors; a new system of laws and political administration was prescribed [b]; and in order to bridle the seditious spirit of the citizens, orders were given to erect a strong citadel, for defraying the expence of which a fine of an hundred and fifty thousand florins was imposed on the inhabitants, together with an annual tax of six thousand florins for the support of the garrison [c]. By these rigorous proceedings, Charles not only punished the citizens of Ghent, but set an awful example of severity before his other subjects in the Netherlands, whose immunities and privileges, partly the effect, partly the cause of their extensive commerce, circumscribed the prerogative of their Sovereign within very narrow bounds, and often stood in the way of measures which he wished to undertake, or fettered and retarded him in his operations.

CHARLES having thus vindicated and re-established his authority in the Low-Countries, and

[b] Les Coutemes & Loix du Compté de Flandre, par Alex. le Grande, 3 tom. fol. Cambray, 1719, tom. i. p. 169.

[c] Haræi Annales Brabantiæ, vol. i. 616.

being now under no neceffity of continuing the fame fcene of falfehood and diffimulation with which he had long amufed Francis, began gradually to throw afide the veil under which he had concealed his intentions with refpect to the Milanefe. At firft, he eluded the demands of the French ambaffadors, when they again reminded him of his promifes; then he propofed, by way of equivalent for the dutchy of Milan, to grant the Duke of Orleans the inveftiture of Flanders, clogging the offer, however, with impracticable conditions, or fuch as he knew would be rejected [d]. At laft, being driven from all his evafions and fubterfuges by their infifting for a categorical anfwer, he peremptorily refufed to give up a territory of fuch value, or voluntarily to make fuch a liberal addition to the ftrength of an enemy by diminifhing his own power [e]. He denied, at the fame time, that he had ever made any promife which could bind him to an action fo foolifh, and fo contrary to his own intereft [f].

OF all the tranfactions in the Emperor's life, this, without doubt, reflects the greateft difhonour on his reputation [g]. Though Charles was not extremely fcrupulous at other times about the means which he employed for accomplifhing his ends, and was not always obfervant of the ftrict pre-

[d] Mem. de Ribier, i. 509. 514.   [e] Ribier, i. 519.
[f] Bellay, 365-6.
[g] Jovii Hift. lib. xxxix. p. 238. a.

cepts

cepts of veracity and honour, he had hitherto maintained some regard for the maxims of that less precise and rigid morality by which Monarchs think themselves entitled to regulate their conduct. But, on this occasion, the scheme that he formed of deceiving a generous and openhearted Prince; the illiberal and mean artifices by which he carried it on; the insensibility with which he received all the marks of his friendship, as well as the ingratitude with which he requited them; are all equally unbecoming the dignity of his character, and inconsistent with the grandeur of his views.

This transaction exposed Francis to as much scorn as it did the Emperor to censure. After the experience of a long reign, after so many opportunities of discovering the duplicity and artifices of his rival, the credulous simplicity with which he trusted him at this juncture seemed to merit no other return than what it actually met with. Francis, however, remonstrated and exclaimed, as if this had been the first instance in which the Emperor had deceived him. Feeling, as is usual, the insult which was offered to his understanding still more sensibly than the injury done to his interest, he discovered such resentment, as made it obvious that he would lay hold on the first opportunity of being revenged, and that a war, no less rancorous than that which had so lately raged, would soon break out anew in Europe.

But

But singular as the transaction which has been related may appear, this year is rendered still more memorable by the establishment of the Order of Jesuits; a body whose influence on ecclesiastical as well as civil affairs hath been so considerable, that an account of the genius of its laws and government justly merits a place in history. When men take a view of the rapid progress of this society towards wealth and power; when they contemplate the admirable prudence with which it has been governed; when they attend to the persevering and systematic spirit with which its schemes have been carried on; they are apt to ascribe such a singular institution to the superior wisdom of its founder, and to suppose that he had formed and digested his plan with profound policy. But the Jesuits, as well as the other monastic orders, are indebted for the existence of their order not to the wisdom of their founder, but to his enthusiasm. Ignatio Loyola, whom I have already mentioned on occasion of the wound which he received in defending Pampeluna [h], was a fanatic distinguished by extravagancies in sentiment and conduct, no less incompatible with the maxims of sober reason, than repugnant to the spirit of true religion. The wild adventures, and visionary schemes, in which his enthusiasm engaged him, equal any thing recorded in the legends of the Romish saints; but are unworthy of notice in history.

[h] Vol. ii. Book ii. p. 192.

BOOK VI.

1540.
Fanaticism of Loyola its founder.

Prompted by this fanatical spirit, or incited by the love of power and distinction, from which such pretenders to superior sanctity are not exempt, Loyola was ambitious of becoming the founder of a religious order. The plan, which he formed of its constitution and laws, was suggested, as he gave out, and as his followers still teach, by the immediate inspiration of heaven[i]. But notwithstanding this high pretension, his design met at first with violent opposition. The Pope, to whom Loyola had applied for the sanction of his authority to confirm the institution, referred his petition to a committee of Cardinals. They represented the establishment to be unnecessary as well as dangerous, and Paul refused to grant his approbation of it. At last, Loyola removed all his scruples by an offer which it was impossible for any Pope to resist.

The Pope's motives for confirming the order.

He proposed that besides the three vows of poverty, of chastity, and of monastic obedience, which are common to all the orders of regulars, the members of his society should take a fourth vow of obedience to the Pope, binding themselves to go whithersoever he should command for the service of religion, and without requiring any thing from the Holy See for their support. At a time when the papal authority had received such a shock by the revolt of so many nations from the Romish church; at a time when every part of the popish system was attacked with so much violence and

[i] Compte rendu des Constitutions des Jesuits, au Parlement de Provence, par M. de Monclar, p. 285.

success,

success, the acquisition of a body of men, thus peculiarly devoted to the See of Rome, and whom it might set in opposition to all its enemies, was an object of the highest consequence. Paul, instantly perceiving this, confirmed the institution of the Jesuits by his bull; granted the most ample privileges to the members of the society; and appointed Loyola to be the first general of the order. The event hath fully justified Paul's discernment, in expecting such beneficial consequences to the See of Rome from this institution. In less than half a century, the society obtained establishments in every country that adhered to the Roman catholic church; its power and wealth increased amazingly; the number of its members became great; their character as well as accomplishments were still greater; and the Jesuits were celebrated by the friends, and dreaded by the enemies, of the Romish faith, as the most able and enterprizing order in the church.

The constitution and laws of the society were perfected by Laynez and Aquaviva, the two generals who succeeded Loyola, men far superior to their master in abilities, and in the science of government. They framed that system of profound and artful policy which distinguishes the order. The large infusion of fanaticism, mingled with its regulations, should be imputed to Loyola its founder. Many circumstances concurred in giving a peculiarity of character to the order of Jesuits, and in forming the members of it not only to take

Its constitution and genius merit particular attention.

BOOK VI.
1540.

The object of the order singular.

take a greater part in the affairs of the world than any other body of monks, but to acquire superior influence in the conduct of them.

THE primary object of almost all the monastic orders is to separate men from the world, and from any concern in its affairs. In the solitude and silence of the cloister, the monk is called to work out his own salvation by extraordinary acts of mortification and piety. He is dead to the world, and ought not to mingle in its transactions. He can be of no benefit to mankind, but by his example and by his prayers. On the contrary, the Jesuits are taught to consider themselves as formed for action. They are chosen soldiers, bound to exert themselves continually in the service of God, and of the Pope, his vicar on earth. Whatever tends to instruct the ignorant; whatever can be of use to reclaim or to oppose the enemies of the Holy See, is their proper object. That they may have full leisure for this active service, they are totally exempted from those functions, the performance of which is the chief business of other monks. They appear in no processions; they practise no rigorous austerities; they do not consume one half of their time in the repetition of tedious offices [k]. But they are required to attend to all the transactions of the world, on account of the influence which these may have upon religion; they are directed to study

[k] Compte rendu, par M. de Monclar, p. xiii. 290. Sur la Destruct. des Jesuites, par M. D'Alembert, p. 42.

study the dispositions of persons in high rank, and to cultivate their friendship[1]; and by the very constitution, as well as genius of the order, a spirit of action and intrigue is infused into all its members.

Peculiarities in the form of its policy, particularly with respect to the power of the general.

As the object of the society of Jesuits differed from that of the other monastic orders, the diversity was no less in the form of its government. The other orders are to be considered as voluntary associations, in which whatever affects the whole body, is regulated by the common suffrage of all its members. The executive power is vested in the persons placed at the head of each convent, or of the whole society; the legislative authority resides in the community. Affairs of moment, relating to particular convents, are determined in conventual chapters; such as respect the whole order are considered in general congregations. But Loyola, full of the ideas of implicit obedience, which he had derived from his military profession, appointed that the government of his order should be purely monarchical. A General, chosen for life by deputies from the several provinces, possessed power that was supreme and independent, extending to every person, and to every case. He, by his sole authority, nominated provincials, rectors, and every other officer employed in the government of the society, and could remove them at pleasure. In him was vested the

---

[1] Compte par M. de Monclar, p. 12.

sovereign administration of the revenues and funds of the order. Every member belonging to it was at his disposal; and by his uncontrolable mandate, he could impose on them any task, or employ them in what service soever he pleased. To his commands they were required not only to yield outward obedience, but to resign up to him the inclinations of their own wills, and the sentiments of their own understandings. They were to listen to his injunctions, as if they had been uttered by Christ himself. Under his direction, they were to be mere passive instruments, like clay in the hands of the potter, or like dead carcases incapable of resistance [m]. Such a singular form of policy could not fail to impress its character on all the members of the order, and to give a peculiar force to all its operations. There is not in the annals of mankind any example of such a perfect despotism, exercised not over monks shut up in the cells of a convent, but over men dispersed among all the nations of the earth.

Circumstances which enable him to exercise it with the greatest advantage.

As the constitutions of the order vest, in the General, such absolute dominion over all its members, they carefully provide for his being perfectly informed with respect to the character and abilities of his subjects. Every novice who offers himself as a candidate for entering into the order, is oblig-

---

[m] Compte rendu au Parlem. de Bretagne, par M. de Chalotais, p. 41, &c. Compte par M. de Monclar, 83. 185. 343.

ed to *manifest his conscience* to the superior, or to a person appointed by him; and in doing this is required to confess not only his sins and defects, but to discover the inclinations, the passions, and the bent of his soul. This manifestation must be renewed every six months [n]. The society, not satisfied with penetrating in this manner into the innermost recesses of the heart, directs each member to observe the words and actions of the novices; they are constituted spies upon their conduct; and are bound to disclose every thing of importance concerning them to the superior. In order that this scrutiny into their character may be as complete as possible, a long noviciate must expire, during which they pass through the several gradations of ranks in the society, and they must have attained the full age of thirty-three years before they can be admitted to take the final vows, by which they become *professed* members [o]. By these various methods, the superiors, under whose immediate inspection the novices are placed, acquire a thorough knowledge of their dispositions and talents. In order that the General, who is the soul that animates and moves the whole society, may have under his eye every thing necessary to inform or direct him, the provincials and heads of the several houses are obliged to transmit to him regular and frequent reports concerning the members under their inspec-

[n] Compte par M. de Monclar, p. 121, &c.
[o] Compte par M. de Moncl. 215. 241. Sur la Destr. des Jes. par M. d'Alemb. p. 39.

BOOK VI.
1540.

tion. In these they descend into minute details with respect to the character of each person, his abilities natural or acquired, his temper, his experience in affairs, and the particular department for which he is best fitted [p]. These reports, when digested and arranged, are entered into registers kept on purpose that the General may, at one comprehensive view, survey the state of the society in every corner of the earth; observe the qualifications and talents of its members; and thus choose, with perfect information, the instruments, which his absolute power can employ

[p] M. de Chalotais has made a calculation of the number of these reports, which the General of the Jesuits must annually receive according to the regulations of the society. These amount in all to 6584. If this sum be divided by 37, the number of provinces in the order, it will appear that 177 reports concerning the state of each province are transmitted to Rome annually. Compte, p. 52. Besides this, there may be extraordinary letters, or such as are sent by the monitors or spies whom the General and Provincials entertain in each house. Compte par M. de Moncl. p. 431. Hist. des Jesuites, Amst. 1761, tom. iv. p. 56. The provincials and heads of houses not only report concerning the members of the society, but are bound to give the General an account of the civil affairs in the country wherein they are settled, as far as their knowlege of these may be of benefit to religion. This condition may extend to every particular, so that the General is furnished with full information concerning the transactions of every Prince and State in the world. Compte par M. de Moncl. 443. Hist. des Jesuit. ibid. p. 58. When the affairs with respect to which the provincials or rectors write are of importance, they are directed to use cyphers; and each of them has a particular cypher from the General. Compte par M. Chalotais, p. 54.

in any service for which he thinks meet to destine them [q].

As it was the professed intention of the order of Jesuits to labour with unwearied zeal in promoting the salvation of men, this engaged them, of course, in many active functions. From their first institution, they considered the education of youth as their peculiar province; they aimed at being spiritual guides and confessors; they preached frequently in order to instruct the people; they set out as missionaries to convert unbelieving nations. The novelty of the institution, as well as the singularity of its objects, procured the order many admirers and patrons. The governors of the society had the address to avail themselves of every circumstance in its favour, and in a short time the number as well as influence of its members increased wonderfully. Before the expiration of the sixteenth century, the Jesuits had obtained the chief direction of the education of youth in every Catholic country in Europe. They had become the confessors of almost all its monarchs, a function of no small importance in any reign, but under a weak Prince, superior even to that of minister. They were the spiritual guides of almost every person eminent for rank or power. They possessed the highest degree of confidence and interest with the papal court, as the most

[q] Compte par M. de Moncl. p. 215. 439.—Compte par M. de Chalotais, p. 52. 222.

THE REIGN OF THE

BOOK VI.
1540.

zealous and able champions for its authority. The advantages which an active and enterprising body of men might derive from all these circumstances are obvious. They formed the minds of men in their youth. They retained an ascendant over them in their advanced years. They possessed, at different periods, the direction of the most considerable courts in Europe. They mingled in all affairs. They took part in every intrigue and revolution. The General, by means of the extensive intelligence which he received, could regulate the operations of the order with the most perfect discernment, and by means of his absolute power could carry them on with the utmost vigour and effect [r].

Progress of its wealth.

TOGETHER with the power of the order, its wealth continued to increase. Various expedients were devised for eluding the obligation of the vow of poverty. The order acquired ample possessions in every Catholic country; and by the number as well as magnificence of its public buildings, together with the value of its property,

[r] When Loyola, in the year 1540, petitioned the Pope to authorize the institution of the order, he had only ten disciples. But in the year 1608, sixty-eight years after their first institution, the number of Jesuits had increased to ten thousand five hundred and eighty-one. In the year 1710, the order possessed twenty-four *professed* houses; fifty-nine houses of probation; three hundred and forty residencies; six hundred and twelve colleges; two hundred missions; one hundred and fifty seminaries and boarding-schools; and consisted of 19,998 Jesuits. Hist. des Jesuites, tom. i. p. 20.

moveable

moveable or real, it vied with the most opulent of the monastic fraternities. Besides the sources of wealth common to all the regular clergy, the Jesuits possessed one which was peculiar to themselves. Under pretext of promoting the success of their missions, and of facilitating the support of their missionaries, they obtained a special licence from the court of Rome, to trade with the nations which they laboured to convert. In consequence of this, they engaged in an extensive and lucrative commerce, both in the East and West Indies. They opened warehouses in different parts of Europe, in which they vended their commodities. Not satisfied with trade alone, they imitated the example of other commercial societies, and aimed at obtaining settlements. They acquired possession accordingly of a large and fertile province in the southern continent of America, and reigned as sovereigns over some hundred thousand subjects [s].

UNHAPPILY for mankind, the vast influence which the order of Jesuits acquired by all these different means, has been often exerted with the most pernicious effect. Such was the tendency of that discipline observed by the society in forming its members, and such the fundamental maxims in its constitution, that every Jesuit was taught to regard the interest of the order as the capital object, to which every consideration was to be sacri-

Pernicious effects of these on civil society.

[s] Hist. des Jes. iv. 168—196, &c.

ficed.

ficed. This spirit of attachment to their order, the most ardent, perhaps, that ever influenced any body of men[t], is the characteristic principle of the Jesuits, and serves as a key to the genius of their policy, as well as to the peculiarities in their sentiments and conduct.

As it was for the honour and advantage of the society, that its members should possess an ascendant over persons in high rank or of great power, the desire of acquiring and preserving such a direction of their conduct, with greater facility, has led the Jesuits to propagate a system of relaxed and pliant morality, which accommodates itself to the passions of men, which justifies their vices, which tolerates their imperfections, which authorizes almost every action that the most audacious or crafty politician would wish to perpetrate.

As the prosperity of the order was intimately connected with the preservation of the papal authority, the Jesuits, influenced by the same principle of attachment to the interests of their society, have been the most zealous patrons of those doctrines, which tend to exalt ecclesiastical power on the ruins of civil government. They have attributed to the court of Rome a jurisdiction as extensive and absolute as was claimed by the most presumptuous pontiffs in the dark ages. They

[t] Compte par M. de Moncl. p. 285.

have contended for the entire independence of ecclesiastics on the civil magistrate. They have published such tenets concerning the duty of opposing Princes who were enemies of the Catholic faith, as countenanced the most atrocious crimes, and tended to dissolve all the ties which connect subjects with their rulers.

As the order derived both reputation and authority from the zeal with which it stood forth in defence of the Romish church against the attacks of the reformers, its members, proud of this distinction, have considered it as their peculiar function to combat the opinions, and to check the progress of the Protestants. They have made use of every art, and have employed every weapon against them. They have set themselves in opposition to every gentle or tolerating measure in their favour. They have incessantly stirred up against them all the rage of ecclesiastical and civil persecution.

Monks of other denominations have, indeed, ventured to teach the same pernicious doctrines, and have held opinions equally inconsistent with the order and happiness of civil society. But they, from reasons which are obvious, have either delivered such opinions with greater reserve, or have propagated them with less success. Whoever recollects the events which have happened in Europe during two centuries, will find that the Jesuits

THE REIGN OF THE

BOOK VI.
1540.

Jesuits may justly be considered as responsible for most of the pernicious effects arising from that corrupt and dangerous casuistry, from those extravagant tenets concerning ecclesiastical power, and from that intolerant spirit, which have been the disgrace of the church of Rome throughout that period, and which have brought so many calamities upon civil society [u].

Some advantages resulting from the institution of this order.

But amidst many bad consequences flowing from the institution of this order, mankind, it must be acknowledged, have derived from it some considerable advantages. As the Jesuits made the education of youth one of their capital objects, and as their first attempts to establish colleges for the reception of students were violently opposed by the universities in different countries, it became necessary for them, as the most effectual method of acquiring the public favour, to surpass their rivals in science and industry.

Particularly to literature.

This prompted them to cultivate the study of ancient literature with extraordinary ardour. This put them upon various methods for facilitating the instruction of youth; and by the improvements which they made in it, they have contributed so much towards the progress of polite learning, that on this account they have merited well of society. Nor has the order of Jesuits been successful only in teaching the elements

[u] Encyclopedie, art. *Jesuites*, tom. viii. 513.

of literature; it has produced likewife eminent mafters in many branches of fcience, and can alone boaft of a greater number of ingenious authors, than all the other religious fraternities taken together [x].

BOOK VI.

1549.

But it is in the new world that the Jefuits have exhibited the moft wonderful difplay of their abilities, and have contributed moft effectually to the benefit of the human fpecies. The conquerors of that unfortunate quarter of the globe acted at firft as if they had nothing in view, but to plunder, to

More efpecially from the fettlement of the Jefuits in Paraguay.

---

[x] M. d'Alembert has obferved, that though the Jefuits have made extraordinary progrefs in erudition of every fpecies; though they can reckon up many of their brethren who have been eminent mathematicians, antiquaries, and critics; though they have even formed fome orators of reputation; yet the order has never produced one man, whofe mind was fo much enlightened with found knowledge, as to merit the name of a philofopher. But it feems to be the unavoidable effect of monaftic education to contract and fetter the human mind. The partial attachment of a monk to the intereft of his order, which is often incompatible with that of other citizens; the habit of implicit obedience to the will of a fuperior, together with the frequent return of the wearifome and frivolous duties of the cloifter, debafe his faculties, and extinguifh that generofity of fentiment and fpirit, which qualifies men for thinking or feeling juftly with refpect to what is proper in life and conduct. Father Paul of Venice is, perhaps, the only perfon educated in a cloifter, that ever was altogether fuperior to its prejudices, or who viewed the tranfactions of men, and reafoned concerning the interefts of fociety, with the enlarged fentiments of a philofopher, with the difcernment of a man converfant in affairs, and with the liberality of a gentleman.

enflave,

enslave, and to exterminate its inhabitants. The Jesuits alone made humanity the object of their settling there. About the beginning of the last century they obtained admission into the fertile province of Paraguay, which stretches across the southern continent of America, from the east side of the immense ridge of the Andes, to the confines of the Spanish and Portuguese settlements on the banks of the river de la Plata. They found the inhabitants in a state little different from that which takes place among men when they first begin to unite together; strangers to the arts; subsisting precariously by hunting or fishing; and hardly acquainted with the first principles of subordination and government. The Jesuits set themselves to instruct and to civilize these savages. They taught them to cultivate the ground, to rear tame animals, and to build houses. They brought them to live together in villages. They trained them to arts and manufactures. They made them taste the sweets of society; and accustomed them to the blessings of security and order. These people became the subjects of their benefactors; who have governed them with a tender attention, resembling that with which a father directs his children. Respected and beloved almost to adoration, a few Jesuits presided over some hundred thousand Indians. They maintained a perfect equality among all the members of the community. Each of them was obliged to labour not for himself alone, but for the public. The produce of their fields, together with the fruits

fruits of their industry of every species, were deposited in common storehouses, from which each individual received every thing necessary for the supply of his wants. By this institution, almost all the passions which disturb the peace of society, and render the members of it unhappy, were extinguished. A few magistrates, chosen from among their countrymen, by the Indians themselves, watched over the public tranquillity, and secured obedience to the laws. The sanguinary punishments frequent under other governments were unknown. An admonition from a Jesuit; a slight mark of infamy; or, on some singular occasion, a few lashes with a whip, were sufficient to maintain good order among these innocent and happy people[y].

BOOK VI.

1540.

But even in this meritorious effort of the Jesuits for the good of mankind, the genius and spirit of their order have mingled and are discernible. They plainly aimed at establishing in Paraguay an independent empire, subject to the society alone, and which, by the superior excellence of its constitution and police, could scarcely have failed to extend its dominion over all the southern continent of America. With this view, in order to prevent the Spaniards or Portuguese in the adjacent settlements, from acquiring any dangerous influence over the people within the

Even here the ambition and policy of the order discernible.

[y] Hist. du Paraguay par Pere de Charlevoix, tom. ii. 42, &c. Voyage au Perou par Don G. Juan & D. Ant. de Ulloa, tom. i. 540, &c. Par. 4to. 1752.

limits

limits of the province subject to the society, the Jesuits endeavoured to inspire the Indians with hatred and contempt of these nations. They cut off all intercourse between their subjects and the Spanish or Portuguese settlements. They prohibited any private trader of either nation from entering their territories. When they were obliged to admit any person in a public character from the neighbouring governments, they did not permit him to have any conversation with their subjects, and no Indian was allowed even to enter the house where these strangers resided, unless in the presence of a Jesuit. In order to render any communication between them as difficult as possible, they industriously avoided giving the Indians any knowledge of the Spanish, or of any other European language; but encouraged the different tribes, which they had civilized, to acquire a certain dialect of the Indian tongue, and laboured to make that the universal language throughout their dominions. As all these precautions, without military force, would have been insufficient to have rendered their empire secure and permanent, they instructed their subjects in the European arts of war. They formed them into bodies of cavalry and infantry, completely armed and regularly disciplined. They provided a great train of artillery, as well as magazines stored with all the implements of war. Thus they established an army so numerous and well-appointed, as to be formidable in a country, where a few sickly and ill-disciplined battalions composed all the military

military force kept on foot by the Spaniards or Portuguese[z].

The Jesuits gained no considerable degree of power during the reign of Charles V. who, with his usual sagacity, discerned the dangerous tendency of the institution, and checked its progress[a]. But as the order was founded in the period of which I write the history, and as the age to which I address this work hath seen its fall, the view which I have exhibited of the laws and genius of this formidable body will not, I hope, be unacceptable to my readers; especially as one circumstance has enabled me to enter into this detail with particular advantage. Europe had observed, for two centuries, the ambition and power of the order. But while it felt many fatal effects of these, it could not fully discern the causes to which they were to be imputed. It was unacquainted with many of the singular regulations in the political constitution or government of the Jesuits, which formed the enterprising spirit of intrigue that distinguished its members, and elevated the body itself to such a height of power. It was a fundamental maxim with the Jesuits, from their first institution, not to publish the rules of their order. These they kept concealed as an impenetrable mystery. They never communi-

Reason for giving so full a view of the government and progress of the order.

[z] Voyage de Juan & de Ulloa, tom. i. 549. Recueil des toutes les Pieces qui ont paru sur les Affaires des Jesuites en Portugal, tom. i. p. 7, &c.
[a] Compte par M. de Moncl. p. 312.

cated

cated them to strangers; nor even to the greater part of their own members. They refused to produce them when required by courts of justice [b]; and by a strange solecism in policy, the civil power in different countries authorised or connived at the establishment of an order of men, whose constitution and laws were concealed with a solicitude, which alone was a good reason for excluding them. During the prosecutions lately carried on against them in Portugal and France, the Jesuits have been so inconsiderate as to produce the mysterious volumes of their institute. By the aid of these authentic records, the principles of their government may be delineated, and the sources of their power investigated with a degree of certainty and precision, which, previous to that event, it was impossible to attain [c]. But as I have pointed out the dangerous tendency of the constitution and spirit of the order with the freedom becoming an historian, the candour and impartiality no less requisite in that

[b] Hist. des Jes. tom. iii. 236, &c. Compte par. M. de Chalot. p. 38.

[c] The greater part of my information concerning the government and laws of the order of Jesuits, I have derived from the reports of M. de Chalotais and M. de Monclar. I rest not my narrative, however, upon the authority even of these respectable magistrates and elegant writers, but upon innumerable passages which they have extracted from the constitutions of the order, deposited in their hands. Hospinian, a Protestant Divine of Zurich, in his *Historia Jesuitica*, printed A. D. 1619, published a small part of the constitutions of the Jesuits. of which by some accident he had got a copy; p. 13—54.

character

character call on me to add one obfervation, That no clafs of regular clergy in the Romifh church has been more eminent for decency, and even purity of manners, than the major part of the order of Jefuits[d]. The maxims of an intriguing, ambitious, interefted policy, might influence thofe who governed the fociety, and might even corrupt the heart, and pervert the conduct of fome individuals, while the greater number, engaged in literary purfuits, or employed in the functions of religion, was left to the guidance of thofe common principles which reftrain men from vice, and excite them to what is becoming and laudable. The caufes which occafioned the ruin of this mighty body, as well as the circumftances and effects with which it has been attended in the different countries of Europe, though objects extremely worthy the attention of every intelligent obferver of human affairs, do not fall within the period of this hiftory.

No fooner had Charles re-eftablifhed order in the Low-Countries, than he was obliged to turn his attention to the affairs in Germany. The Proteftants prefled him earneftly to appoint that conference between a felect number of the divines of each party, which had been ftipulated in the convention at Francfort. The Pope confidered fuch an attempt to examine into the points in difpute, or to decide concerning them, as derogatory to his

[d] Sur la Destruct. des Jef. par M. D'Alembert, p. 55.

right of being the supreme judge in controversy; and being convinced that such a conference would either be ineffectual by determining nothing, or prove dangerous by determining too much, he employed every art to prevent it. The Emperor, however, finding it more for his interest to sooth the Germans than to gratify Paul, paid little regard to his remonstrances. In a diet held at Haguenaw, matters were ripened for the conference. In another diet assembled at Worms, the conference was begun, Melancthon on the one side and Eckius on the other, sustaining the principal part in the dispute; but after they had made some progress, though without concluding any thing, it was suspended by the Emperor's command, that it might be renewed with greater solemnity in his own presence in a diet summoned to meet at Ratisbon. This assembly was opened with great pomp, and with a general expectation that its proceedings would be vigorous and decisive. By the consent of both parties, the Emperor was entrusted with the power of nominating the persons who should manage the conference, which it was agreed should be conducted not in the form of a public disputation, but as a friendly scrutiny or examination into the articles which had given rise to the present controversies. He appointed Eckius, Gropper, and Pflug, on the part of the Catholics; Melancthon, Bucer, and Pistorius, on that of the Protestants; all men of distinguished reputation among their own adherents, and, except Eckius, all eminent for moderation, as well as desirous of peace.

peace. As they were about to begin their confultations, the Emperor put into their hands a book, compofed, as he faid, by a learned divine in the Low-Countries, with fuch extraordinary perfpicuity and temper, as, in his opinion, might go far to unite and comprehend the two contending parties. Gropper, a canon of Cologne, whom he had named among the managers of the conference, a man of addrefs as well as of erudition, was afterwards fufpected to be the author of this fhort treatife. It contained pofitions with regard to twenty-two of the chief articles in theology, which included moft of the queftions then agitated in the controverfy between the Lutherans and the church of Rome. By ranging his fentiments in a natural order, and expreffing them with great fimplicity; by employing often the very words of fcripture, or of the primitive fathers; by foftening the rigour of fome opinions, and explaining away what was abfurd in others; by conceffions, fometimes on one fide, and fometimes on the other; and efpecially by banifhing as much as poffible fcholaftic phrafes, thofe words and terms of art in controverfy, which ferve as badges of diftinction to different fects, and for which theologians often contend more fiercely than for opinions themfelves; he at laft framed his work in fuch a manner, as promifed fairer than any thing that had hitherto been attempted to compofe and to terminate religious diffentions [e].

[e] Goldaft. Conftit. Imper. ii. p. 182.

BUT the attention of the age was turned, with such acute observation, towards theological controversies, that it was not easy to impose on it by any gloss, how artful or specious soever. The length and eagerness of the dispute had separated the contending parties so completely, and had set their minds at such variance, that they were not to be reconciled by partial concessions. All the zealous Catholics, particularly the ecclesiastics who had a seat in the diet, joined in condemning Gropper's treatise as too favourable to the Lutheran opinion, the poison of which heresy it conveyed, as they pretended, with greater danger, because it was in some degree disguised. The rigid Protestants, especially Luther himself, and his patron the Elector of Saxony, were for rejecting it as an impious compound of error and truth, craftily prepared that it might impose on the weak, the timid, and the unthinking. But the divines, to whom the examination of it was committed, entered upon that business with greater deliberation and temper. As it was more easy in itself, as well as more consistent with the dignity of the church, to make concessions, and even alterations with regard to speculative opinions, the discussion whereof is confined chiefly to schools, and which present nothing to the people that either strikes their imagination or affects their senses, they came to an accommodation about these without much labour, and even defined the great article concerning justification to their mutual satisfaction. But, when they proceeded to points

points of jurifdiction, where the intereft and authority of the Roman See were concerned, or to the rites and forms of external worfhip, where every change that could be made muft be public, and draw the obfervation of the people, there the Catholics were altogether untractable; nor could the church either with fafety or with honour abolifh its ancient inftitutions. All the articles relative to the power of the Pope, the authority of councils, the adminiftration of the facraments, the worfhip of faints, and many other particulars, did not, in their nature, admit of any temperament; fo that after labouring long to bring about an accommodation with refpect to thefe, the Emperor found all his endeavours ineffectual. Being impatient, however, to clofe the diet, he at laft prevailed on a majority of the members to approve of the following recefs; "That the articles concerning which the divines had agreed in the conference, fhould be held as points decided, and be obferved inviolably by all; that the other articles about which they had differed, fhould be referred to the determination of a general council, or if that could not be obtained, to a national fynod of Germany; and if it fhould prove impracticable, likewife, to affemble a fynod, that a general diet of the Empire fhould be called within eighteen months, in order to give fome final judgment upon the whole controverfy; that the Emperor fhould ufe all his intereft and authority with the Pope, to procure the meeting either

BOOK VI.

1541.

Recefs of the diet of Ratifbon in favour of a general council, July 28.

BOOK VI.
1541.

gives offence both to Papists and Protestants.

Charles courts the Protestants.

either of a general council or synod; that, in the mean time, no innovations should be attempted, no endeavours should be employed to gain proselytes; and neither the revenues of the church, nor the rights of monasteries, should be invaded [f].

ALL the proceedings of this diet, as well as the recess in which they terminated, gave great offence to the Pope. The power which the Germans had assumed of appointing their own divines to examine and determine matters of controversy, he considered as a very dangerous invasion of his rights; the renewing of their ancient proposal concerning a national synod, which had been so often rejected by him and his predecessors, appeared extremely undutiful; but the bare mention of allowing a diet, composed chiefly of laymen, to pass judgment with respect to articles of faith, was deemed no less criminal and profane, than the worst of those heresies which they seemed zealous to suppress. On the other hand, the Protestants were no less dissatisfied with a recess, that considerably abridged the liberty which they enjoyed at that time. As they murmured loudly against it, Charles, unwilling to leave any seeds of discontent in the Empire, granted them a private declaration in the most ample terms, exempting them from whatever they thought op-

[f] Sleidan, 267, &c. Pallav. l. iv. c. 11. p. 136. F. Paul, p. 86. Seckend. l. iii. 256.

pressive

pressive or injurious in the recess, and ascertaining to them the full possession of all the privileges which they had ever enjoyed [g].

Affairs of Hungary.

Extraordinary as these concessions may appear, the situation of the Emperor's affairs at this juncture made it necessary for him to grant them. He foresaw a rupture with France to be not only unavoidable, but near at hand, and durst not give any such cause of disgust or fear to the Protestants, as might force them, in self-defence, to court the protection of the French King, from whom, at present, they were much alienated. The rapid progress of the Turks in Hungary, was a more powerful and urgent motive to that moderation which Charles discovered. A great revolution had happened in that kingdom; John Zapol Scæpus having chosen, as has been related, rather to possess a tributary kingdom, than to renounce the royal dignity to which he had been accustomed, had, by the assistance of his mighty protector Solyman, wrested from Ferdinand a great part of the country, and left him only the precarious possession of the rest. But being a prince of pacific qualities, the frequent attempts of Ferdinand, or of his partisans among the Hungarians, to recover what they had lost, greatly disquieted him; and the necessity on these occasions, of calling in the Turks, whom he considered

[g] Sleid. 283. Seckend. 366. Dumont Corps Diplom. iv. p. ii. p. 210.

and felt to be his masters rather than auxiliaries, was hardly less mortifying. In order, therefore, to avoid these distresses, as well as to secure quiet and leisure for cultivating the arts and enjoying amusements in which he delighted, he secretly came to an agreement with his competitor, on this condition; That Ferdinand should acknowledge him as King of Hungary, and leave him, during life, the unmolested possession of that part of the kingdom now in his power; but that, upon his demise, the sole right of the whole should devolve upon Ferdinand [h]. As John had never been married, and was then far advanced in life, the terms of the contract seemed very favourable to Ferdinand. But, soon after, some of the Hungarian nobles, solicitous to prevent a foreigner from ascending their throne, prevailed on John to put an end to a long celibacy, by marrying Isabella, the daughter of Sigismond King of Poland. John had the satisfaction, before his death, which happened within less than a year after his marriage, to see a son born to inherit his kingdom. To him, without regarding his treaty with Ferdinand, which he considered, no doubt, as void, upon an event not foreseen when it was concluded, he bequeathed his crown; appointing the Queen and George Martinuzzi, bishop of Waradin, guardians of his son, and regents of the kingdom. The greater part of the Hungarians immediately acknowledged the young Prince as King, to whom, in

Death of the King of Hungary.

[g] Istuanhaffii Hist. Hung. lib. xii. p. 135.

EMPEROR CHARLES V. 217

memory of the founder of their monarchy, they gave the name of Stephen[1].

Ferdinand, though extremely disconcerted by this unexpected event, resolved not to abandon the kingdom which he flattered himself with having acquired by his compact with John. He sent ambassadors to the Queen to claim possession, and to offer the province of Transylvania as a settlement for her son, preparing at the same time to assert his right by force of arms. But John had committed the care of his son to persons, who had too much spirit to give up the crown tamely, and who possessed abilities sufficient to defend it. The Queen, to all the address peculiar to her own sex, added a masculine courage, ambition, and magnanimity. Martinuzzi, who had raised himself from the lowest rank in life to his present dignity, was one of those extraordinary men, who, by the extent as well as variety of their talents, are fitted to act a superior part in bustling and factious times. In discharging the functions of his ecclesiastical office, he put on the semblance of an humble and austere sanctity. In civil transactions, he discovered industry, dexterity, and boldness. During war he laid aside the cassock, and appeared on horseback with his scymitar and buckler, as active, as ostentatious, and as gallant as any of his countrymen. Amidst all these different and contradictory forms which he could assume, an insa-

Ferdinand's efforts to obtain the crown.

Character and power of Martinuzzi.

---
[1] Jovii Hist. lib. xxxix. p. 239, a. &c.

tiable

tiable desire of dominion and authority was conspicuous. From such persons it was obvious what answer Ferdinand had to expect. He soon perceived that he must depend on arms alone for recovering Hungary. Having levied for this purpose a considerable body of Germans, whom his partisans among the Hungarians joined with their vassals, he ordered them to march into that part of the kingdom which adhered to Stephen. Martinuzzi, unable to make head against such a powerful army in the field, satisfied himself with holding out the towns, all of which, especially Buda, the place of greatest consequence, he provided with every thing necessary for defence; and in the mean time he sent ambassadors to Solyman, beseeching him to extend towards the son, the same Imperial protection which had so long maintained the father on his throne. The Sultan, though Ferdinand used his utmost endeavours to thwart this negociation, and even offered to accept of the Hungarian crown on the same ignominious condition of paying tribute to the Ottoman Porte, by which John had held it, saw such prospects of advantage from espousing the interest of the young King, that he instantly promised him his protection; and commanding one army to advance forthwith towards Hungary, he himself followed with another. Meanwhile the Germans, hoping to terminate the war by the reduction of a city in which the King and his mother were shut up, had formed the siege of Buda. Martinuzzi, having drawn thither the strength of

the

the Hungarian nobility, defended the town with such courage and skill, as allowed the Turkish forces time to come up to its relief. They instantly attacked the Germans, weakened by fatigue, diseases, and desertion, and defeated them with great slaughter [k].

Solyman soon after joined his victorious troops, and being weary of so many expensive expeditions undertaken in defence of dominions which were not his own, or being unable to resist this alluring opportunity of seizing a kingdom, while possessed by an infant, under the guardianship of a woman and a priest, he allowed interested confiderations to triumph with too much facility over the principles of honour and the sentiments of humanity. What he planned ungenerously, he executed by fraud. Having prevailed on the Queen to send her son, whom he pretended to be desirous of seeing, into his camp, and having, at the same time, invited the chief of the nobility to an entertainment there, while they, suspecting no treachery, gave themselves up to the mirth and jollity of the feast, a select band of troops by the Sultan's orders seized one of the gates of Buda. Being thus master of the capital, of the King's person, and of the leading men among the nobles, he gave orders to conduct the Queen, together with her son, to Transylvania, which province he allotted to them, and appointing a

Solyman's ungenerous conduct.

[k] Istuanhaffii Hist. Hung. lib. xiv. p. 150.

Basha

Basha to preside in Buda with a large body of soldiers, annexed Hungary to the Ottoman empire. The tears and complaints of the unhappy Queen had no influence to change his purpose, nor could Martinuzzi either resist his absolute and uncontroulable command, or prevail on him to recall it¹.

Ferdinand's overtures to Solyman.

BEFORE the account of this violent usurpation reached Ferdinand, he was so unlucky as to have dispatched other ambassadors to Solyman with a fresh representation of his right to the crown of Hungary, as well as a renewal of his former overture to hold the kingdom of the Ottoman Porte, and to pay for it an annual tribute. This ill-timed proposal was rejected with scorn. The Sultan, elated with success, and thinking that he might prescribe what terms he pleased to a Prince who voluntarily proffered conditions so unbecoming his own dignity, declared that he would not suspend the operations of war, unless Ferdinand instantly evacuated all the towns which he still held in Hungary, and consented to the imposition of a tribute upon Austria, in order to reimburse the sums which his presumptuous invasion of Hungary had obliged the Ottoman Porte to expend in defence of that kingdom ᵐ.

---

¹ Istuanhaffii Hist. Hung. lib. xiv. p. 56. Jovii Histor. lib. xxxix. p. 2476, &c.

ᵐ Istuanhaffii Hist. Hung. lib. xiv. p. 158.

EMPEROR CHARLES V.

IN this state were the affairs of Hungary. As the unfortunate events there had either happened before the dissolution of the diet at Ratisbon, or were dreaded at that time, Charles saw the danger of irritating and inflaming the minds of the Germans, while a formidable enemy was ready to break into the Empire; and perceived that he could not expect any vigorous assistance either towards the recovery of Hungary, or the defence of the Austrian frontier, unless he courted and satisfied the Protestants. By the concessions which have been mentioned, he gained this point, and such liberal supplies both of men and money were voted for carrying on the war against the Turks, as left him under little anxiety about the security of Germany during next campaign[n].

IMMEDIATELY upon the conclusion of the diet, the Emperor set out for Italy. As he passed through Lucca he had a short interview with the Pope; but nothing could be concluded concerning the proper method of composing the religious disputes in Germany, between two Princes, whose views and interest with regard to that matter were at this juncture so opposite. The Pope's endeavours to remove the causes of discord between Charles and Francis, and to extinguish those mutual animosities which threatened to break out suddenly into open hostility, were not more successful.

[n] Sleid. 283.

THE

THE Emperor's thoughts were bent so entirely, at that time, on the great enterprize which he had concerted against Algiers, that he listened with little attention to the Pope's schemes or overtures, and hastened to join his army and fleet [o].

ALGIERS still continued in that state of dependence on the Turkish empire to which Barbarossa had subjected it. Ever since he, as Captain Basha, commanded the Ottoman fleet, Algiers had been governed by Hascen-Aga, a renegado eunuch, who, by passing through every station in the Corsair's service, had acquired such experience in war, that he was well fitted for a station which required a man of tried and daring courage. Hascen, in order to shew how well he deserved that dignity, carried on his piratical depredations against the Christian States with amazing activity, and outdid, if possible, Barbarossa himself in boldness and cruelty. The commerce of the Mediterranean was greatly interrupted by his cruisers, and such frequent alarms given to the coast of Spain, that there was a necessity of erecting watch-towers at proper distances, and of keeping guards constantly on foot, in order to descry the approach of his squadrons, and to protect the inhabitants from their descents [p]. Of this the Emperor had received repeated and clamorous complaints from his subjects, who represented it as an enterprise corresponding to

[o] Sandov. Histor. tom. ii. 298.
[p] Jovii Hist. l. xl. p. 266.

his power, and becoming his humanity, to reduce Algiers, which, since the conquest of Tunis, was the common receptacle of all the free-booters; and to exterminate that lawless race, the implacable enemies of the Christian name. Moved partly by their entreaties, and partly allured by the hope of adding to the glory which he had acquired by his last expedition into Africa, Charles, before he left Madrid, in his way to the Low-Countries, had issued orders both in Spain and Italy to prepare a fleet and army for this purpose. No change in circumstances, since that time, could divert him from this resolution, or prevail on him to turn his arms towards Hungary; though the success of the Turks in that country seemed more immediately to require his presence there; though many of his most faithful adherents in Germany urged that the defence of the Empire ought to be his first and peculiar care; though such as bore him no good-will ridiculed his preposterous conduct in flying from an enemy almost at hand, that he might go in quest of a remote and more ignoble foe. But to attack the Sultan in Hungary, how splendid soever that measure might appear, was an undertaking which exceeded his power, and was not consistent with his interest. To draw troops out of Spain or Italy, to march them into a country so distant as Hungary, to provide the vast apparatus necessary for transporting thither the artillery, ammunition, and baggage of a regular army, and to push the war in that quarter, where there was little prospect of bringing it to an issue during several campaigns,

campaigns, were undertakings so expensive and unwieldy as did not correspond with the low condition of the Emperor's treasury. While his principal force was thus employed, his dominions in Italy and the Low-Countries must have lain open to the French King, who would not have allowed such a favourable opportunity of attacking them to go unimproved. Whereas the African expedition, the preparations for which were already finished, and almost the whole expence of it defrayed, would depend upon a single effort; and besides the security and satisfaction which the success of it must give his subjects, would detain him during so short a space, that Francis could hardly take advantage of his absence, to invade his dominions in Europe.

His preparations.

ON all these accounts, Charles adhered to his first plan, and with such determined obstinacy, that he paid no regard to the Pope, who advised, or to Andrew Doria who conjured him not to expose his whole armament to almost unavoidable destruction, by venturing to approach the dangerous coast of Algiers at such an advanced season of the year, and when the autumnal winds were so violent. Having embarked on board Doria's gallies at Porto-Venere in the Genoese territories, he soon found that this experienced sailor had not judged wrong concerning the element with which he was so well acquainted; for such a storm arose that it was with the utmost difficulty and danger he reached Sardinia, the place of general rendezvous.

vous. But as his courage was undaunted, and his temper often inflexible, neither the renewed remonstrances of the Pope and Doria, nor the danger to which he had already been exposed by disregarding their advice, had any other effect than to confirm him in his fatal resolution. The force, indeed, which he had collected, was such as might have inspired a Prince less adventurous, and less confident in his own schemes, with the most sanguine hopes of success. It consisted of twenty thousand foot, and two thousand horse, Spaniards, Italians, and Germans, mostly veterans, together with three thousand volunteers, the flower of the Spanish and Italian nobility, fond of paying court to the Emperor by attending him in his favourite expedition, and eager to share in the glory which they believed he was going to reap; to these were added a thousand soldiers sent from Malta by the order of St. John, led by an hundred of its most gallant Knights.

Lands in Africa.

THE voyage, from Majorca to the African coast, was not less tedious, or full of hazard, than that which he had just finished. When he approached the land, the roll of the sea, and vehemence of the winds, would not permit the troops to disembark. But at last, the Emperor, seizing a favourable opportunity, landed them without opposition, not far from Algiers, and immediately advanced towards the town. To oppose this mighty army, Hascen had only eight hundred Turks, and five thousand Moors, partly natives

BOOK VI.
1541.

of Africa, and partly refugees from Granada. He returned, however, a fierce and haughty anſwer when ſummoned to ſurrender. But with ſuch a handful of ſoldiers, neither his deſperate courage, nor conſummate ſkill in war, could have long reſiſted forces ſuperior to thoſe which had defeated Barbaroſſa at the head of ſixty thouſand men, and which had reduced Tunis, in ſpite of all his endeavours to ſave it.

The diſaſters which befel his army,

But how far ſoever the Emperor might think himſelf beyond the reach of any danger from the enemy, he was ſuddenly expoſed to a more dreadful calamity, and one againſt which human prudence and human efforts availed nothing. On the ſecond day after his landing, and before he had time for any thing but to diſperſe ſome light-armed Arabs who moleſted his troops on their march, the clouds began to gather, and the heavens to appear with a fierce and threatening aſpect. Towards evening, rain began to fall, accompanied with violent wind; and the rage of the tempeſt increaſing, during the night, the ſoldiers, who had brought nothing aſhore but their arms, remained expoſed to all its fury, without tents, or ſhelter, or cover of any kind. The ground was ſoon ſo wet that they could not lie down on it; their camp being in a low ſituation was overflowed with water, and they ſunk at every ſtep to the ankles in mud; while the wind blew with ſuch impetuoſity, that, to prevent their falling, they were obliged to thruſt their ſpears into the ground,

and

and to support themselves by taking hold of them. Hascen was too vigilant an officer to allow an enemy in such distress to remain unmolested. About the dawn of morning, he sallied out with soldiers, who having been screened from the storm under their own roofs, were fresh and vigorous. A body of Italians, who were stationed nearest the city, dispirited and benumbed with cold, fled at the approach of the Turks. The troops at the post behind them discovered greater courage; but as the rain had extinguished their matches, and wet their powder, their muskets were useless, and having scarcely strength to handle their other arms, they were soon thrown into confusion. Almost the whole army, with the Emperor himself in person, was obliged to advance, before the enemy could be repulsed, who, after spreading such general consternation, and killing a considerable number of men, retired at last in good order.

BUT all feeling or remembrance of this loss and danger were quickly obliterated by a more dreadful as well as affecting spectacle. It was now broad day; the hurricane had abated nothing of its violence, and the sea appeared agitated with all the rage of which that destructive element is capable; all the ships, on which alone the whole army knew that their safety and subsistence depended, were seen driven from their anchors, some dashing against each other, some beat to pieces on the rocks, many forced ashore, and not a few

few sinking in the waves. In less than an hour, fifteen ships of war, and an hundred and forty transports with eight thousand men, perished; and such of the unhappy crews as escaped the fury of the sea, were murdered without mercy by the Arabs, as soon as they reached land. The Emperor stood in silent anguish and astonishment beholding this fatal event, which at once blasted all his hopes of success, and buried in the depths the vast stores which he had provided, as well for annoying the enemy, as for subsisting his own troops. He had it not in his power to afford them any other assistance or relief than by sending some troops to drive away the Arabs, and thus delivering a few who were so fortunate as to get ashore from the cruel fate which their companions had met with. At last the wind began to fall, and to give some hopes that as many ships might escape, as would be sufficient to save the army from perishing by famine, and transport them back to Europe. But these were only hopes; the approach of evening covered the sea with darkness; and it being impossible for the officers aboard the ships which had outlived the storm, to send any intelligence to their companions who were ashore, they remained during the night in all the anguish of suspense and uncertainty. Next day, a boat dispatched by Doria, made shift to reach land, with information, that having weathered out the storm, to which, during fifty years knowledge of the sea, he had never seen any equal in fierceness and horror,

ror, he had found it neceffary to bear away with his fhattered fhips to Cape Metafuz. He advifed the Emperor, as the face of the fky was ftill lowering and tempeftuous, to march with all fpeed to that place, where the troops could re-embark with greater eafe.

Obliged to retreat. WHATEVER comfort this intelligence afforded Charles, from being affured that part of his fleet had efcaped, was balanced by the new cares and perplexity in which it involved him with regard to his army. Metafuz was at leaft three days march from his prefent camp; all the provifions which he had brought afhore at his firft landing were now confumed; his foldiers, worn out with fatigue, were hardly able for fuch a march, even in a friendly country; and being difpirited by a fucceffion of hardfhips, which victory itfelf would fcarcely have rendered tolerable, they were in no condition to undergo new toils. But the fituation of the army was fuch, as allowed not one moment for deliberation, nor left it in the leaft doubtful what to choofe. They were ordered inftantly to march, the wounded, the fick, and the feeble, being placed in the centre; fuch as feemed moft vigorous were ftationed in the front and rear. Then the fad effects of what they had fuffered began to appear more manifeftly than ever, and new calamities were added to all thofe which they had already endured. Some could hardly bear the weight of their arms; others, fpent with the toil of forcing their way through deep and almoft impaffable roads, funk down

down and died; many perished by famine, as the whole army subsisted chiefly on roots and berries, or the flesh of horses, killed by the Emperor's order, and distributed among the several battalions; many were drowned in brooks, which were swoln so much by the excessive rains, that in passing them they waded up to the chin; not a few were killed by the enemy, who, during the greatest part of their retreat, alarmed, harassed, and annoyed them night and day. At last they arrived at Metafuz; and the weather being now so calm as to restore their communication with the fleet, they were supplied with plenty of provisions, and cheered with the prospect of safety.

His fortitude of mind.

DURING this dreadful series of calamities, the Emperor discovered great qualities, many of which a long continued flow of prosperity had scarcely afforded him an opportunity of displaying. He appeared conspicuous for firmness and constancy of spirit, for magnanimity, fortitude, humanity, and compassion. He endured as great hardships as the meanest soldier; he exposed his own person wherever danger threatened; he encouraged the desponding; visited the sick and wounded; and animated all by his words and example. When the army embarked, he was among the last who left the shore, although a body of Arabs hovered at no great distance, ready to fall on the rear. By these virtues, Charles atoned, in some degree, for his obstinacy and presumption in undertaking an expedition so fatal to his subjects.

THE calamities which attended this unfortunate enterprize did not end here; for no sooner were the forces got on board, than a new storm arising, though less furious than the former, scattered the fleet, and obliged them, separately, to make towards such ports in Spain or Italy as they could first reach; thus spreading the account of their disasters, with all the circumstances of aggravation and horror, which their imagination, still under the influence of fear, suggested. The Emperor himself, after escaping great dangers, and being forced into the port of Bugia in Africa, where he was obliged by contrary winds to remain several weeks, arrived at last in Spain, in a condition very different from that in which he had returned from his former expedition against the Infidels [z].

[z] Carol. V. Expeditio ad Argyriam, per Nicolaum Villagnonem Equitem Rhodium, ap. Scardium, v. ii. 365. Jovii Hist. l. xl. p. 269, &c. Vera y Zuniga Vida de Carlos V. p. 83. Sandov. Histor. ii. 299, &c.

THE HISTORY

OF THE

REIGN

OF THE

EMPEROR CHARLES V.

BOOK VII.

THE calamities which the Emperor suffered in his unfortunate enterprize against Algiers were great; and the account of these, which augmented in proportion as it spread at a greater distance from the scene of his disasters, encouraged Francis to begin hostilities, on which he had been for some time resolved. But he did not think it prudent to produce, as the motives of this resolution, either his ancient pretensions to the dutchy of Milan, or the Emperor's disingenuity in violating his repeated promises with regard to the restitution of that country. The former might have been a good reason against concluding the truce of Nice, but was none for breaking it; the latter could not be urged without exposing his own

1541. Renewal of hostilities by Francis, and his motives for it.

own credulity as much as the Emperor's want of integrity. A violent and unwarrantable action of one of the Imperial generals furnished him with a reason to justify his taking arms, which was of greater weight than either of these, and such as would have roused him, if he had been as desirous of peace as he was eager for war. Francis, by signing the treaty of truce at Nice, without consulting Solyman, gave (as he foresaw) great offence to that haughty Monarch, who considered an alliance with him as an honour of which a Christian prince had cause to be proud. The friendly interview of the French King with the Emperor in Provence, followed by such extraordinary appearances of union and confidence which distinguished the reception of Charles when he passed through the dominions of Francis to the Low-Countries, induced the Sultan to suspect that the two rivals had at last forgotten their ancient enmity, in order that they might form such a general confederacy against the Ottoman power, as had been long wished for in Christendom, and often attempted in vain. Charles, with his usual art, endeavoured to confirm and strengthen these suspicions, by instructing his emissaries at Constantinople, as well as in those courts with which Solyman held any intelligence, to represent the concord between him and Francis to be so entire, that their sentiments, views, and pursuits, would be the same for the future [a]. It was not without difficulty

---

[a] Mem. de Ribier, tom. i. p. 502.

culty that Francis effaced thefe impreffions; but the addrefs of Rincon, the French ambaffador at the Porte, together with the manifeft advantage of carrying on hoftilities againft the houfe of Auftria in concert with France, prevailed at length on the Sultan not only to banifh his fufpicions, but to enter into a clofer conjunction with Francis than ever. Rincon returned into France, in order to communicate to his mafter a fcheme of the Sultan's, for gaining the concurrence of the Venetians in their operations againft the common enemy. Solyman having lately concluded a peace with that republic, to which the mediation of Francis and the good offices of Rincon had greatly contributed, thought it not impoffible to allure the fenate by fuch advantages, as, together with the example of the French Monarch, might overbalance any fcruples arifing either from decency or caution, that could operate on the other fide. Francis, warmly approving of this meafure, difpatched Rincon back to Conftantinople, and, directing him to go by Venice along with Fregofo, a Genoefe exile, whom he appointed his ambaffador to that republic, empowered them to negociate the matter with the fenate, to whom Solyman had fent an envoy for the fame purpofe [b]. The marquis del Guafto, governor of the Milanefe, an officer of great abilities, but capable of attempting and executing the moft atrocious actions, got intelligence of the motions and deftination of thefe ambaffadors. As he

[b] Hift. de Venet. de Paruta, iv. 125.

The murder of his ambassadors his pretext for this.

knew how much his master wished to discover the intentions of the French King, and of what consequence it was to retard the execution of his measures, he employed some soldiers belonging to the garrison of Pavia to lie in wait for Rincon and Fregoso as they sailed down the Po, who murdered them and most of their attendants, and seized their papers. Upon receiving an account of this barbarous outrage, committed, during the subsistence of a truce, against persons held sacred by the most uncivilized nations, Francis's grief for the unhappy fate of two servants whom he loved and trusted, his uneasiness at the interruption of his schemes by their death, and every other passion, were swallowed up and lost in the indignation which this insult on the honour of his crown excited. He exclaimed loudly against Guasto, who, having drawn upon himself all the infamy of assassination without making any discovery of importance, as the ambassadors had left their instructions and other papers of consequence behind them, now boldly denied his being accessary in any wise to the crime. He sent an ambassador to the Emperor, to demand suitable reparation for an indignity, which no prince, how inconsiderable or pusillanimous soever, could tamely endure: and when Charles, impatient at that time to set out on his African expedition, endeavoured to put him off with an evasive answer, he appealed to all the courts in Europe, setting forth the heinousness of the injury, the spirit of moderation with which he had applied for redress, and the iniquity

quity of the Emperor in disregarding this just request.

NOTWITHSTANDING the confidence with which Guasto asserted his own innocence, the accusations of the French gained greater credit than all his protestations; and Bellay, the French commander in Piedmont, procured, at length, by his industry and address, such a minute detail of the transaction, with the testimony of so many of the parties concerned, as amounted almost to a legal proof of the marquis's guilt. In consequence of this opinion of the public, confirmed by such strong evidence, Francis's complaints were universally allowed to be well founded, and the steps which he took towards renewing hostilities, were ascribed not merely to ambition or resentment, but to the unavoidable necessity of vindicating the honour of his crown [c].

HOWEVER just Francis might esteem his own cause, he did not trust so much to that, as to neglect the proper precautions for gaining other allies besides the Sultan, by whose aid he might counterbalance the Emperor's superior power. But his negociations to this effect were attended with very little success. Henry VIII. eagerly bent at that time upon schemes against Scotland, which he knew would at once dissolve his union with France, was inclinable rather to take part

[c] Bellay, 367, &c. Jovii Hist. lib. xl. 268.

with

with the Emperor, than to contribute in any degree towards favouring the operations againſt him. The Pope adhered inviolably to his ancient ſyſtem of neutrality. The Venetians, notwithſtanding Solyman's ſolicitations, imitated the Pope's example. The Germans, ſatisfied with the religious liberty which they enjoyed, found it more their intereſt to gratify than to irritate the Emperor; ſo that the Kings of Denmark and Sweden, who on this occaſion were firſt drawn in to intereſt themſelves in the quarrels of the more potent Monarchs of the ſouth, and the duke of Cleves, who had a diſpute with the Emperor about the poſſeſſion of Gueldres, were the only confederates whom Francis ſecured. But the dominions of the two former lay at ſuch a diſtance, and the power of the latter was ſo inconſiderable, that he gained little by their alliance.

<small>Francis's induſtry in preparing for war.</small>

But Francis by vigorous efforts of his own activity ſupplied every defect. Being afflicted at this time with a diſtemper, which was the effect of his irregular pleaſures, and which prevented his purſuing them with the ſame licentious indulgence, he applied to buſineſs with more than his uſual induſtry. The ſame cauſe which occaſioned this extraordinary attention to his affairs, rendered him moroſe and diſſatisfied with the miniſters whom he had hitherto employed. This accidental peeviſhneſs being ſharpened by reflecting on the falſe ſteps into which he had lately been betrayed, as well as the inſults to which he had been expoſed, ſome of thoſe

EMPEROR CHARLES V.

those in whom he had usually placed the greatest confidence felt the effects of this change in his temper, and were deprived of their offices. At last he disgraced Montmorency himself, who had long directed affairs, as well civil as military, with all the authority of a minister no less beloved than trusted by his master; and Francis being fond of shewing that the fall of such a powerful favourite did not affect the vigour or prudence of his administration, this was a new motive to redouble his diligence in preparing to open the war by some splendid and extraordinary effort.

BOOK VII.

1541.

He accordingly brought into the field five armies. One to act in Luxembourg under the duke of Orleans, accompanied by the duke of Lorraine as his instructor in the art of war. Another commanded by the dauphin marched towards the frontiers of Spain. A third led by Van Rossem the marshal of Gueldres, and composed chiefly of the troops of Cleves, had Brabant allotted for the theatre of its operations. A fourth, of which the duke of Vendome was general, hovered on the borders of Flanders. The last, consisting of the forces cantoned in Piedmont, was destined for the Admiral Annebaut. The dauphin and his brother were appointed to command where the chief exertions were intended, and the greatest honour to be reaped; the army of the former amounted to forty thousand, that of the latter to thirty thousand men. Nothing appears more surprising than that Francis did not pour

1542. He brings five armies into the field.

with

with these numerous and irresistible armies into the Milanese, which had so long been the object of his wishes as well as enterprizes; and that he should choose rather to turn almost his whole strength into another direction, and towards new conquests. But the remembrance of the disasters which he had met with in his former expeditions into Italy, together with the difficulty of supporting a war carried on at such a distance from his own dominions, had gradually abated his violent inclination to obtain footing in that country, and made him willing to try the fortune of his arms in another quarter. At the same time he expected to make such a powerful impression on the frontier of Spain, where there were few towns of any strength, and no army assembled to oppose him, as might enable him to recover possession of the country of Roussillon, lately dismembered from the French crown, before Charles could bring into the field any force able to obstruct his progress. The necessity of supporting his ally the duke of Cleves, and the hope of drawing a considerable body of soldiers out of Germany by his means, determined him to act with vigour in the Low-Countries.

June. Their operations.

THE dauphin and duke of Orleans opened the campaign much about the same time; the former laying siege to Perpignan the capital of Roussillon, and the latter entering Luxembourg. The duke of Orleans pushed his operations with the greatest rapidity and success, one town falling after

after another, until no place in that large dutchy remained in the Emperor's hands but Thionville. Nor could he have failed of over-running the adjacent provinces with the same ease, if he had not voluntarily stopt short in this career of victory. But a report prevailing that the Emperor had determined to hazard a battle in order to save Perpignan, on a sudden the duke, prompted by youthful ardour, or moved, perhaps, by jealousy of his brother, whom he both envied and hated, abandoned his own conquest, and hastened towards Roussillon, in order to divide with him the glory of the victory.

On his departure some of his troops were disbanded, others deserted their colours, and the rest, cantoned in the towns which he had taken, remained inactive. By this conduct, which leaves a dishonourable imputation either on his understanding or his heart, or on both, he not only renounced whatever he could have hoped from such a promising commencement of the campaign, but gave the enemy an opportunity of recovering, before the end of summer, all the conquests which he had gained. On the Spanish frontier, the Emperor was not so inconsiderate as to venture on a battle, the loss of which might have endangered his kingdom. Perpignan, though poorly fortified, and briskly attacked, having been largely supplied with ammunition and provisions by the vigilance of Doria[d], was defended so long

[d] Sigonii Vita A. Doriæ, p. 1191.

and so vigorously by the duke of Alva, the persevering obstinacy of whose temper fitted him admirably for such a service, that at last the French, after a siege of three months, wasted by diseases, repulsed in several assaults, and despairing of success, relinquished the undertaking, and retired into their own country [e]. Thus all Francis's mighty preparations, either from some defect in his own conduct, or from the superior power and prudence of his rival, produced no effects which bore any proportion to his expence and efforts, or such as gratified, in any degree, his own hopes, or answered the expectation of Europe. The only solid advantage of the campaign was the acquisition of a few towns in Piedmont, which Bellay gained rather by stratagem and address, than by force of arms [f].

1543. Preparations for another campaign.

THE Emperor and Francis, though both considerably exhausted by such great but indecisive efforts, discovering no abatement of their mutual animosity, employed all their attention, tried every expedient, and turned themselves towards every quarter, in order to acquire new allies, together with such a reinforcement of strength as would give them the superiority in the ensuing campaign. Charles, taking advantage of the terror and resentment of the Spaniards, upon the sudden invasion of their country, prevailed on the Cortes of the several kingdoms to grant him subsidies with a

[e] Sandov. Hist. tom. ii. 315.
[f] Sandov. Hist. ii. 318. Bellay, 387, &c. Ferrer. ix. 237.

more

more liberal hand than ufual. At the fame time he borrowed a large fum from John King of Portugal, and, by way of fecurity for his repayment, put him in poffeffion of the Molucca Ifles in the Eaft Indies, with the gainful commerce of precious fpices, which that fequeftered corner of the globe yields. Not fatisfied with this, he negociated a marriage between Philip his only fon, now in his fixteenth year, and Mary daughter of that Monaach, with whom her father, the moft opulent prince in Europe, gave a large dower; and having likewife perfuaded the Cortes of Aragon and Valencia to recognife Philip as the heir of thefe crowns, he obtained from them the donative ufual on fuch occafions[g]. Thefe extraordinary fupplies enabled him to make fuch additions to his forces in Spain, that he could detach a great body into the Low-Countries, and yet referve as many as were fufficient for the defence of the kingdom. Having thus provided for the fecurity of Spain, and committed the government of it to his fon, he failed for Italy, in his way to Germany. But how attentive foever to raife the funds for carrying on the war, or eager to grafp at any new expedient for that purpofe, he was not fo inconfiderate as to accept of an overture which Paul, knowing his neceffities, artfully threw out to him. That ambitious Pontiff, no lefs fagacious to difcern, than watchful to feize opportunities of aggrandizing his family, folicited

[g] Ferreras, ix. 238. 241. Jovii Hift. lib. xlii. 298. 6.

him to grant Octavio his grandchild, whom the Emperor had admitted to the honour of being his son-in-law, the investure of the dutchy of Milan, in return for which he promised such a sum of money as would have gone far towards supplying all his present exigencies. But Charles, as well from unwillingness to alienate a province of so much value, as from disgust at the Pope, who had hitherto refused to join in the war against Francis, rejected the proposal. His dissatisfaction with Paul at that juncture was so great, that he even refused to approve his alienating Parma and Placentia from the patrimony of St. Peter, and settling them on his son and grandson as a fief to be held of the Holy See. As no other expedient for raising money among the Italian states remained, he consented to withdraw the garrisons which he had hitherto kept in the citadels of Florence and Leghorn; in consideration for which he received a large present from Cosmo di Medici, who by this means secured his own independence, and got possession of two forts, which were justly called the fetters of Tuscany [h].

The Emperor's negociations with Henry VIII.

But Charles, while he seemed to have turned his whole attention towards raising the sums necessary for defraying the expences of the year, had not been negligent of objects more distant, though no less important, and had concluded a

[h] Adriani Istoria, i. 195. Sleid. 312. Jovii Hist. lib. xliii. p. 301. Vita di Cos. Medici di Baldini, p. 34.

league

league offensive and defensive with Henry VIII. from which he derived, in the end, greater advantage than from all his other preparations. Several slight circumstances which have already been mentioned, had begun to alienate the affections of that Monarch from Francis, with whom he had been for some time in close alliance; and new incidents of greater moment had occurred to increase his disgust and animosity. Henry, desirous of establishing an uniformity in religion in both the British kingdoms, as well as fond of making proselytes to his own opinions, had formed a scheme of persuading his nephew the King of Scots to renounce the Pope's supremacy, and to adopt the same system of reformation, which he had introduced into England. This measure he pursued with his usual eagerness and impetuosity, making such advantageous offers to James, whom he considered as not over-scrupulously attached to any religious tenets, that he hardly doubted of success. His propositions were accordingly received in such a manner, that he flattered himself with having gained his point. But the Scottish ecclesiastics, foreseeing how fatal the union of their Sovereign with England must prove both to their own power, and to the established system of religion; and the partisans of France, no less convinced that it would put an end to the influence of that crown upon the public councils of Scotland; combined together, and by their insinuations defeated Henry's scheme at the very moment when he expected it to have taken effect[i]. Too

Henry's rupture with France and Scotland.

---

[i] Hist. of Scotl. vol. i. p. 71, &c. 9th edit. 8vo.

haughty to brook such a disappointment, which he imputed as much to the arts of the French, as to the levity of the Scottish Monarch, he took arms against Scotland, threatening to subdue the kingdom, since he could not gain the friendship of its King. At the same time, his resentment against Francis quickened his negociations with the Emperor, an alliance with whom he was now as forward to accept as the other could be to offer it. During this war with Scotland, and before the conclusion of his negociations with Charles, James V. died, leaving his crown to Mary his only daughter, an infant a few days old. Upon this event, Henry altered at once his whole system with regard to Scotland, and abandoning all thoughts of conquering it, aimed at what was more advantageous as well as more practicable, an union with that kingdom by a marriage between Edward his only son and the young Queen. But here, too, he apprehended a vigorous opposition from the French faction in Scotland, which began to bestir itself in order to thwart the measure. The necessity of crushing this party among the Scots, and of preventing Francis from furnishing them any effectual aid, confirmed Henry's resolution of breaking with France, and pushed him on to put a finishing hand to the treaty of confederacy with the Emperor.

Feb. 11. Alliance between Charles and Henry.

In this league were contained first of all, articles for securing their future amity and mutual defence; then were enumerated the demands which they were respectively to make upon Francis;

cis; and the plan of their operations was fixed, if he should refuse to grant them satisfaction. They agreed to require that Francis should not only renounce his alliance with Solyman, which had been the source of infinite calamities to Christendom, but also that he should make reparation for the damages which that unnatural union had occasioned; that he should restore Burgundy to the Emperor; that he should desist immediately from hostilities, and leave Charles at leisure to oppose the common enemy of the Christian faith; and that he should immediately pay the sums due to Henry, or put some towns in his hands as security to that effect. If, within forty days, he did not comply with these demands, they then engaged to invade France each with twenty thousand foot and five thousand horse, and not to lay down their arms until they had recovered Burgundy, together with the towns on the Somme, for the Emperor, and Normandy and Guienne, or even the whole realm of France, for Henry[k]. Their heralds, acccordingly, set out with these haughty requisitions; and though they were not permitted to enter France, the two Monarchs held themselves fully entitled to execute whatever was stipulated in their treaty.

FRANCIS, on his part, was not less diligent in preparing for the approaching campaign. Having early observed symptoms of Henry's dis-

Francis's negociations with Solyman.

[k] Rym. xiv. 768. Herb. 238.

BOOK VII.
1543.

gust and alienation, and finding all his endeavours to sooth and reconcile him ineffectual, he knew his temper too well not to expect that open hostilities would quickly follow upon this cessation of friendship. For this reason he redoubled his endeavours to obtain from Solyman such aid as might counterbalance the great accession of strength which the Emperor would receive by his alliance with England. In order to supply the place of the two ambassadors who had been murdered by Guasto, he sent as his envoy, first to Venice, and then to Constantinople, Paulin, who, though in no higher rank than a captain of foot, was deemed worthy of being raised to this important station, to which he was recommended by Bellay, who had trained him to the arts of negociation, and made trial of his talents and address on several occasions. Nor did he belie the opinion conceived of his courage and abilities. Hastening to Constantinople, without regarding the dangers to which he was exposed, he urged his master's demands with such boldness, and availed himself of every circumstance with such dexterity, that he soon removed all the Sultan's difficulties. As some of the Bashaws, swayed either by their own opinion, or influenced by the Emperor's emissaries, who had made their way even into this court, had declared in the Divan against acting in concert with France, he found means either to convince or silence them[k].

[k] Sandov. Histor. tom. ii. 346. Jovii Hist. lib. xli. 285, &c. 300, &c. Brantome.

At

At last he obtained orders for Barbarossa to sail with a powerful fleet, and to regulate all his operations by the directions of the French King. Francis was not equally successful in his attempts to gain the Princes of the Empire. The extraordinary rigour with which he thought it necessary to punish such of his subjects as had embraced the Protestant opinions, in order to give some notable evidence of his own zeal for the Catholic faith, and to wipe off the imputations to which he was liable from his confederacy with the Turks, placed an insuperable barrier between him and such of the Germans as interest or inclination would have prompted most readily to join him[1]. His chief advantage, however, over the Emperor, he derived on this, as on other occasions, from the contiguity of his dominions, as well as from the extent of the royal authority in France, which exempted him from all the delays and disappointments unavoidable wherever popular assemblies provide for the expences of government by occasional and frugal subsidies. Hence his domestic preparations were always carried on with vigour and rapidity, while those of the Emperor, unless when quickened by some foreign supply, or some temporary expedient, were extremely slow and dilatory.

Long before any army was in readiness to oppose him, Francis took the field in the Low Countries, *Operations in the Low-Countries.*

[1] Seck. lib. iii. 493.

Countries, against which he turned the whole weight of the war. He made himself master of Landrecy, which he determined to keep as the key to the whole province of Hainault; and ordered it to be fortified with great care. Turning from thence to the right, he entered the dutchy of Luxembourg, and found it in the same defenceless state as in the former year. While he was thus employed, the Emperor having drawn together an army, composed of all the different nations subject to his government, entered the territories of the Duke of Cleves, on whom he had vowed to inflict exemplary vengeance. This prince, whose conduct and situation were similar to that of Robert de la Mark in the first war between Charles and Francis, resembled him likewise in his fate. Unable, with his feeble army, to face the Emperor, who advanced at the head of forty-four thousand men, he retired at his approach; and the Imperialists being at liberty to act as they pleased, immediately invested Duren. That town, though gallantly defended, was taken by assault; all the inhabitants were put to the sword, and the place itself reduced to ashes. This dreadful example of severity struck the people of the country with such general terror, that all the other towns, even such as were capable of resistance, sent their keys to the Emperor; and before a body of French, detached to his assistance, could come up, the Duke himself was obliged to make his submission to Charles in the most abject manner. Being admitted into the Imperial presence, he

The Emperor becomes master of the Dutchy of Cleves, August 24.

he kneeled, together with eight of his principal subjects, and implored mercy. The Emperor allowed him to remain in that ignominious posture, and eyeing him with an haughty and severe look, without deigning to answer a single word, remitted him to his ministers. The conditions, however, which they prescribed were not so rigoous as he had reason to have expected after such a reception. He was obliged to renounce his alliance with France and Denmark; to resign all his pretensions to the dutchy of Gueldres; to enter into perpetual amity with the Emperor and King of the Romans. In return for which, all his hereditary dominions were restored, except two towns which the Emperor kept as pledges of the Duke's fidelity during the continuance of the war; and he was reinstated in his privileges as a Prince of the Empire. Not long after, Charles, as a proof of the sincerity of his reconcilement, gave him in marriage one of the daughters of his brother Ferdinand[m].

HAVING thus chastised the presumption of the Duke of Cleves, detached one of his allies from Francis, and annexed to his own dominions in the Low-Countries a considerable province which lay contiguous to them, Charles advanced towards Hainault, and laid siege to Landrecy. There, as the first fruits of his alliance with Henry, he was

[m] Haræi Annal. Brabant. t. i. 628. Recueil des Traitez, t. ii. 226.

joined by six thousand English under Sir John Wallop. The garrison, consisting of veteran troops commanded by De la Lande and Dessé, two officers of reputation, made a vigorous resistance. Francis approached with all his forces to relieve that place; Charles covered the siege; both were determined to hazard an engagement; and all Europe expected to see this contest, which had continued so long, decided at last by a battle between two great armies, led by their respective Monarchs in person. But the ground which separated their two camps was such, as put the disadvantage manifestly on his side who should venture to attack, and neither of them chose to run that risque. Amidst a variety of movements, in order to draw the enemy into the snare, or to avoid it themselves, Francis, with admirable conduct and equal good fortune, threw first a supply of fresh troops, and then a convoy of provisions, into the town, so that the Emperor, despairing of success, withdrew into winter-quarters[n], in order to preserve his army from being entirely ruined by the rigour of the season.

November. Solyman invades Hungary.

DURING this campaign, Solyman fulfilled his engagements to the French King with great punctuality. He himself marched into Hungary with a numerous army; and as the Princes of the Empire made no great effort to save a country which Charles, by employing his own force against Francis, seemed willing to sacrifice, there was no ap-

[n] Bellay, 405, &c.

pearance of any body of troops to oppose his progress. He besieged, one after another, Quinque Ecclesiæ, Alba, and Gran, the three most considerable towns in the kingdom, of which Ferdinand had kept possession. The first was taken by storm; the other two surrendered; and the whole kingdom, a small corner excepted, was subjected to the Turkish yoke[o]. About the same time, Barbarossa sailed with a fleet of an hundred and ten gallies, and coasting along the shore of Calabria, made a descent at Rheggio, which he plundered and burnt; and advancing from thence to the mouth of the Tiber, he stopt there to water. The citizens of Rome, ignorant of his destination, and filled with terror, began to fly with such general precipitation, that the city would have been totally deserted, if they had not resumed courage upon letters from Paulin the French envoy, assuring them that no violence or injury would be offered by the Turks to any state in alliance with the King his master[p]. From Ostia, Barbarossa sailed to Marseilles, and being joined by the French fleet with a body of land forces on board, under the count d'Enguien, a gallant young prince of the house of Bourbon, they directed their course towards Nice, the sole retreat of the unfortunate Duke of Savoy. There, to the astonishment and scandal of all Christendom, the Lilies of France and Crescent of Mahomet appeared in conjunction

Barbarossa's descent on Italy.

August 10.

[o] Istuanhaff. Histor. Hung. l. xv. 167.
[p] Jovii Hist. l. xliii. 304, &c. Pallavic. 160.

against

against a fortress on which the Cross of Savoy was displayed. The town, however, was bravely defended against their combined force by Montfort a Savoyard gentleman, who stood a general assault, and repulsed the enemy with great loss, before he retired into the castle. That fort, situated upon a rock, on which the artillery made no impression, and which could not be undermined, he held out so long, that Doria had time to approach with his fleet, and the Marquis del Guasto to march with a body of troops from Milan. Upon intelligence of this, the French and Turks raised the siege [q]; and Francis had not even the consolation of success, to render the infamy which he drew on himself by calling in such an auxiliary, more pardonable.

Preparations for a new campaign.

FROM the small progress of either party during this campaign, it was obvious to what a length the war might be drawn out between two princes, whose power was so equally balanced, and who, by their own talents or activity, could so vary and multiply their resources. The trial which they had now made of each other's strength might have taught them the imprudence of persisting in a war, wherein there was greater appearance of their distressing their own dominions than of conquering those of their adversary, and should have disposed both to wish for peace. If Charles and Francis

[q] Guichenon Histoire de Savoye, t. i. p. 651. Bellay, 425, &c.

had

had been influenced by confiderations of intereft or prudence alone, this, without doubt, muft have been the manner in which they would have reafoned. But the perfonal animofity, which mingled itfelf in all their quarrels, had grown to be fo violent and implacable, that, for the pleafure of gratifying it, they difregarded every thing elfe; and were infinitely more folicitous how to hurt each other, than how to fecure what would be of advantage to themfelves. No fooner then did the feafon force them to fufpend hoftilities, than, without paying any attention to the Pope's repeated endeavours or paternal exhortations to re-eftablifh peace, they began to provide for the operations of the next year with new vigour, and an activity increafing with their hatred. Charles turned his chief attention towards gaining the Princes of the Empire, and endeavoured to roufe the formidable but unwieldy ftrength of the Germanic body againft Francis. In order to underftand the propriety of the fteps which he took for that purpofe, it is neceffary to review the chief tranfactions in that country fince the diet of Ratifbon in the year one thoufand five hundred and forty-one.

Affairs of Germany.

Much about the time that affembly broke up, Maurice fucceeded his father Henry in the government of that part of Saxony which belonged to the Albertine branch of the Saxon family. This young prince, then only in his twentieth year, had, even at that early period, begun to difcover the great ta-

Maurice of Saxony fucceeds his father.

BOOK VII.
1543.

The views and conduct of this young prince.

lents which qualified him for acting such a distinguished part in the affairs of Germany. As soon as he entered upon the administration, he struck out into such a new and singular path, as shewed that he aimed, from the beginning, at something great and uncommon. Though zealously attached to the Protestant opinions, both from education and principle, he refused to accede to the league of Smalkalde, being determined, as he said, to maintain the purity of religion, which was the original object of that confederacy, but not to entangle himself in the political interests or combinations to which it had given rise. At the same time, foreseeing a rupture between Charles and the confederates of Smalkalde, and perceiving which of them was most likely to prevail in the contest, instead of that jealousy and distrust which the other Protestants expressed of all the Emperor's designs, he affected to place in him an unbounded confidence; and courted his favour with the utmost assiduity. When the other Protestants, in the year fifteen hundred and forty-two, either declined assisting Ferdinand in Hungary, or afforded him reluctant and feeble aid, Maurice marched thither in person, and rendered himself conspicuous by his zeal and courage. From the same motive, he had led to the Emperor's assistance, during the last campaign, a body of his own troops; and the gracefulness of his person, his dexterity in all military exercises, together with his intrepidity, which courted and delighted in danger, did not distinguish

guish him more in the field, than his great abilities and infinuating addrefs won upon the Emperor's confidence and favour [r]. While by this conduct, which appeared extraordinary to thofe who held the fame opinions with him concerning religion, Maurice endeavoured to pay court to the Emperor, he began to difcover fome degree of jealoufy of his coufin the Elector of Saxony. This, which proved in the fequel fo fatal to the Elector, had almoft occafioned an open rupture between them; and foon after Maurice's acceffion to the government, they both took arms with equal rage, upon account of a difpute about the right of jurifdiction over a paltry town fituated on the Moldaw. They were prevented, however, from proceeding to action by the mediation of the Landgrave of Heffe, whofe daughter Maurice had married, as well as by the powerful and authoritative admonitions of Luther [s].

BOOK VII.

1543.

AMIDST thefe tranfactions, the Pope, though extremely irritated at the Emperor's conceffions to the Proteftants at the diet of Ratifbon, was fo warmly folicited on all hands, by fuch as were moft devoutly attached to the See of Rome, no lefs than by thofe whofe fidelity or defigns he fufpected, to fummon a general council, that he found it impoffible to avoid any longer calling that affembly. The impatience for its meeting,

The Pope propofes to hold a general council at Trent.

[r] Sleid. 317. Seck. l. iii. 371. 386. 428.
[s] Sleid. 292. Seck. l. iii. 403.

and the expectations of great effects from its decisions, seemed to grow in proportion to the difficulty of obtaining it. He still adhered, however, to his original resolution of holding it in some town of Italy, where, by the number of ecclesiastics, retainers to his court, and depending on his favour, who could repair to it without difficulty or expence, he might influence and even direct all its proceedings. This proposition, though often rejected by the Germans, he instructed his nuncio to the diet held at Spires, in the year one thousand five hundred and forty-two, to renew once more; and if he found it gave no greater satisfaction than formerly, he empowered him, as a last concession, to propose for the place of meeting, Trent, a city in the Tyrol, subject to the King of the Romans, and situated on the confines between Germany and Italy. The Catholic princes in the diet, after giving it as their opinion that the council might have been held with greater advantage in Ratisbon, Cologne, or some of the great cities of the Empire, were at length induced to approve of the place which the Pope had named. The Protestants unanimously expressed their dissatisfaction, and protested that they would pay no regard to a council held beyond the precincts of the Empire, called by the Pope's authority, and in which he assumed the right of presiding[t].

THE Pope, without taking any notice of their objections, published the bull of intimation, named

[t] Sleid. 291. Seck. l. iii. 283.

three

three cardinals to preside as his legates, and appointed them to repair to Trent before the first of November, the day he had fixed for opening the council. But if Paul had desired the meeting of a council as sincerely as he pretended, he would not have pitched on such an improper time for calling it. Instead of that general union and tranquillity, without which the deliberations of a council could neither be conducted with security, nor attended with authority, such a fierce war was just kindled between the Emperor and Francis, as rendered it impossible for the ecclesiastics from many parts of Europe to resort thither in safety. The legates, accordingly, remained several months at Trent; but as no person appeared there, except a few prelates from the ecclesiastical state, the Pope, in order to avoid the ridicule and contempt which this drew upon him from the enemies of the church, recalled them and prorogued the council [u].

Obliged to prorogue it.

UNHAPPILY for the authority of the papal see, at the very time that the German Protestants took every occasion of pouring contempt upon it, the Emperor and King of the Romans found it necessary not only to connive at their conduct, but to court their favour by repeated acts of indulgence. In the same diet of Spires, in which they had protested in the most disrespectful terms against assembling a council at Trent, Ferdinand, who de-

The Emperor courts the Protestants.

[u] F. Paul, p. 97. Sleid. 296.

pended

BOOK VII.
1543.

pended on their aid for the defence of Hungary, not only permitted that protestation to be inserted in the records of the diet, but renewed in their favour all the Emperor's concessions at Ratisbon, adding to them whatever they demanded for their farther security. Among other particulars, he granted a suspension of a decree of the Imperial chamber against the city of Goslar (one of those which had entered into the league of Smalkalde), on account of its having seized the ecclesiastical revenues within its domains, and enjoined Henry Duke of Brunswick to desist from his attempts to carry that decree into execution. But Henry, a furious bigot, and no less obstinate than rash in all his undertakings, continuing to disquiet the people of Goslar by his incursions, the Elector of Saxony and Landgrave of Hesse, that they might not suffer any member of the Smalkaldic body to be oppressed, assembled their forces, declared war in form against Henry, and in the space of a few weeks, stripping him entirely of his dominions, drove him as a wretched exile to take refuge in the court of Bavaria. By this act of vengeance, no less severe than sudden, they filled all Germany with dread of their power, and the confederates of Smalkalde appeared, by this first effort of their arms, to be as ready as they were able to protect those who had joined their association [x].

Their vigorous proceedings.

[x] Sleid. 296. Commemoratio succincta Causarum Belli, &c. a Smalkaldicis contra Henr. Brunsw. ab iisdem edita: ap. Scardium, tom. ii. 307.

EMPEROR CHARLES V.

EMBOLDENED by so many concessions in their favour, as well as by the progress which their opinions daily made, the princes of the league of Smalkalde took a solemn protest against the Imperial chamber, and declined its jurisdiction for the future, because that court had not been visited or reformed according to the decree of Ratisbon, and continued to discover a most indecent partiality in all its proceedings. Not long after this, they ventured a step farther; and protesting against the recess of a diet held at Nuremberg, which provided for the defence of Hungary, refused to furnish their contingent for that purpose, unless the Imperial chamber were reformed, and full security were granted them in every point with regard to religion [y].

SUCH were the lengths to which the Protestants had proceeded, and such their confidence in their own power, when the Emperor returned from the Low-Countries, to hold a diet, which he had summoned to meet at Spires. The respect due to the Emperor, as well as the importance of the affairs which were to be laid before it, rendered this assembly extremely full. All the Electors, a great number of princes ecclesiastical and secular, with the deputies of most of the cities, were present. Charles soon perceived that this was not a time to offend the jealous spirit of the Protestants, by asserting in any high tone the authority and doctrines of the church, or by abridging, in the smallest ar-

[y] Sleid. 304. 307. Seck. l. iii. 404. 416.

ticle, the liberty which they now enjoyed; but that, on the contrary, if he expected any support from them, or wished to preserve Germany from intestine disorders while he was engaged in a foreign war, he must sooth them by new concessions, and a more ample extension of their religious privileges. He began, accordingly, with courting the Elector of Saxony, and Landgrave of Hesse, the heads of the Protestant party, and by giving up some things in their favour, and granting liberal promises with regard to others, he secured himself from any danger of opposition on their part. Having gained this capital point, he then ventured to address the diet with greater freedom. He began by representing his own zeal, and unwearied efforts with regard to two things most essential to Christendom, the procuring of a general council in order to compose the religious dissensions which had unhappily arisen in Germany, and the providing some proper means for checking the formidable progress of the Turkish arms. But he observed, with deep regret, that his pious endeavours had been entirely defeated by the unjustifiable ambition of the French King, who having wantonly kindled the flame of war in Europe, which had been so lately extinguished by the truce of Nice, rendered it impossible for the fathers of the church to assemble in council, or to deliberate with security; and obliged him to employ those forces in his own defence, which, with greater satisfaction to himself, as well as more honour to Christendom, he would have turned against the Infidels: That Francis, not thinking

thinking it enough to have called him off from opposing the Mahometans, had, with unexampled impiety, invited them into the heart of Christendom, and, joining his arms to theirs, had openly attacked the Duke of Savoy a member of the Empire: That Barbaroffa's fleet was now in one of the ports of France, waiting only the return of spring to carry terror and defolation to the coaft of fome Chriftian ftate: That in fuch a fituation it was folly to think of diftant expeditions againft the Turk, or of marching to oppofe his armies in Hungary, while fuch a powerful ally received him into the centre of Europe, and gave him footing there. It was a dictate of prudence, he added, to oppofe the neareft and moft imminent danger, firft of all, and by humbling the power of France, to deprive Solyman of the advantages, which he derived from the unnatural confederacy formed between him and a Monarch who ftill arrogated the name of Moft Chriftian: That, in truth, a war againft the French King and the Sultan ought to be confidered as the fame thing; and that every advantage gained over the former, was a fevere and fenfible blow to the latter: On all thefe accounts, he concluded with demanding their aid againft Francis, not merely as an enemy of the Germanic body, or of him who was its head, but as an avowed ally of the Infidels, and a public enemy to the Chriftian name.

In order to give greater weight to this violent invective of the Emperor, the King of the Romans man's stood up, and related the rapid conquests of the Sultan in Hungary, occasioned, as he said, by the fatal necessity imposed on his brother, of employing his arms against France. When he had finished, the ambassador of Savoy gave a detail of Barbarossa's operations at Nice, and of the ravages which he had committed on that coast. All these, added to the general indignation which Francis's unprecedented union with the Turks excited in Europe, made such an impression on the diet as the Emperor wished, and disposed most of the members to grant him such effectual aid as he had demanded. The ambassadors whom Francis had sent to explain the motives of his conduct, were not permitted to enter the bounds of the Empire; and the apology which they published for their master, vindicating his alliance with Solyman, by examples drawn from Scripture, and the practice of Christian princes, was little regarded by men who were irritated already, or prejudiced against him to such a degree, as to be incapable of allowing their proper weight to any arguments in his behalf.

His vast concessions in order to gain the Protestants.

SUCH being the favourable disposition of the Germans, Charles perceived that nothing could now obstruct his gaining all that he aimed at, but the fears and jealousies of the Protestants, which he determined to quiet by granting every thing that the utmost solicitude of these passions could desire for the security of their religion. With this view, he consented to a recess, whereby all the rigorous edicts hitherto issued against the Protestants

testants were suspended; a council either general or national to be assembled in Germany was declared necessary, in order to re-establish peace in the church; until one of these should be held (which the Emperor undertook to bring about as soon as possible), the free and public exercise of the Protestant religion was authorized; the Imperial chamber was enjoined to give no molestation to the Protestants; and when the term, for which the present judges in that court were elected, should expire, persons duly qualified were then to be admitted as members, without any distinction on account of religion. In return for these extraordinary acts of indulgence, the Protestants concurred with the other members of the diet, in declaring war against Francis in name of the empire; in voting the Emperor a body of twenty-four thousand foot and four thousand horse, to be maintained at the public expence for six months, to be employed against France; and at the same time the diet imposed a poll-tax to be levied throughout all Germany on every person without exception, for the support of the war against the Turks.

BOOK VII.

1544.

Aid granted by the diet.

CHARLES, while he gave the greatest attention to the minute and intricate detail of particulars necessary towards conducting the deliberations of a numerous and divided assembly to such a successful period, negociated a separate peace with the King of Denmark; who, though he had hitherto performed nothing considerable in consequence

Charles's negociations with Denmark and England.

quence of his alliance with Francis, had it in his power, however, to make a troublesome diversion in favour of that Monarch [z]. At the same time, he did not neglect proper applications to the King of England, in order to rouse him to more vigorous efforts against their common enemy. Little, indeed, was wanting to accomplish this; for such events had happened in Scotland as inflamed Henry to the most violent pitch of resentment against Francis. Having concluded with the parliament of Scotland a treaty of marriage between his son and their young Queen, by which he reckoned himself secure of effecting the union of the two kingdoms, which had been long desired, and often attempted without success by his predecessors, Mary of Guise the Queen-mother, cardinal Beatoun, and other partizans of France, found means not only to break off the match, but to alienate the Scottish nation entirely from the friendship of England, and to strengthen its ancient attachment to France. Henry, however, did not abandon an object of so much importance; and as the humbling of Francis, besides the pleasure of taking revenge upon an enemy who had disappointed a favourite measure, appeared the most effectual method of bringing the Scots to accept once more of the treaty which they had relinquished, he was so eager to accomplish this, that he was ready to second whatever the Emperor could propose to be attempted against the French king.

---

[z] Dumont Corps Diplom. t. iv. p. ii. p. 274.

king. The plan, accordingly, which they concerted, was such, if it had been punctually executed, as must have ruined France in the first place, and would have augmented so prodigiously the Emperor's power and territories, as might in the end have proved fatal to the liberties of Europe. They agreed to invade France each with an army of twenty-five thousand men, and, without losing time in besieging the frontier towns, to advance directly towards the interior provinces, and to join their forces near Paris [a].

FRANCIS stood alone in opposition to all the enemies whom Charles was mustering against him. Solyman had been the only ally who did not desert him; but the assistance which he received from him had rendered him so odious to all Christendom, that he resolved rather to forego all the advantages of his friendship, than to become, on that account, the object of general detestation. For this reason, he dismissed Barbarossa as soon as winter was over, who, after ravaging the coast of Naples and Tuscany, returned to Constantinople. As Francis could not hope to equal the forces of so many powers combined against him, he endeavoured to supply that defect by dispatch, which was more in his power, and to get the start of them in taking the field. Early in the spring the count d'Enguien invested Carignan, a town in Piedmont, which the marquis del Guasto the Imperial general-

The French take the field in Piedmont.

Invest Carignan.

---

[a] Herbert, 245. Bellay, 448.

ral having surprised the former year, considered as of so much importance, that he had fortified it at great expence. The count pushed the siege with such vigour, that Guasto, fond of his own conquest, and seeing no other way of saving it from falling into the hands of the French, resolved to hazard a battle in order to relieve it. He began his march from Milan for this purpose, and as he was at no pains to conceal his intention, it was soon known in the French camp. Enguien, a gallant and enterprising young man, wished passionately to try the fortune of a battle; his troops desired it with no less ardour; but the peremptory injunction of the King not to venture a general engagement, flowing from a prudent attention to the present situation of affairs, as well as from the remembrance of former disasters, restrained him from venturing upon it. Unwilling, however, to abandon Carignan, when it was just ready to yield, and eager to distinguish his command by some memorable action, he dispatched Monluc to court, in order to lay before the King the advantages of fighting the enemy, and the hopes which he had of victory. The King referred the matter to his privy council; all the ministers declared, one after another, against fighting, and supported their sentiments by reasons extremely plausible. While they were delivering their opinions, Monluc, who was permitted to be present, discovered such visible and extravagant symptoms of impatience to speak, as well as such dissatisfaction with what he heard, that

Francis,

Francis, diverted with his appearance, called on him to declare what he could offer in reply to sentiments which seemed to be as just as they were general. Upon this, Monluc, a plain but spirited soldier, and of known courage, represented the good condition of the troops, their eagerness to meet the enemy in the field, their confidence in their officers, together with the everlasting infamy which the declining of a battle would bring on the French arms; and he urged his arguments with such lively impetuosity, and such a flow of military eloquence, as gained over to his opinion, not only the King, naturally fond of daring actions, but several of the council. Francis, catching the same enthusiasm which had animated his troops, suddenly started up, and having lifted his hands to Heaven, and implored the Divine protection, he then addressed himself to Monluc, "Go, says he, return to Piedmont, and fight in the name of God [b]."

Battle of Cerisoles.

No sooner was it known that the King had given Enguien leave to fight the Imperialists, than such was the martial ardour of the gallant and high-spirited gentlemen of that age, that the court was quite deserted, every person desirous of reputation, or capable of service, hurrying to Piedmont, in order to share, as volunteers, in the danger and glory of the action. Encouraged by the arrival of so many brave officers, Enguien

[b] Memoires de Monluc.

immediately prepared for battle, nor did Guasto decline the combat. The number of cavalry was almost equal, but the Imperial infantry exceeded the French by at least ten thousand men. They met near Cerisoles, in an open plain, which afforded to neither any advantage of ground, and both had full time to form their army in proper order. The shock was such as might have been expected between veteran troops, violent and obstinate. The French cavalry rushing forward to the charge with their usual vivacity, bore down every thing that opposed them; but, on the other hand, the steady and disciplined valour of the Spanish infantry having forced the body which they encountered to give way, victory remained in suspense, ready to declare for whichever general could make the best use of that critical moment. Guasto, engaged in that part of his army which was thrown into disorder, and afraid of falling into the hands of the French, whose vengeance he dreaded on account of the murder of Rincon and Fregoso, lost his presence of mind, and forgot to order a large body of reserve to advance; whereas Enguien, with admirable courage and equal conduct, supported, at the head of his gens d'armes, such of his battalions as began to yield; and at the same time he ordered the Swiss in his service, who had been victorious wherever they fought, to fall upon the Spaniards. This motion proved decisive. All that followed was confusion and slaughter. The marquis del Guasto, wounded in the thigh, escaped only by the swiftness of his horse. The victory of the French was complete, ten thousand of the Imperialists being slain, and a considerable number, with all their tents, baggage, and artillery, taken. On the part of the conquerors, their joy was without allay, a few only being killed, and among these no officer of distinction [c].

THIS splendid action, beside the reputation with which it was attended, delivered France from an imminent danger, as it ruined the army with which Guasto had intended to invade the country between the Rhone and Saone, where there were neither fortified towns nor regular forces to oppose his progress. But it was not in Francis's power to pursue the victory with such vigour as to reap all the advantages which it might have yielded; for though the Milanese remained now almost defenceless; though the inhabitants, who had long murmured under the rigour of the Imperial government, were ready to throw off the yoke; though Enguien, flushed with success, urged the King to seize this happy opportunity of recovering a country, the acquisition of which had been long his favourite object; yet, as the Emperor and King of England were preparing to break in upon the opposite frontier of France with numerous armies, it became necessary to sacrifice all thoughts of conquest to the public safety, and to recal

Effects of it.

[c] Bellay, 429, &c. Memoires de Monluc. Jovii Hist. l. xliv. p. 327. 6.

twelve

twelve thousand of Enguien's best troops to be employed in defence of the kingdom. Enguien's subsequent operations were, of consequence, so languid and inconsiderable, that the reduction of Carignan and some other towns in Piedmont, was all that he gained by his great victory at Cerisoles [d].

Operations in the Low-Countries.

June.

THE Emperor, as usual, was late in taking the field, but he appeared, towards the beginning of June, at the head of an army more numerous and better appointed than any which he had hitherto led against France. It amounted almost to fifty thousand men, and part of it having reduced Luxembourg and some other towns in the Netherlands, before he himself joined it, he now marched with the whole towards the frontiers of Champagne. Charles, according to his agreement with the King of England, ought to have advanced directly towards Paris; and the Dauphin, who commanded the only army to which Francis trusted for the security of his dominions in that quarter, was in no condition to oppose him. But the success with which the French had defended Provence in the year one thousand five hundred and thirty-six, had taught them the most effectual method of distressing an invading enemy. Champagne, a country abounding more in vines than corn, was incapable of maintaining a great army; and before the Emperor's approach, whatever could be

[d] Bellay, 438, &c.

of any use to his troops had been carried off or destroyed. This rendered it necessary for him to be master of some places of strength in order to secure the convoys, on which alone he now perceived that he must depend for subsistence; and he found the frontier towns so ill provided for defence, that he hoped it would not be a work either of much time or difficulty to reduce them. Accordingly Ligny and Commercy, which he first attacked, surrendered after a short resistance. He then invested St. Disier, which, though it commanded an important pass on the Marne, was destitute of every thing necessary for sustaining a siege. But the count de Sancerre and M. de la Lande, who had acquired such reputation by the defence of Landrecy, generously threw themselves into the town, and undertook to hold it out to the last extremity. The emperor soon found how capable they were of making good their promise, and that he could not expect to take the town without besieging it in form. This accordingly he undertook; and as it was his nature never to abandon any enterprise in which he had once engaged, he persisted in it with an inconsiderate obstinacy.

The Emperor invests St. Disier. July 8.

THE King of England's preparations for the campaign were complete long before the Emperor's; but as he did not choose, on the one hand, to encounter alone the whole power of France, and was unwilling, on the other, that his troops should remain inactive, he took that

Henry VIII. invests Boulogne.

VOL. III.   T   oppor-

opportunity of chastising the Scots, by sending his fleet, together with a considerable part of his infantry, under the earl of Hertford, to invade their country. Hertford executed his commission with vigour, plundered and burnt Edinburgh and Leith, laid waste the adjacent country, and reimbarked his men with such dispatch that they joined their sovereign soon after his landing in France*. When Henry arrived in that kingdom, he found the Emperor engaged in the siege of St. Disier; an ambassador, however, whom he sent to congratulate the English Monarch on his safe arrival on the continent, solicited him to march, in terms of the treaty, directly to Paris. But Charles had set his ally such an ill example of fulfilling the conditions of their confederacy with exactness, that Henry, observing him employ his time and forces in taking towns for his own behoof, saw no reason why he should not attempt the reduction of some places that lay conveniently for himself. Without paying any regard to the Emperor's remonstrances, he immediately invested Boulogne, and commanded the duke of Norfolk to press the siege of Montreuil, which had been begun before his arrival, by a body of Flemings, in conjunction with some English troops. While Charles and Henry shewed such attention each to his own interest, they both neglected the common cause. Instead of the union and confidence requisite towards conducting the great plan that they had formed, they early

* Hist. Scotland, i. 112.

discovered

discovered a mutual jealousy of each other, which, by degrees, begot distrust, and ended in open hatred[e].

By this time, Francis had, with unwearied industry, drawn together an army, capable, as well from the number as from the valour of the troops, of making head against the enemy. But the dauphin, who still acted as general, prudently declining a battle, the loss of which would have endangered the kingdom, satisfied himself with harassing the Emperor with his light troops, cutting off his convoys, and laying waste the country around him. Though extremely distressed by these operations, Charles still pressed the siege of St. Disier, which Sancerre defended with astonishing fortitude and conduct. He stood repeated assaults, repulsing the enemy in them all; and undismayed even by the death of his brave associate De la Lande, who was killed by a cannon-ball, he continued to shew the same bold countenance and obstinate resolution. At the end of five weeks, he was still in a condition to hold out some time longer, when an artifice of Granvelle's induced him to surrender. That crafty politician, having intercepted the key to the cypher which the Duke of Guise used in communicating intelligence to Sancerre, forged a letter in his name, authorizing Sancerre to capitulate, as the King, though highly satisfied with his behaviour, thought it imprudent to hazard a battle for his relief. This letter

Gallant defence of St. Disier.

[e] Herbert.

he conveyed into the town in a manner which could raise no suspicion, and the governor fell into the snare. Even then, he obtained such honourable conditions as his gallant defence merited, and among others, a cessation of hostilities for eight days, at the expiration of which he bound himself to open the gates, if Francis, during that time, did not attack the Imperial army, and throw fresh troops into the town[f]. Thus Sancerre, by detaining the Emperor so long before an inconsiderable place, afforded his sovereign full time to assemble all his forces, and what rarely falls to the lot of an officer in such an inferior command, acquired the glory of having saved his country.

August 17. The Emperor penetrates into the heart of France.

As soon as St. Disier surrendered, the Emperor advanced into the heart of Champagne, but Sancerre's obstinate resistance had damped his sanguine hopes of penetrating to Paris, and led him seriously to reflect on what he might expect before towns of greater strength, and defended by more numerous garrisons. At the same time, the procuring subsistence for his army was attended with great difficulty, which increased in proportion as he withdrew farther from his own frontier. He had lost a great number of his best troops in the siege of St. Disier, and many fell daily in skirmishes, which it was not in his power to avoid, though they wasted his army insensibly,

[f] Brantome, tom. vi. 489.

without

without leading to any decisive action. The season advanced apace, and he had not yet the command either of a sufficient extent of territory, or of any such considerable town as rendered it safe to winter in the enemy's country. Great arrears too were now due to his soldiers, who were upon the point of mutinying for their pay, while he knew not from what funds to satisfy them. All these considerations induced him to listen to the overtures of peace, which a Spanish Dominican, the confessor of his sister the Queen of France, had secretly made to his confessor, a monk of the same order. In consequence of this, plenipotentiaries were named on both sides, and began their conferences in Chauffe, a small village near Chalons. At the same time, Charles, either from a desire of making one great final effort against France, or merely to gain a pretext for deserting his ally, and concluding a separate peace, sent an ambassador formally to require Henry, according to the stipulation in their treaty, to advance towards Paris. While he expected a return from him, and waited the issue of the conferences at Chauffe, he continued to march forward, though in the utmost distress from scarcity of provisions. But at last, by a fortunate motion on his part, or through some neglect or treachery on that of the French, he surprised first Esperney and then Chateau Thierry, in both which were considerable magazines. No sooner was it known that these towns, the latter of which is not two days march from Paris, were in the hands of the enemy, than that great capital, defenceless, and susceptible of any violent alarm in proportion to its greatness, was filled with consternation. The inhabitants, as if the Emperor had been already at their gates, fled in the wildest confusion and despair, many sending their wives and children down the Seine to Roüen, others to Orleans, and the towns upon the Loire. Francis himself, more afflicted with this than with any other event during his reign, and sensible as well of the triumph that his rival would enjoy in insulting his capital, as of the danger to which the kingdom was exposed, could not refrain from crying out, in the first emotion of his surprise and sorrow, " How dear, O my God, do I pay for this crown, which I thought thou hadst granted me freely [g]!" But recovering in a moment from this sudden sally of peevishness and impatience, he devoutly added, " Thy will, however, be done;" and proceeded to issue the necessary orders for opposing the enemy with his usual activity and presence of mind. The dauphin detached eight thousand men to Paris, which revived the courage of the affrighted citizens; he threw a strong garrison into Meaux, and by a forced march got into Fertè, between the Imperialists and the capital.

Obliged to retire.

UPON this, the Emperor, who began again to feel the want of provisions, perceiving that the dauphin still prudently declined a battle, and not

[g] Brantome, tom. vi. 381.

daring to attack his camp with forces so much shattered and reduced by hard service, turned suddenly to the right, and began to fall back towards Soissons. Having about this time received Henry's answer, whereby he refused to abandon the sieges of Boulogne and Montreuil, of both which he expected every moment to get possession, he thought himself absolved from all obligations of adhering to the treaty with him, and at full liberty to consult his own interest in what manner soever he pleased. He consented, therefore, to renew the conference, which the surprise of Esperney had broken off. To conclude a peace between two princes, one of whom greatly desired, and the other greatly needed it, did not require a long negociation. It was signed at Crespy, a small town near Meaux, on the eighteenth of September. The chief articles of it were, That all the conquests which either party had made since the truce of Nice shall be restored; That the Emperor shall give in marriage to the Duke of Orleans, either his own eldest daughter, or the second daughter of his brother Ferdinand; That if he chose to bestow on him his own daughter, he shall settle on her all the provinces of the Low-Countries, to be erected into an independent state, which shall descend to the male issue of the marriage; That if he determined to give him his niece, he shall, with her, grant him the investiture of Milan and its dependencies; That he shall within four months declare which of these two Princesses he had pitched upon, and fulfil

Peace between him and Francis concluded at Crespy.

the respective conditions upon the consummation of the marriage, which shall take place within a year from the date of the treaty; That as soon as the Duke of Orleans is put in possession either of the Low-Countries or of Milan, Francis shall restore to the Duke of Savoy all that he now possesses of his territories, except Pignerol and Montmilian; That Francis shall renounce all pretensions to the kingdom of Naples, or to the sovereignty of Flanders and Artois, and Charles shall give up his claim to the dutchy of Burgundy and county of Charolois; That Francis shall give no aid to the exiled King of Navarre; That both Monarchs shall join in making war upon the Turk, towards which the King shall furnish, when required by the Emperor and Empire, six hundred men at arms, and ten thousand foot [h].

Motives of concluding it.

BESIDES the immediate motives to this peace, arising from the distress of his army through want of provisions; from the difficulty of retreating out of France, and the impossibility of securing winter-quarters there; the Emperor was influenced by other considerations, more distant indeed, but not less weighty. The Pope was offended to a great degree, as well at his concessions to the Protestants in the late diet, as at his consenting to call a council, and to admit of public disputations in Germany with a view of

[h] Recueil des Traitez, t. i. 227. Belius de Caufis Pacis Crepiac. in Actis Erudit. Lipf. 1763.

determining the doctrines in controversy. Paul considering both these steps as sacrilegious encroachments on the jurisdiction as well as privileges of the Holy See, had addressed to the Emperor a remonstrance rather than a letter on this subject, written with such acrimony of language, and in a style of such high authority, as discovered more of an intention to draw on a quarrel than of a desire to reclaim him. This ill humour was not a little inflamed by the Emperor's league with Henry of England, which being contracted with an heretic, excommunicated by the apostolic see, appeared to the Pope a profane alliance, and was not less dreaded by him than that of Francis with Solyman. Paul's son and grandson, highly incensed at the Emperor for having refused to gratify them with regard to the alienation of Parma and Placentia, contributed by their suggestions to sour and disgust him still more. To all which was added the powerful operation of the flattery and promises which Francis incessantly employed to gain him. Though from his desire of maintaining a neutrality, the Pope had hitherto suppressed his own resentment, had eluded the artifices of his own family, and resisted the solicitations of the French King, it was not safe to rely much on the steadiness of a man whom his passions, his friends, and his interest combined to shake. The union of the Pope with France, Charles well knew, would instantly expose his dominions in Italy to be attacked. The Venetians, he foresaw, would probably follow the example of a Pontiff, who was

consider-

considered as a model of political wisdom among the Italians; and thus, at a juncture when he felt himself hardly equal to the burden of the present war, he would be overwhelmed with the weight of a new confederacy against him [i]. At the same time, the Turks, almost unresisted, made such progress in Hungary, reducing town after town, that they approached near to the confines of the Austrian provinces [k]. Above all these, the extraordinary progress of the Protestant doctrines in Germany, and the dangerous combination into which the Princes of that profession had entered, called for his immediate attention. Almost one half of Germany had revolted from the established church; the fidelity of the rest was much shaken; the nobility of Austria had demanded of Ferdinand the free exercise of religion [l]; the Bohemians, among whom some seeds of the doctrines of Huss still remained, openly favoured the new opinions; the archbishop of Cologne, with a zeal which is seldom found among ecclesiastics, had begun the reformation of his diocese; nor was it possible, unless some timely and effectual check were given to the spirit of innovation, to foresee where it would end. He himself had been a witness, in the late diet, to the peremptory and decisive tone which the Protestants had now assumed. He had seen how, from confidence in their number and union,

[i] P. Paul, 100. Pallavic. 163.
[k] Istuanhaffii Hist. Hung. 177.
[l] Sleid. 285.

they

they had forgotten the humble style of their first petitions, and had grown to such boldness as openly to despise the Pope, and to shew no great reverence for the Imperial dignity itself. If, therefore, he wished to maintain either the ancient religion or his own authority, and would not choose to dwindle into a mere nominal head of the Empire, some vigorous and speedy effort was requisite on his part, which could not be made during a war that required the greatest exertion of his strength against a foreign and powerful enemy.

Such being the Emperor's inducements to peace, he had the address to frame the treaty of Crespy so as to promote all the ends which he had in view. By coming to an agreement with Francis, he took from the Pope all prospect of advantage in courting the friendship of that Monarch in preference to his. By the proviso with regard to a war with the Turks, he not only deprived Solyman of a powerful ally, but turned the arms of that ally against him. By a private article, not inserted in the treaty, that it might not raise any unseasonable alarm, he agreed with Francis that both should exert all their influence and power in order to procure a general council, to assert its authority, and to exterminate the Protestant heresy out of their dominions. This cut off all chance of assistance which the confederates of Smalkalde might expect from the French King [m]; and left

[m] Seck. l. iii. 496.

BOOK VII.
1544.

their solicitations, or his jealousy of an ancient rival, should hereafter tempt Francis to forget this engagement, he left him embarrassed with a war against England, which would put it out of his power to take any considerable part in the affairs of Germany.

War continues between France and England.

HENRY, possessed at all times with an high idea of his own power and importance, felt, in the most sensible manner, the neglect with which the Emperor had treated him in concluding a separate peace. But the situation of his affairs was such as somewhat alleviated the mortification which this occasioned. For though he was obliged to recall the Duke of Norfolk from the siege of Montreuil, because the Flemish troops received orders to retire, Boulogne had surrendered before the negociations at Crespy were brought to an issue. While elated with vanity on account of this conquest, and inflamed with indignation against the Emperor, the ambassadors whom Francis sent to make overtures of peace, found him too arrogant to grant what was moderate or equitable. His demands were indeed extravagant, and made in the tone of a conqueror; that Francis should renounce his alliance with Scotland, and not only pay up the arrears of former debts, but reimburse the money which Henry had expended in the present war. Francis, though sincerely desirous of peace, and willing to yield a great deal in order to obtain it, being now free from the pressure of the Imperial arms, rejected these ignominious propositions with

Sept. 14.

with disdain; and Henry departing for England, hostilities continued between the two nations[n].

1544.

The dauphin dissatisfied with the peace of Crespy.

THE treaty of peace, how acceptable soever to the people of France, whom it delivered from the dread of an enemy who had penetrated into the heart of the kingdom, was loudly complained of by the dauphin. He considered it as a manifest proof of the King his father's extraordinary partiality towards his younger brother, now Duke of Orleans, and complained that, from his eagerness to gain an establishment for a favourite son, he had sacrificed the honour of the kingdom, and renounced the most ancient as well as valuable rights of the crown. But as he durst not venture to offend the King by refusing to ratify it, though extremely desirous at the same time of securing to himself the privilege of reclaiming what was now alienated so much to his detriment, he secretly protested, in presence of some of his adherents, against the whole transaction; and declared whatever he should be obliged to do in order to confirm it, null in itself, and void of all obligation. The parliament of Thoulouse, probably by the instigation of his partisans, did the same[o]. But Francis, highly pleased as well with having delivered his subjects from the miseries of an invasion, as with the prospect of acquiring an independent settlement for his son at no greater price than that

[n] Mem. de Ribier, t. i. p. 572. Herbert, 244.
[o] Recueil des Traitez, t. ii. 235. 238.

of renouncing conquests to which he had no just claim; titles which had brought so much expence and so many disasters upon the nation; and rights grown obsolete and of no value; ratified the treaty with great joy. Charles, within the time prescribed by the treaty, declared his intention of giving Ferdinand's daughter in marriage to the Duke of Orleans, together with the dutchy of Milan as her dowry [p]. Every circumstance seemed to promise the continuance of peace. The Emperor, cruelly afflicted with the gout, appeared to be in no condition to undertake any enterprise where great activity was requisite, or much fatigue to be endured. He himself felt this, or wished at least that it should be believed; and being so much disabled by this excruciating distemper, when a French ambassador followed him to Brussels, in order to be present at his ratification of the treaty of peace, that it was with the utmost difficulty that he signed his name, he observed, that there was no great danger of his violating these articles, as a hand that could hardly hold a pen, was little able to brandish a lance.

The Emperor's schemes with respect to Germany.

THE violence of his disease confined the Emperor several months in Brussels, and was the apparent cause of putting off the execution of the great scheme which he had formed in order to humble the Protestant party in Germany. But there were other reasons for this delay. For,

[p] Recueil des Traitez, t. ii. 238.

however

however prevalent the motives were which determined him to undertake this enterprife, the nature of that great body which he was about to attack, as well as the fituation of his own affairs, made it neceffary to deliberate long, to proceed with caution, and not too fuddenly to throw afide the veil under which he had hitherto concealed his real fentiments and fchemes. He was fenfible that the Proteftants, confcious of their own ftrength, but under continual apprehenfions of his defigns, had all the boldnefs of a powerful confederacy joined to the jealoufy of a feeble faction; and were no lefs quick-fighted to difcern the firft appearance of danger, than ready to take arms in order to repel it. At the fame time, he ftill continued involved in a Turkifh war; and though, in order to deliver himfelf from this incumbrance, he had determined to fend an envoy to the Porte with moft advantageous and even fubmiffive overtures of peace, the refolutions of that haughty court were fo uncertain, that before thefe were known, it would have been highly imprudent to have kindled the flames of civil war in his own dominions.

UPON this account, he appeared diffatisfied with a bull iffued by the Pope immediately after the peace of Crefpy, fummoning the council to affemble at Trent early next fpring, and exhorting all Chriftian Princes to embrace the opportunity that the prefent happy interval of tranquillity afforded them, of fuppreffing thofe herefies which threatened to

The Pope fummons a general council to meet at Trent, Nov. 19.

fubvert

subvert whatever was sacred or venerable among Christians. But after such a slight expression of dislike, as was necessary in order to cover his designs, he determined to countenance the council, which might become no inconsiderable instrument towards accomplishing his projects, and therefore not only appointed ambassadors to appear there in his name, but ordered the ecclesiastics in his dominions to attend at the time prefixed [q].

Such were the Emperor's views, when the Imperial diet, after several prorogations, was opened at Worms. The Protestants, who enjoyed the free exercise of their religion by a very precarious tenure, having no other security for it than the recess of the last diet, which was to continue in force only until the meeting of a council, wished earnestly to establish that important privilege upon some firmer basis, and to hold it by a perpetual not a temporary title. But instead of offering them any additional security, Ferdinand opened the diet with observing, that there were two points, which chiefly required consideration, the prosecution of the war against the Turks, and the state of religion; that the former was the most urgent, as Solyman, after conquering the greatest part of Hungary, was now ready to fall upon the Austrian provinces; that the Emperor, who, from the beginning of his reign, had neglected no op-

[q] F. Paul, 104.

portunity of annoying this formidable enemy, and with the hazard of his own person had resisted his attacks, being animated still with the same zeal, had now consented to stop short in the career of his success against France, that, in conjunction with his ancient rival, he might turn his arms with greater vigour against the common adversary of the Christian faith; that it became all the members of the Empire to second those pious endeavours of its head; that, therefore, they ought, without delay, to vote him such effectual aid as not only their duty but their interest called upon them to furnish; that the controversies about religion were so intricate, and of such difficult discussion, as to give no hope of its being possible to bring them at present to any final issue; that by perseverance and repeated solicitations the Emperor had at length prevailed on the Pope to call a council, for which they had so often wished and petitioned; that the time appointed for its meeting was now come, and both parties ought to wait for its decrees, and submit to them as the decisions of the universal church.

Ferdinand requires the Germans to acknowledge the council.

The popish members of the diet received this declaration with great applause, and signified their entire acquiescence in every particular which it contained. The Protestants expressed great surprise at propositions, which were so manifestly repugnant to the recess of the former diet; they insisted that the questions with regard to religion, as first in dignity and importance, ought to come first

first under deliberation; that, alarming as the progress of the Turks was to all Germany, the securing the free exercise of their religion touched them still more nearly, nor could they prosecute a foreign war with spirit, while solicitous and uncertain about their domestic tranquillity; that if the latter were once rendered firm and permanent, they would concur with their countrymen in pushing the former, and yield to none of them in activity or zeal. But if the danger from the Turkish arms was indeed so imminent, as not to admit of such a delay as would be occasioned by an immediate examination of the controverted points in religion, they required that a diet should be instantly appointed, to which the final settlement of their religious disputes should be referred; and that in the mean time the decree of the former diet concerning religion should be explained in a point which they deemed essential. By the recess of Spires it was provided, that they should enjoy unmolested the public exercise of their religion, until the meeting of a legal council; but as the Pope had now called a council, to which Ferdinand had required them to submit, they began to suspect that their adversaries might take advantage of an ambiguity in the terms of the recess, and pretending that the event therein mentioned had now taken place, might pronounce them to be no longer entitled to the same indulgence. In order to guard against this interpretation, they renewed their former remonstrances against a council called to meet without the bounds of the Empire,

Empire, fummoned by the Pope's authority, and in which he affumed the right of prefiding; and declared that, notwithftanding the convocation of any fuch illegal affembly, they ftill held the recefs of the late diet to be in full force.

A<small>T</small> other junctures, when the Emperor thought it of advantage to footh and gain the Proteftants, he had devifed expedients for giving them fatisfaction with regard to demands feemingly more extravagant; but his views at prefent being very different, Ferdinand, by his command, adhered inflexibly to his firft propofitions, and would make no conceffions which had the moft remote tendency to throw difcredit on the council, or to weaken its authority. The Proteftants, on their part, were no lefs inflexible; and after much time fpent in fruitlefs endeavours to convince each other, they came to no agreement. Nor did the prefence of the Emperor, who upon his recovery arrived at Worms, contribute in any degree to render the Proteftants more compliant. Fully convinced that they were maintaining the caufe of God and of truth, they fhewed themfelves fuperior to the allurements of intereft, or the fuggeftions of fear; and in proportion as the Emperor redoubled his folicitations, or difcovered his defigns, their boldnefs feems to have increafed. At laft they openly declared, that they would not even deign to vindicate their tenets in prefence of a council, affembled not to examine, but to condemn them; and that they would pay no regard

Marginalia: BOOK VII. 1545. — Emperor arrives at Worms. — May 15. — The Proteftants difclaim all connexion with the council of Trent.

to an assembly held under the influence of a Pope, who had already precluded himself from all title to act as a judge, by his having stigmatized their opinions with the name of heresy, and denounced against them the heaviest censures, which, in the plenitude of his usurped power, he could inflict [r].

Conduct of Maurice of Saxony in this diet.

WHILE the Protestants, with such union as well as firmness, rejected all intercourse with the council, and refused their assent to the Imperial demands in respect to the Turkish war, Maurice of Saxony alone shewed an inclination to gratify the Emperor with regard to both. Though he professed an inviolable regard for the Protestant religion, he assumed an appearance of moderation peculiar to himself, by which he confirmed the favourable sentiments which the Emperor already entertained of him, and gradually paved the way for executing the ambitious designs which always occupied his active and enterprising mind [s]. His example, however, had little influence upon such as agreed with him in their religious opinions; and Charles perceived that he could not hope either to procure present aid from the Protestants against the Turks, or to quiet their fears and jealousies on account of their religion. But, as his schemes were not yet ripe for execution, nor his preparations so far advanced that he could force

[r] Sleid. 343, &c. Seck. iii. 543, &c. Thuan. Histor. lib. ii. p. 56.
[s] Seck. iii. 571.

the compliance of the Proteſtants, or puniſh their obſtinacy, he artfully concealed his own intentions. That he might augment their ſecurity, he appointed a diet to be held at Ratiſbon early next year, in order to adjuſt what was now left undetermined; and previous to it, he agreed that a certain number of divines of each party ſhould meet, in order to confer upon the points in diſpute [t].

But, how far ſoever this appearance of a deſire to maintain the preſent tranquillity might have impoſed upon the Proteſtants, the Emperor was incapable of ſuch uniform and thorough diſſimulation, as to hide altogether from their view the dangerous deſigns which he was meditating againſt them. Herman count de Wied, Archbiſhop and Elector of Cologne, a prelate conſpicuous for his virtue and primitive ſimplicity of manners, though not more diſtinguiſhed for learning than the other deſcendants of noble families, who in that age poſſeſſed moſt of the great benefices in Germany, having become a proſelyte to the doctrines of the Reformers, had begun in the year one thouſand five hundred and forty-three, with the aſſiſtance of Melancthon and Bucer, to aboliſh the ancient ſuperſtition in his dioceſe, and to introduce in its place the rites eſtabliſhed among the Proteſtants. But the canons of his cathedral, who were not poſſeſſed with the ſame ſpirit of innovation, and who foreſaw how fatal

[t] Sleid. 351.

the levelling genius of the new sect would prove to their dignity and wealth, opposed, from the beginning, this unprecedented enterprise of their Archbishop, with all the zeal flowing from reverence for old institutions, heightened by concern for their own interest. This opposition, which the Archbishop considered only as a new argument to demonstrate the necessity of a reformation, neither shook his resolution, nor slackened his ardour in prosecuting his plan. The canons, perceiving all their endeavours to check his career to be ineffectual, solemnly protested against his proceedings, and appealed for redress to the Pope and Emperor, the former as his ecclesiastical, the latter as his civil superior. This appeal being laid before the Emperor, during his residence in Worms, he took the canons of Cologne under his immediate protection; enjoined them to proceed with rigour against all who revolted from the established church; prohibited the Archbishop to make any innovation in his diocese; and summoned him to appear at Brussels within thirty days, to answer the accusations which should be preferred against him [u].

To this clear evidence of his hostile intentions against the Protestant party, Charles added other proofs still more explicit. In his hereditary dominions of the Low-Countries, he persecuted all who were suspected of Lutheranism with unrelent-

[u] Sleid. 310. 340. 351. Seckend. iii. 443. 553.

ing rigour. As soon as he arrived at Worms, he silenced the Protestant preachers in that city. He allowed an Italian monk to inveigh against the Lutherans from the pulpit of his chapel, and to call upon him, as he regarded the favour of God, to exterminate that pestilent heresy. He dispatched the embassy, which has been already mentioned, to Constantinople, with overtures of peace, that he might be free from any apprehensions of danger or interruption from that quarter. Nor did any of these steps, or their dangerous tendency, escape the jealous observation of the Protestants, or fail to alarm their fears, and to excite their solicitude for the safety of their sect.

MEANWHILE, Charles's good fortune, which predominated on all occasions over that of his rival Francis, extricated him out of a difficulty, from which, with all his sagacity and address, he would have found it no easy matter to have disentangled himself. Just about the time when the Duke of Orleans should have received Ferdinand's daughter in marriage, and together with her the possession of the Milanese, he died of a malignant fever. By this event, the Emperor was freed from the necessity of giving up a valuable province into the hands of an enemy, or from the indecency of violating a recent and solemn engagement, which must have occasioned an immediate rupture with France. He affected, however, to express great sorrow for the untimely death of a young Prince, who was to have been

BOOK VII.
1545.

so nearly allied to him; but he carefully avoided entering into any fresh discussions concerning the Milanese; and would not listen to a proposal which came from Francis of new-modelling the treaty of Crespy, so as to make him some reparation for the advantages which he had lost by the demise of his son. In the more active and vigorous part of Francis's reign, a declaration of war would have been the certain and instantaneous consequence of such a flat refusal to comply with a demand seemingly so equitable; but the declining state of his own health, the exhausted condition of his kingdom, together with the burden of the war against England, obliged him, at present, to dissemble his resentment, and to put off thoughts of revenge to some other juncture. In consequence of this event, the unfortunate Duke of Savoy lost all hope of obtaining the restitution of his territories; and the rights or claims relinquished by the treaty of Crespy, returned in full force to the crown of France, to serve as pretexts for future wars [x].

The Pope grants the dutchies of Parma and Piacentia to his son.

Upon the first intelligence of the Duke of Orleans's death, the confederates of Smalkalde flattered themselves that the essential alterations which appeared to be unavoidable consequences of it could hardly fail of producing a rupture, which would prove the means of their safety. But they were not more disappointed with regard to this, than in their

[x] Belcarii Comment. 769. Paruta, Hist. Venet. iv. p. 177.

expect-

expectations from an event which seemed to be the certain prelude of a quarrel between the Emperor and the Pope. When Paul, whose passion for aggrandizing his family increased as he advanced in years, and as he saw the dignity and power which they derived immediately from him becoming more precarious, found that he could not bring Charles to approve of his ambitious schemes, he ventured to grant his son Peter Lewis the investiture of Parma and Placentia, though at the risk of incurring the displeasure of the Emperor. At a time when a great part of Europe inveighed openly against the corrupt manners and exorbitant power of Ecclesiastics, and when a council was summoned to reform the disorders in the church, this indecent grant of such a principality, to a son of whose illegitimate birth the Pope ought to have been ashamed, and whose licentious morals all good men detested, gave general offence. Some Cardinals in the Imperial interest remonstrated against such an unbecoming alienation of the patrimony of the church; the Spanish ambassador would not be present at the solemnity of his infeofment; and upon pretext that these cities were part of the Milanese state, the Emperor peremptorily refused to confirm the deed of investiture. But both the Emperor and Pope being intent upon one common object in Germany, they sacrificed their particular passions to that public cause, and suppressed the emotions of jealousy or resentment which were rising on this occasion,

that

that they might jointly pursue what each deemed to be of greater importance^y.

Henry of Brunswick kindles a war in Germany.

ABOUT this time the peace of Germany was disturbed by a violent but short eruption of Henry Duke of Brunswick. This Prince, though still stript of his dominions, which the Emperor held in sequestration, until his differences with the confederates of Smalkalde should be adjusted, possessed however so much credit in Germany, that he undertook to raise for the French King a considerable body of troops to be employed in the war against England. The money stipulated for this purpose was duly advanced by Francis; the troops were levied; but Henry, instead of leading them towards France, suddenly entered his own dominions at their head, in hopes of recovering possession of them before any army could be assembled to oppose him. The confederates were not more surprised at this unexpected attack, than the King of France was astonished at a mean thievish fraud, so unbecoming the character of a Prince. But the Landgrave of Hesse, with incredible expedition, collected as many men as put a stop to the progress of Henry's undisciplined forces, and being joined by his son-in-law, Maurice, and by some troops belonging to the Elector of Saxony, he gained such advantages over Henry, who was rash and bold in forming his schemes, but feeble

^y Paruta, Hist. Venet. iv. 178. Pallavic. 180.

and

EMPEROR CHARLES V. 299

and undetermined in executing them, as obliged him to disband his army, and to surrender himself, together with his eldest son, prisoners at discretion. He was kept in close confinement, until a new reverse of affairs procured him liberty [z].

As this defeat of Henry's wild enterprise added new reputation to the arms of the Protestants, the establishment of the Protestant religion in the Palatinate brought a great accession of strength to their party. Frederick, who succeeded his brother Lewis in that Electorate, had long been suspected of a secret propensity to the doctrines of the Reformers, which, upon his accession to the principality, he openly manifested. But as he expected that something effectual towards a general and legal establishment of religion, would be the fruit of so many diets, conferences, and negociations, he did not, at first, attempt any public innovation in his dominions. Finding all these issue in nothing, he thought himself called, at length, to countenance by his authority the system which he approved of, and to gratify the wishes of his subjects, who, by their intercourse with the Protestant states, had almost universally imbibed their opinions. As the warmth and impetuosity which accompanied the spirit of Reformation in its first efforts, had somewhat abated, this change was made with great order and regularity; the ancient rites were abolished, and new forms introduced, without any acts of violence, or

The Reformation of the Palatinate.

Jan. 10.

[z] Sleid. 352. Seck. iii. 567.

symptom of discontent. Though Frederick adopted the religious system of the Protestants, he imitated the example of Maurice, and did not accede to the league of Smalkalde [a].

The council assembles at Trent.

A FEW weeks before this revolution in the Palatinate, the general council was opened with the accustomed solemnities at Trent. The eyes of the Catholic states were turned with much expectation towards an assembly, which all had considered as capable of applying an effectual remedy for the disorders of the church when they first broke out, though many were afraid that it was now too late to hope for great benefit from it, when the malady, by being suffered to increase during twenty-eight years, had become inveterate, and grown to such extreme violence. The Pope, by his last bull of convocation, had appointed the first meeting to be held in March. But his views, and those of the Emperor, were so different, that almost the whole year was spent in negociations. Charles, who foresaw that the rigorous decrees of the council against the Protestants would soon drive them, in self-defence as well as from resentment, to some desperate extreme, laboured to put off its meeting until his warlike preparations were so far advanced, that he might be in a condition to second its decisions by the force of his arms. The Pope, who had early sent to Trent the legates who were to preside

[a] Sleid. 356. Seck. l. iii. 616.

preside in his name, knowing to what contempt it would expose his authority, and what suspicions it would beget of his intentions, if the fathers of the council should remain in a state of inactivity, when the church was in such danger as to require their immediate and vigorous interposition, insisted either upon translating the council to some city in Italy, or upon suspending altogether its proceedings at that juncture, or upon authorizing it to begin its deliberations immediately. The Emperor rejected the two former expedients as equally offensive to the Germans of every denomination; but finding it impossible to elude the latter, he proposed that the council should begin with reforming the disorders in the church, before it proceeded to examine or define articles of faith. This was the very thing which the court of Rome dreaded most, and which had prompted it to employ so many artifices in order to prevent the meeting of such a dangerous judicatory. Paul, though more compliant than some of his predecessors with regard to calling a council, was no less jealous than they had been of its jurisdiction, and saw what matter of triumph such a method of proceeding would afford the heretics. He apprehended consequences not only humbling but fatal to the papal see, if the council came to consider an inquest into abuses as their only business; or if inferior prelates were allowed to gratify their own envy and peevishness, by prescribing rules to those who were exalted above them in dignity and power.

BOOK
VII.
1546.

power. Without listening, therefore, to this insidious proposal of the Emperor, he instructed his legates to open the council.

Jan. 18.
Its proceedings.

THE first session was spent in matters of form. In a subsequent one, it was agreed that the framing a confession of faith, wherein should be contained all the articles which the church required its members to believe, ought to be the first and principal business of the council; but that, at the same time, due attention should be given to what was necessary towards the reformation of manners and discipline. From this first symptom of the spirit with which the council was animated, from the high tone of authority which the legates who presided in it assumed, and from the implicit deference with which most of the members followed their directions, the Protestants conjectured with ease what decisions they might expect. It astonished them, however, to see forty prelates (for no greater number were yet assembled) assume authority as representatives of the universal church, and proceed to determine the most important points of doctrine in its name. Sensible of this indecency, as well as of the ridicule with which it might be attended, the council advanced slowly in its deliberations, and all its proceedings were for some time languishing and feeble [b]. As soon as the confederates of Smalkalde received inform-

[b] F. Paul, 120, &c. Pallavic. p. 180, &c.

ation of the opening of the council, they published a long manifesto, containing a renewal of their protest against its meeting, together with the reasons which induced them to decline its jurisdictions[c]. The Pope and Emperor, on their part, were so little solicitous to quicken or add vigour to its operations, as plainly discovered that some object of greater importance occupied and interested them.

Apprehensions of the Protestants.

THE Protestants were not inattentive or unconcerned spectators of the motions of the sovereign Pontiff and of Charles, and they entertained every day more violent suspicions of their intentions, in consequence of intelligence received from different quarters of the machinations carrying on against them. The King of England informed them, that the Emperor having long resolved to exterminate their opinions, would not fail to employ this interval of tranquillity which he now enjoyed, as the most favourable juncture for carrying his design into execution. The merchants of Augsburg, which was at that time a city of extensive trade, received advice, by means of their correspondents in Italy, among whom were some who secretly favoured the Protestant cause[d], that a dangerous confederacy against it was forming between the Pope and Emperor. In confirmation of this, they heard from the Low-Countries that Charles had issued orders, though with every precaution which could

[c] Seckend. l. iii. 602, &c. [d] Seck. l. iii. 579.

keep the measure concealed, for raising troops both there and in other parts of his dominions. Such a variety of information, corroborating all that their own jealousy or observation led them to apprehend, left the Protestants little reason to doubt of the Emperor's hostile intentions. Under this impression, the deputies of the confederates of Smalkalde assembled at Francfort, and by communicating their intelligence and sentiments to each other, reciprocally heightened their sense of the impending danger. But their union was not such as their situation required, or the preparations of their enemies rendered necessary. Their league had now subsisted ten years. Among so many members, whose territories were intermingled with each other, and who, according to the custom of Germany, had created an infinite variety of mutual rights and claims by intermarriages, alliances, and contracts of different kinds, subjects of jealousy and discord had unavoidably arisen. Some of the confederates, being connected with the Duke of Brunswick, were highly disgusted with the Landgrave, on account of the rigour with which he had treated that rash and unfortunate Prince. Others taxed the Elector of Saxony and Landgrave, the heads of the league, with having involved the members in unnecessary and exorbitant expences by their profuseness or want of œconomy. The views, likewise, and temper of those two Princes, who, by their superior power and authority, influenced and directed the whole body, being extremely different, rendered all its motions

tions languid, at a time when the utmost vigour and dispatch were requisite. The Landgrave, of a violent and enterprising temper, but not forgetful, amidst his zeal for religion, of the usual maxims of human policy, insisted that, as the danger which threatened them was manifest and unavoidable, they should have recourse to the most effectual expedient for securing their own safety, by courting the protection of the Kings of France and England, or by joining in alliance with the Protestant cantons of Swisserland, from whom they might expect such powerful and present assistance as their situation demanded. The Elector, on the other hand, with the most upright intentions of any Prince in that age, and with talents which might have qualified him abundantly for the administration of government in any tranquil period, was possessed with such superstitious veneration for all the parts of the Lutheran system, and such bigoted attachment to all its tenets, as made him averse to an union with those who differed from him in any article of faith, and rendered him very incapable of undertaking its defence in times of difficulty and danger. He seemed to think, that the concerns of religion were to be regulated by principles and maxims totally different from those which apply to the common affairs of life; and being swayed too much by the opinions of Luther, who was not only a stranger to the rules of political conduct, but despised them; he often discovered an uncomplying spirit, that proved of the greatest detriment to the cause which he wished to support. Influenced, on this occasion,

sion, by the severe and rigid notions of that Reformer, he refused to enter into any confederacy with Francis, because he was a persecutor of the truth; or to solicit the friendship of Henry, because he was no less impious and profane than the Pope himself; or even to join in alliance with the Swiss, because they differed from the Germans in several essential articles of faith. This dissension, about a point of such consequence, produced its natural effects. Each secretly censured and reproached the other. The Landgrave considered the Elector as fettered by narrow prejudices, unworthy of a Prince called to act a chief part in a scene of such importance. The Elector suspected the Landgrave of loose principles and ambitious views, which corresponded ill with the sacred cause wherein they were engaged. But though the Elector's scruples prevented their timely application for foreign aid; and the jealousy or discontent of the other Princes defeated a proposal for renewing their original confederacy, the term during which it was to continue in force being on the point of expiring; yet the sense of their common danger induced them to agree with regard to other points, particularly that they would never acknowledge the assembly of Trent as a lawful council, nor suffer the archbishop of Cologne to be oppressed on account of the steps which he had taken towards the reformation of his diocese [e].

[e] Seck. l. iii. 566. 576. 613. Sleid. 355.

EMPEROR CHARLES V.

1546. Their negociations with the Emperor.

THE Landgrave, about this time, desirous of penetrating to the bottom of the Emperor's intentions, wrote to Granvelle, whom he knew to be thoroughly acquainted with all his master's schemes, informing him of the several particulars which raised the suspicions of the Protestants, and begging an explicit declaration of what they had to fear or to hope. Granvelle, in return, assured them, that the intelligence which they had received of the Emperor's military preparations was exaggerated, and all their suspicions destitute of foundation; that though, in order to guard his frontiers against any insult of the French or English, he had commanded a small body of men to be raised in the Low-Countries, he was as solicitous as ever to maintain tranquillity in Germany [f].

BUT the Emperor's actions did not correspond with these professions of his minister. For, instead of appointing men of known moderation and a pacific temper to appear in defence of the Catholic doctrines at the conference which had been agreed on, he made choice of fierce bigots, attached to their own system with a blind obstinacy, that rendered all hope of a reconcilement desperate. Malvenda, a Spanish divine, who took upon him the conduct of the debate on the part of the Catholics, managed it with all the subtle dexterity of a scholastic metaphysician, more studious to perplex his

[f] Sleid. 356.

BOOK VII.
1546.

adversaries than to convince them, and more intent on palliating error than on discovering truth. The Protestants, filled with indignation, as well at his sophistry as at some regulations which the Emperor endeavoured to impose on the disputants, broke off the conference abruptly, being now fully convinced that, in all his late measures, the Emperor could have no other view than to amuse them, and to gain time for ripening his own schemes [g].

[g] Sleid. 358. Seck. l. iii. 620.

THE HISTORY
OF THE
REIGN
OF THE
EMPEROR CHARLES V.

BOOK VIII.

WHILE appearances of danger daily increased, and the tempest which had been so long a gathering was ready to break forth in all its violence against the Protestant church, Luther was saved, by a seasonable death, from feeling or beholding its destructive rage. Having gone, though in a declining state of health, and during a rigorous season, to his native city of Eysleben, in order to compose, by his authority, a dissension among the counts of Mansfield, he was seized with a violent inflammation in his stomach, which in a few days put an end to his life, in the sixty-third year of his age. As he was raised up by Providence to be the author of one of the greatest and most interesting revolutions recorded in history, there is not any person perhaps whose character

BOOK VIII.
1546.
Death of Luther.

Feb. 18.

racter has been drawn with such opposite colours. In his own age, one party, struck with horror and inflamed with rage, when they saw with what a daring hand he overturned every thing which they held to be sacred, or valued as beneficial, imputed to him not only all the defects and vices of a man, but the qualities of a dæmon. The other, warmed with the admiration and gratitude, which they thought he merited as the restorer of light and liberty to the Christian church, ascribed to him perfections above the condition of humanity, and viewed all his actions with a veneration bordering on that which should be paid only to those who are guided by the immediate inspiration of Heaven. It is his own conduct, not the undistinguishing censure or the exaggerated praise of his contemporaries, that ought to regulate the opinions of the present age concerning him. Zeal for what he regarded as truth, undaunted intrepidity to maintain his own system, abilities, both natural and acquired, to defend his principles, and unwearied industry in propagating them, are virtues which shine so conspicuously in every part of his behaviour, that even his enemies must allow him to have possessed them in an eminent degree. To these may be added, with equal justice, such purity and even austerity of manners, as became one who assumed the character of a Reformer; such sanctity of life as suited the doctrine which he delivered; and such perfect disinterestedness as affords no slight presumption of his sincerity. Superior to all selfish considerations,

tions, a stranger to the elegancies of life, and despising its pleasures, he left the honours and emoluments of the church to his disciples, remaining satisfied himself in his original state of professor in the university, and pastor of the town of Wittemberg, with the moderate appointments annexed to these offices. His extraordinary qualities were allayed with no inconsiderable mixture of human frailty and human passions. These, however, were of such a nature, that they cannot be imputed to malevolence or corruption of heart, but seem to have taken their rise from the same source with many of his virtues. His mind, forcible and vehement in all its operations, roused by great objects, or agitated by violent passions, broke out, on many occasions, with an impetuosity which astonishes men of feebler spirits, or such as are placed in a more tranquil situation. By carrying some praise-worthy dispositions to excess, he bordered sometimes on what was culpable, and was often betrayed into actions which exposed him to censure. His confidence that his own opinions were well founded, approached to arrogance; his courage in asserting them, to rashness; his firmness in adhering to them, to obstinacy; and his zeal in confuting his adversaries, to rage and scurrility. Accustomed himself to consider every thing as subordinate to truth, he expected the same deference for it from other men; and, without making any allowances for their timidity or prejudices, he poured forth against such as disappointed him in this particular, a torrent of invective mingled with contempt. Regardless of any distinction of rank or character when his doctrines were attacked, he chastised all his adversaries indiscriminately, with the same rough hand; neither the royal dignity of Henry VIII. nor the eminent learning and abilities of Erasmus, screened them from the same gross abuse with which he treated Tetzel or Eccius.

But these indecencies of which Luther was guilty, must not be imputed wholly to the violence of his temper. They ought to be charged in part on the manners of the age. Among a rude people, unacquainted with those maxims, which by putting continual restraint on the passions of individuals, have polished society, and rendered it agreeable, disputes of every kind were managed with heat, and strong emotions were uttered in their natural language without reserve or delicacy. At the same time, the works of learned men were all composed in Latin, and they were not only authorized, by the example of eminent writers in that language, to use their antagonists with the most illiberal scurrility; but, in a dead tongue, indecencies of every kind appear less shocking than in a living language, whose idioms and phrases seem gross, because they are familiar.

In paffing judgment upon the characters of men, we ought to try them by the principles and maxims of their own age, not by thofe of another. For, although virtue and vice are at all times the fame, manners and cuftoms vary continually. Some parts of Luther's behaviour, which to us appear moft culpable, gave no difguft to his contemporaries. It was even by fome of thofe qualities, which we are now apt to blame, that he was fitted for accomplifhing the great work which he undertook. To roufe mankind, when funk in ignorance or fuperftition, and to encounter the rage of bigotry armed with power, required the utmoft vehemence of zeal, as well as a temper daring to excefs. A gentle call would neither have reached, nor have excited thofe to whom it was addreffed. A fpirit more amiable, but lefs vigorous than Luther's, would have fhrunk back from the dangers which he braved and furmounted. Towards the clofe of Luther's life, though without any perceptible diminution of his zeal or abilities, the infirmities of his temper increafed upon him, fo that he grew daily more peevifh, more irafcible, and more impatient of contradiction. Having lived to be a witnefs of his own amazing fuccefs; to fee a great part of Europe embrace his doctrines; and to fhake the foundation of the papal throne, before which the mightieft Monarchs had trembled, he difcovered, on fome occafions, fymptoms of vanity and felf-applaufe. He muft have been, indeed, more than man, if, upon contemplating all that he actually accom-

accomplished, he had never felt any sentiment of this kind rising in his breast *.

SOME time before his death he felt his strength declining, his constitution being worn out by a prodigious multiplicity of business, added to the labour of discharging his ministerial function with unremitting diligence, to the fatigue of constant study, besides the composition of works as voluminous as if he had enjoyed uninterrupted leisure and retirement. His natural intrepidity did not forsake him at the approach of death; his last conversation with his friends was concerning the happiness reserved for good men in a future life, of which he spoke with the fervour and delight natural to one who expected and wished to enter

* A remarkable instance of this, as well as of a certain singularity and elevation of sentiment, is found in his Last Will. Though the effects which he had to bequeath were very inconsiderable, he thought it necessary to make a Testament, but scorned to frame it with the usual legal formalities. Notus sum, says he, in coelo, in terra, & inferno, & auctoritatem ad hoc sufficientem habeo, ut mihi soli credatur, cum Deus mihi, homini licet damnabili, et miserabili peccatori, ex paterna misericordia Evangelium filii sui crediderit, dederitque ut in eo verax & fidelis fuerim, ita ut multi in mundo illud per me acceperint, & me pro Doctore veritatis agnoverint, spreto banno Papæ, Cæsaris, Regum, Principum & sacerdotum, immo omnium dæmonum odio. Quidni, igitur, ad dispositionem hanc, in re exigua, sufficiat, si adsit manus meæ testimonium, & dici possit, hæc scripsit D. Martinus Luther, Notarius Dei, & testis Evangelii ejus. Sec. l. iii. p. 651.

soon

soon upon the enjoyment of it[a]. The account of his death filled the Roman Catholic party with excessive as well as indecent joy, and damped the spirits of all his followers; neither party sufficiently considering that his doctrines were now so firmly rooted, as to be in a condition to flourish independent of the hand which had first planted them. His funeral was celebrated by order of the Elector of Saxony with extraordinary pomp. He left several children by his wife Catherine a Boria, who survived him. Towards the end of the last century, there were in Saxony some of his descendants in decent and honourable stations[b].

The Emperor, meanwhile, pursued the plan of dissimulation with which he had set out, employing every art to amuse the Protestants, and to quiet their fears and jealousies. For this purpose he contrived to have an interview with the Landgrave of Hesse, the most active of all the confederates, and the most suspicious of his designs. To him he made such warm professions of his concern for the happiness of Germany, and of his aversion to all violent measures; he denied in such express terms, his having entered into any league, or having begun any military preparations which should give any just cause of alarm to the Protestants, as seem to have dispelled all the Landgrave's doubts and apprehensions, and sent him

The Emperor endeavours to amuse and deceive the Protestants.

March 28.

[a] Sleid. 362. Seck. lib. iii. 632, &c.
[b] Seck. l. iii. 651.

away

away fully satisfied of his pacific intentions. This artifice was of great advantage, and effectually answered the purpose for which it was employed. The Landgrave, upon his leaving Spires, where he had been admitted to this interview, went to Worms, where the Smalkaldic confederates were assembled, and gave them such a flattering representation of the Emperor's favourable disposition towards them, that they, who were too apt, as well from the temper of the German nation, as from the genius of all great associations or bodies of men, to be slow, and dilatory, and undecisive in their deliberations, thought there was no necessity of taking any immediate measures against danger, which appeared to be distant or imaginary [c].

Proceedings of the council against the Protestants.

SUCH events, however, soon occurred, as staggered the credit which the Protestants had given to the Emperor's declarations. The council of Trent, though still composed of a small number of Italian and Spanish prelates, without a single deputy from many of the kingdoms which it assumed a right of binding by its decrees, being ashamed of its long inactivity, proceeded now to settle articles of the greatest importance. Having begun with examining the first and chief point in controversy between the church of Rome and the Reformers, concerning the rule which should be held as supreme and decisive in matters of faith, the council, by its infallible authority, determined,

[c] Sleid. Hist. 367. 373.

mined, "That the books to which the designation of *Apocryphal* hath been given, are of equal authority with those which were received by the Jews and primitive Christians into the sacred canon; that the traditions handed down from the apostolic age, and preserved in the church, are entitled to as much regard as the doctrines and precepts which the inspired authors have committed to writing; that the Latin translation of the Scriptures, made or revised by St. Jerome, and known by the name of the *Vulgate* translation, should be read in churches, and appealed to in the schools as authentic and canonical." Against all who disclaimed the truth of these tenets, anathemas were denounced in the name and by the authority of the Holy Ghost. The decision of these points, which undermined the main foundation of the Lutheran system, was a plain warning to the Protestants what judgment they might expect when the council should have leisure to take into consideration the particular and subordinate articles of their creed[d].

This discovery of the council's readiness to condemn the opinions of the Protestants, was soon followed by a striking instance of the Pope's resolution to punish such as embraced them. The appeal of the canons of Cologne against their Archbishop having been carried to Rome, Paul eagerly seized on that opportunity, both of dis-

---

[d] F. Paul, 141. Pallav. 206.

playing the extent of his own authority, and of teaching the German ecclesiastics the danger of revolting from the established church. As no person appeared in behalf of the Archbishop, he was held to be convicted of the crime of heresy, and a Papal bull was issued, depriving him of his ecclesiastical dignity, inflicting on him the sentence of excommunication, and absolving his subjects from the oath of allegiance which they had taken to him as their civil superior. The countenance which he had given to the Lutheran heresy was the only crime imputed to him, as well as the only reason assigned to justify the extraordinary severity of this decree. The Protestants could hardly believe that Paul, how zealous soever he might be to defend the established system, or to humble those who invaded it, would have ventured to proceed to such extremities against a Prince and Elector of the Empire, without having previously secured such powerful protection as would render his censure something more than an impotent and despicable sally of resentment. They were of course deeply alarmed at this sentence against the Archbishop, considering it as a sure indication of the malevolent intentions not only of the Pope, but of the Emperor, against the whole party [d].

Charles about to commence hostilities against the Protestants.

UPON this fresh revival of their fears, with such violence as is natural to men roused from a

[d] Sleid. 354. F. Paul, 155. Pallavic. 224.

false

false security, and conscious of their having been deceived, Charles saw that now it became necessary to throw aside the mask, and to declare openly what part he determined to act. By a long series of artifice and fallacy, he had gained so much time, that his measures, though not altogether ripe for execution, were in great forwardness. The Pope, by his proceedings against the Elector of Cologne, as well as by the decrees of the council, had precipitated matters into such a situation, as rendered a breach between the Emperor and the Protestants almost unavoidable. Charles had therefore no choice left him, but either to take part with them in overturning what the See of Rome had determined, or to support the authority of the church openly by force of arms. Nor did the Pope think it enough to have brought the Emperor under a necessity of acting; he pressed him to begin his operations immediately, and to carry them on with such vigour as could not fail of securing success. Transported by his zeal against heresy, Paul forgot all the prudent and cautious maxims of the Papal See, with regard to the danger of extending the Imperial authority beyond due bounds; and in order to crush the Lutherans, he was willing to contribute towards raising up a master that might one day prove formidable to himself as well as to the rest of Italy.

Negociates with the Pope.

But, besides the certain expectation of assistance from the Pope, Charles was now secure from any

Concludes a truce with Solyman.

any danger of interruption to his designs by the Turkish arms. His negociations at the Porte, which he had carried on with great assiduity since the peace of Crespy, were on the point of being terminated in such a manner as he desired. Solyman, partly in compliance with the French King, who, in order to avoid the disagreeable obligation of joining the Emperor against his ancient ally, laboured with great zeal to bring about an accommodation between them, and partly from its being necessary to turn his arms towards the east, where the Persians threatened to invade his dominions, consented without difficulty to a truce for five years. The chief article of it was, That each should retain possession of what he now held in Hungary; and Ferdinand, as a sacrifice to the pride of the Sultan, submitted to pay an annual tribute of fifty thousand crowns [e].

Gains Maurice, and other Princes in Germany.

BUT it was upon the aid and concurrence of the Germans themselves that the Emperor relied with the greatest confidence. The Germanic body, he knew, was of such vast strength, as to be invincible if it were united, and that it was only by employing its own force that he could hope to subdue it. Happily for him, the union of the several members in this great system was so feeble, the whole frame was so loosely compacted, and its different parts tended so violently towards se-

[e] Istuanhaffii Hist. Hun. 180. Mem. de Ribier, tom. i. 582.

paration from each other, that it was almost impossible for it, on any important emergence, to join in a general or vigorous effort. In the present juncture, the sources of discord were as many, and as various, as had been known on any occasion. The Roman Catholics, animated with zeal in defence of their religion proportional to the fierceness with which it had been attacked, were eager to second any attempt to humble those innovators, who had overturned it in many provinces, and endangered it in more. John and Albert of Brandenburg, as well as several other Princes, incensed at the haughtiness and rigour with which the Duke of Brunswick had been treated by the confederates of Smalkalde, were impatient to rescue him, and to be revenged on them. Charles observed, with satisfaction, the working of those passions in their minds, and counting on them as sure auxiliaries whenever he should think it proper to act, he found it, in the mean time, more necessary to moderate than to inflame their rage.

Such was the situation of affairs, such the discernment with which the Emperor foresaw and provided for every event, when the diet of the Empire met at Ratisbon. Many of the Roman Catholic members appeared there in person, but most of the confederates of Smalkalde, under pretence of being unable to bear the expence occasioned by the late unnecessary frequency of such assem-

Holds a diet at Ratisbon.

assemblies, sent only deputies. Their jealousy of the Emperor, together with an apprehension that violence might, perhaps, be employed, in order to force their approbation of what he should propose in the diet, was the true cause of their absence. The speech with which the Emperor opened the diet was extremely artful. After professing, in common form, his regard for the prosperity of the Germanic body, and declaring, that, in order to bestow his whole attention upon the re-establishment of its order and tranquillity, he had at present abandoned all other cares, rejected the most pressing solicitations of his other subjects to reside among them, and postponed affairs of the greatest importance; he took notice, with some disapprobation, that his disinterested example had not been imitated; many members of chief consideration having neglected to attend an assembly to which he had repaired with such manifest inconvenience to himself. He then mentioned their unhappy dissensions about religion; lamented the ill success of his past endeavours to compose them; complained of the abrupt dissolution of the late conference, and craved their advice with regard to the best and most effectual method of restoring union to the churches of Germany, together with that happy agreement in articles of faith, which their ancestors had found to be of no less advantage to their civil interest, than becoming their Christian profession.

By this gracious and popular method of consulting the members of the diet, rather than of obtruding upon them any opinion of his own, besides the appearance of great moderation, and the merit of paying much respect to their judgment, the Emperor dexterously avoided discovering his own sentiments, and reserved to himself, as his only part, that of carrying into execution what they should recommend. Nor was he less secure of such a decision as he wished to obtain, by referring it wholly to themselves. The Roman Catholic members, prompted by their own zeal, or prepared by his intrigues, joined immediately in representing that the authority of the council now met at Trent ought to be supreme in all matters of controversy; that all Christians should submit to its decrees as the infallible rule of their faith; and therefore they besought him to exert the power, with which he was invested by the Almighty, in protecting that assembly, and in compelling the Protestants to acquiesce in its determinations. The Protestants, on the other hand, presented a memorial, in which, after repeating their objections to the council of Trent, they proposed, as the only effectual method of deciding the points in dispute, that either a free general council should be assembled in Germany, or a national council of the Empire should be called, or a select number of divines should be appointed out of each party to examine and define articles of faith. They mentioned the recesses of several diets favourable to this proposition, and which had afforded them the prospect of terminating all their differences in this amicable manner; they now conjured the Emperor not to depart from his former plan, and by offering violence to their consciences, to bring calamities upon Germany, the very thought of which must fill every lover of his country with horror. The Emperor receiving this paper with a contemptuous smile, paid no farther regard to it. Having already taken his final resolution, and perceiving that nothing but force could compel them to acquiesce in it, he dispatched the Cardinal of Trent to Rome, in order to conclude an alliance with the Pope, the terms of which were already agreed on; he commanded a body of troops, levied on purpose in the Low-Countries, to advance towards Germany; he gave commissions to several officers for raising men in different parts of the Empire; he warned John and Albert of Brandenburg, that now was the proper time of exerting themselves, in order to rescue their ally, Henry of Brunswick, from captivity [f].

The Protestants alarmed.

ALL these things could not be transacted without the observation and knowledge of the Protestants. The secret was now in many hands; under whatever veil the Emperor still affected to conceal his designs, his officers kept no such mysterious reserve; and his allies and subjects spoke out his intentions plainly. Alarmed with reports

[f] Sleid. 374. Seck. iii. 658.

of this kind from every quarter, as well as with the preparations for war which they could not but obferve, the deputies of the confederates demanded audience of the Emperor, and, in the name of their mafters, required to know whether thefe military preparations were carried on by his command, and for what end, and againſt what enemy? To a queſtion put in fuch a tone, and at a time when facts were become too notorious to be denied, it was neceſſary to give an explicit anfwer, Charles owned the orders which he had iſſued, and profeſſing his purpoſe not to moleſt on account of religion thofe who ſhould act as dutiful fubjects; declared, that he had nothing in view but to maintain the rights and prerogatives of the Imperial dignity, and, by puniſhing fome factious members, to preferve the ancient conſtitution of the Empire from being impaired or diſſolved by their irregular and licentious conduct. Though the Emperor did not name the perfons whom he charged with fuch high crimes, and deſtined to be the objects of his vengeance, it was obvious that he had the Elector of Saxony and Landgrave of Heſſe in view. Their deputies confidering what he had faid, as a plain declaration of his hoſtile intentions, immediately retired from Ratiſbon[g].

The Cardinal of Trent found it no difficult matter to treat with the Pope, who having at length

The Emperor's treaty with the Pope.

[g] Sleid. 376.

length brought the Emperor to adopt that plan which he had long recommended, assented with eagerness to every article that he proposed. The league was signed a few days after the Cardinal's arrival at Rome. The pernicious heresies which abounded in Germany, the obstinacy of the Protestants in rejecting the holy council assembled at Trent, and the necessity of maintaining sound doctrine, together with good order in the church, are mentioned as the motives of this union between the contracting parties. In order to check the growth of these evils, and to punish such as had impiously contributed to spread them, the Emperor, having long and without success made trial of gentler remedies, engaged instantly to take the field with a sufficient army, that he might compel all who disowned the council, or had apostatized from the religion of their forefathers, to return into the bosom of the church, and submit with due obedience to the Holy See. He likewise bound himself not to conclude a peace with them during six months without the Pope's consent, nor without assigning him his share in any conquests which should be made upon them; and that even after this period he should not agree to any accommodation which might be detrimental to the church, or to the interest of religion. On his part, the Pope stipulated to deposit a large sum in the bank of Venice towards defraying the expence of the war; to maintain, at his own charge, during the space of six months, twelve thousand foot, and five hundred horse; to grant the

the Emperor, for one year, half of the ecclesiastical revenues throughout Spain; to authorize him, by a bull, to alienate as much of the lands, belonging to religious houses in that country, as would amount to the sum of five hundred thousand crowns; and to employ not only spiritual censures, but military force, against any Prince who should attempt to interrupt or defeat the execution of this treaty [h].

Notwithstanding the explicit terms in which the extirpation of heresy was declared to be the object of the war which was to follow upon this treaty, Charles still endeavoured to persuade the Germans that he had no design to abridge their religious liberty, but that he aimed only at vindicating his own authority, and repressing the insolence of such as had encroached upon it. With this view, he wrote circular letters in the same strain with his answer to the deputies at Ratisbon, to most of the free cities, and to several of the Princes who had embraced the Protestant doctrines. In these he complained loudly, but in general terms, of the contempt into which the Imperial dignity had fallen, and of the presumptuous as well as disorderly behaviour of some members of the Empire. He declared that he now took arms, not in a religious, but in a civil quarrel; not to oppress any who continued to behave as quiet and dutiful subjects, but to

[h] Sleid. 381. Pallav. 255. Dumont Corps Diplom. 11.

humble the arrogance of such as had thrown off all sense of that subordination in which they were placed under him as head of the Germanic body. Gross as this deception was, and manifest as it might have appeared to all who considered the Emperor's conduct with attention, it became necessary for him to make trial of its effect; and such was the confidence and dexterity with which he employed it, that he derived the most solid advantages from this artifice. If he had avowed at once an intention of overturning the Protestant church, and of reducing all Germany under its former state of subjection to the Papal See, none of the cities or Princes who had embraced the new opinions could have remained neutral after such a declaration, far less could they have ventured to assist the Emperor in such an enterprize. Whereas by concealing, and even disclaiming any intention of that kind, he not only saved himself from the danger of being overwhelmed by a general confederacy of all the Protestant states, but he furnished the timid with an excuse for continuing inactive, and the designing or interested with a pretext for joining him, without exposing themselves to the infamy of abandoning their own principles, or taking part openly in suppressing them. At the same time the Emperor well knew, that if, by their assistance, he were enabled to break the power of the Elector of Saxony and the Landgrave; he might afterwards prescribe what terms he pleased to the feeble remains of a party without union, and destitute of leaders,

leaders, who would then regret, too late, their miſtaken confidence in him, and their inconſiderate deſertion of their aſſociates.

THE Pope, by a ſudden and unforeſeen diſplay of his zeal, had well nigh diſconcerted this plan which the Emperor had formed with ſo much care and art. Proud of having been the author of ſuch a formidable league againſt the Lutheran hereſy, and happy in thinking that the glory of extirpating it was reſerved for his Pontificate, he publiſhed the articles of his treaty with the Emperor, in order to demonſtrate the pious intention of their confederacy, as well as to diſplay his own zeal, which prompted him to make ſuch extraordinary efforts for maintaining the faith in its purity. Not ſatisfied with this, he ſoon after iſſued a bull, containing moſt liberal promiſes of indulgence to all who ſhould engage in this holy enterprize, together with warm exhortations to ſuch as could not bear a part in it themſelves, to increaſe the fervour of their prayers, and the ſeverity of their mortifications, that they might draw down the bleſſing of Heaven upon thoſe who undertook it[i]. Nor was it zeal alone which puſhed the Pope to make declarations ſo inconſiſtent with the account which the Emperor himſelf gave of his motives for taking arms. He was much ſcandalized at Charles's diſſimulation in ſuch a cauſe; at his ſeeming to

The Pope diſconcerts his plan.

[i] Du Mont Corps Diplom.

be ashamed of owning his zeal for the church, and at his endeavours to make that pass for a political contest, which he ought to have gloried in as a war that had no other object than the defence of religion. With as much solicitude, therefore, as the Emperor laboured to disguise the purpose of the confederacy, did the Pope endeavour to publish their real plan, in order that they might come at once to an open rupture with the Protestants, that all hope of reconcilement might be cut off, and that Charles might be under fewer temptations, and have it less in his power than at present, to betray the interests of the church by any accommodation beneficial to himself[k].

The Emperor, though not a little offended at the Pope's indiscretion or malice in making this discovery, continued boldly to pursue his own plan, and to assert his intentions to be no other than what he had originally avowed. Several of the Protestant states, whom he had previously gained, thought themselves justified, in some measure, by his declarations, for abandoning their associates, and even for giving assistance to him.

The preparation of the Protestants for their own defence.

But these artifices did not impose on the greater and sounder part of the Protestant confederates. They clearly perceived it to be against the reformed religion that the Emperor had taken arms,

[k] F. Paul, 188. Thuan. Hist. i. 61.

and that not only the suppression of it, but the extinction of the German liberties, would be the certain consequence of his obtaining such an entire superiority as would enable him to execute his schemes in their full extent. They determined, therefore, to prepare for their own defence, and neither to renounce those religious truths, to the knowledge of which they had attained by means so wonderful, nor to abandon those civil rights which had been transmitted to them by their ancestors. In order to give the necessary directions for this purpose, their deputies met at Ulm, soon after their abrupt departure from Ratisbon. Their deliberations were now conducted with such vigour and unanimity, as the imminent danger which threatened them required. The contingent of troops, which each of the confederates was to furnish, having been fixed by the original treaty of union, orders were given for bringing them immediately into the field. Being sensible, at last, that through the narrow prejudices of some of their members, and the imprudent security of others, they had neglected too long to strengthen themselves by foreign alliances, they now applied with great earnestness to the Venetians and Swiss.

To the Venetians they represented the Emperor's intention of overturning the present system of Germany, and of raising himself to absolute power in that country by means of foreign force furnished

They solicit the aid of the Venetians.

furnished by the Pope; they warned them how fatal this event would prove to the liberties of Italy, and that by suffering Charles to acquire unlimited authority in the one country, they would soon feel his dominion to be no less despotic in the other; they besought them, therefore, not to grant a passage through their territories to those troops, which ought to be treated as common enemies, because by subduing Germany they prepared chains for the rest of Europe. These reflections had not escaped the sagacity of those wise republicans. They had communicated their sentiments to the Pope, and had endeavoured to divert him from an alliance, which tended to render irresistible the power of a potentate, whose ambition he already knew to be boundless. But they had found Paul so eager in the prosecution of his own plan, that he disregarded all their remonstrances[1]. This attempt to alarm the Pope having proved unsuccessful, they declined doing any thing more towards preventing the dangers which they foresaw; and in return to the application from the confederates of Smalkalde, they informed them, that they could not obstruct the march of the Pope's troops through an open country, but by levying an army strong enough to face them in the field; and that this would draw upon themselves the whole weight of his as well as of the Emperor's indignation. For the same reason they declined lending a sum of money, which the

[1] Adriani Istoria di suoi Tempi, liv. v. p. 332.

Elector of Saxony and Landgrave propofed to borrow of them, towards carrying on the war[m].

The demands of the confederates upon the Swifs were not confined to the obftructing of the entrance of foreigners into Germany; they required of them, as the neareft neighbours and clofeft allies of the Empire, to interpofe with their wonted vigour for the prefervation of its liberties, and not to ftand as inactive fpectators, while their brethren were oppreffed and enflaved. But with whatever zeal fome of the Cantons might have been difpofed to act when the caufe of the Reformation was in danger, the Helvetic body was fo divided with regard to religion, as to render it unfafe for the Proteftants to take any ftep without confulting their Catholic affociates; and among them the emiffaries of the Pope and Emperor had fuch influence, that a refolution of maintaining an exact neutrality between the contending parties, was the utmoft which could be procured[n].

Being difappointed in both thefe applications, the Proteftants, not long after, had recourfe to the Kings of France and England; the approach of danger either overcoming the Elector of Saxony's fcruples, or obliging him to yield to the importunities of his affociates. The fituation of

Of the Swifs.

Of Francis I. and Henry VIII.

[m] Sleid. 381. Paruta Iftor. Venet. tom. iv. 180. Lambertus Hortenfius de Bello Germanico, apud Scardium, vol. ii. p. 547.
[n] Sleid. 392.

the two Monarchs flattered them with hopes of succefs. Though hoftilities between them had continued for some time after the peace of Crespy, they became weary at laft of a war, attended with no glory or advantage to either, and had lately terminated all their differences by a peace concluded at Campe near Ardres. Francis having with great difficulty procured his allies, the Scots, to be included in the treaty, in return for that conceffion he engaged to pay a great fum, which Henry demanded as due to him on feveral accounts, and he left Boulogne in the hands of the Englifh, as a pledge for his faithful performance of that article. But though the re-eftablifhment of peace feemed to leave the two Monarchs at liberty to turn their attention towards Germany, fo unfortunate were the Proteftants, that they derived no immediate advantage from this circumftance. Henry appeared unwilling to enter into any alliance with them, but on fuch conditions as would render him not only the head, but the fupreme director of their league; a pre-eminence which, as the bonds of union or intereft between them were but feeble, and as he differed from them fo widely in his religious fentiments, they had no inclination to admit °. Francis, more powerfully inclined by political confiderations to afford them affiftance, found his kingdom fo much exhaufted by a long war, and was fo much afraid of irritating the Pope, by entering into clofe union with excom-

° Rymer, xv. 93. Herbert, 258.

municated

municated heretics, that he durſt not undertake the protection of the Smalkaldic league. By this ill-timed caution, or by a ſuperſtitious deference to ſcruples, to which at other times he was not much addicted, he loſt the moſt promiſing opportunity of mortifying and diſtreſſing his rival, which preſented itſelf during his whole reign.

BUT, notwithſtanding their ill ſucceſs in their negociations with foreign courts, the confederates found no difficulty at home, in bringing a ſufficient force into the field. Germany abounded at that time in inhabitants; the feudal inſtitutions, which ſubſiſted in full force, enabled the nobles to call out their numerous vaſſals, and to put them in motion on the ſhorteſt warning; the martial ſpirit of the Germans, not broken or enervated by the introduction of commerce and arts, had acquired additional vigour during the continual wars in which they had been employed, for half a century, either in the pay of the Emperors, or the Kings of France. Upon every opportunity of entering into ſervice, they were accuſtomed to run eagerly to arms; and to every ſtandard that was erected, volunteers flocked from all quarters [p]. Zeal ſeconded, on this occaſion, their native ardour. Men on whom the doctrines of the Reformation had made that deep impreſſion which accompanies truth when firſt diſcovered, prepared to maintain it with proportional vigour; and

[p] Seck. l. iii. 161.

among a warlike people, it appeared infamous to remain inactive, when the defence of religion was the motive for taking arms. Accident combined with all these circumstances in facilitating the levy of soldiers among the confederates. A considerable number of Germans, in the pay of France, being dismissed by the King on the prospect of peace with England, joined in a body the standard of the Protestants [q]. By such a concurrence of causes, they were enabled to assemble in a few weeks an army composed of seventy thousand foot and fifteen thousand horse, provided with a train of an hundred and twenty cannon, eight hundred ammunition waggons, eight thousand beasts of burden, and six thousand pioneers [r]. This army, one of the most numerous, and undoubtedly the best appointed, of any which had been levied in Europe during that century, did not require the united effort of the whole Protestant body to raise it. The Elector of Saxony, the Landgrave of Hesse, the Duke of Wurtemberg, the Princes of Anhalt, and the Imperial cities of Ausbourg, Ulm, and Strasburg, were the only powers which contributed towards this great armament: the Electors of Cologne, of Brandenburg, and the Count Palatine, overawed by the Emperor's threats, or deceived by his professions, remained neuter. John marquis of Brandenburg Bareith,

[q] Thuan. l. i. 68.
[r] Thuan. l. i. 601. Ludovici ab Avila & Zuniga Commentariorum de Bel. Germ. lib. duo, Antw. 1550. 12mo. p. 13, a.

and Albert of Brandenburg Anspach, though both early converts to Lutheranism, entered openly into the Emperor's service, under pretext of having obtained his promise for the security of the Protestant religion; and Maurice of Saxony soon followed their example.

The number of their troops, as well as the amazing rapidity wherewith they had assembled them, astonished the Emperor, and filled him with the most disquieting apprehensions. He was, indeed, in no condition to resist such a mighty force. Shut up in Ratisbon, a town of no great strength, whose inhabitants, being mostly Lutherans, would have been more ready to betray than to assist him, with only three thousand Spanish foot, who had served in Hungary, and about five thousand Germans who had joined him from different parts of the Empire, he must have been overwhelmed by the approach of such a formidable army, which he could not fight, nor could he even hope to retreat from it in safety. The Pope's troops, though in full march to his relief, had hardly reached the frontiers of Germany; the forces which he expected from the Low-Countries had not yet begun to move, and were even far from being complete [s]. His situation, however, called for more immediate succour, nor did it seem practicable for him to wait for such distant auxiliaries, with whom his junction was so precarious.

[s] Sleid. 389. Avila, 8, a.

BOOK
VIII.

1546.
They imprudently negociate instead of acting.

But it happened fortunately for Charles, that the confederates did not avail themselves of the advantage which lay so full in their view. In civil wars, the first steps are commonly taken with much timidity and hesitation. Men are solicitous, at that time, to put on the semblance of moderation and equity; they strive to gain partisans by seeming to adhere strictly to known forms; nor can they be brought, at once, to violate those established institutions, which in times of tranquillity they have been accustomed to reverence; hence their proceedings are often feeble or dilatory, when they ought to be most vigorous and decisive. Influenced by those considerations, which, happily for the peace of society, operate powerfully on the human mind, the confederates could not think of throwing off that allegiance which they owed to the head of the Empire, or of turning their arms against him without one solemn appeal more to his candour, and to the impartial judgment of their fellow-subjects.

July 15.

For this purpose, they addressed a letter to the Emperor, and a manifesto to all the inhabitants of Germany. The tenour of both was the same. They represented their own conduct with regard to civil affairs as dutiful and submissive; they mentioned the inviolable union in which they had lived with the Emperor, as well as the many and recent marks of his good-will and gratitude wherewithal they had been honoured; they asserted religion to be the sole cause of the violence which the Emperor now meditated against them; and in

proof

proof of this produced many arguments to convince those who were so weak as to be deceived by the artifices with which he endeavoured to cover his real intentions; they declared their own resolution to risk every thing in maintenance of their religious rights, and foretold the dissolution of the German constitution, if the Emperor should finally prevail against them [t].

CHARLES, though in such a perilous situation as might have inspired him with moderate sentiments, appeared as inflexible and haughty as if his affairs had been in the most prosperous state. His only reply to the address and manifesto of the Protestants, was to publish the ban of the Empire against the Elector of Saxony and Landgrave of Hesse, their leaders, and against all who should dare to assist them. By this sentence, the ultimate and most rigorous one which the German jurisprudence has provided for the punishment of traitors, or enemies to their country, they were declared rebels and outlaws, and deprived of every privilege which they enjoyed as members of the Germanic body; their goods were confiscated; their subjects absolved from their oath of allegiance; and it became not only lawful but meritorious to invade their territories. The nobles, and free cities, who framed or perfected the constitution of the German government, had not been so negligent of their own safety and privileges as to

[t] Sleid. 384.

trust the Emperor with this formidable jurisdiction. The authority of a diet of the Empire ought to have been interposed before any of its members could be put under the ban. But Charles overlooked that formality, well knowing that, if his arms were crowned with success, there would remain none who would have either power or courage to call in question what he had done[a]. The Emperor, however, did not found his sentence against the Elector and Landgrave on their revolt from the established church, or their conduct with regard to religion; he affected to assign for it reasons purely civil, and those too expressed in such general and ambiguous terms, without specifying the nature or circumstances of their guilt, as rendered it more like an act of despotic power than of a legal and limited jurisdiction. Nor was it altogether from choice, or to conceal his intentions, that Charles had recourse to the ambiguity of general expressions; but he durst not mention too particularly the causes of his sentence, as every action which he could have charged upon the Elector and Landgrave as a crime, might have been employed with equal justice to condemn many of the Protestants whom he still pretended to consider as faithful subjects, and whom it would have been extremely imprudent to alarm or disgust.

[a] Sleid. 386. Du Mont Corps Diplom. iv. p. 11. 314. Pfeffel Hist. Abregè du Droit Publ. 168. 736. 158.

The confederates, now perceiving all hopes of accommodation to be at an end, had only to choose whether they would submit without reserve to the Emperor's will, or proceed to open hostilities. They were not destitute either of public spirit, or of resolution to make the proper choice. A few days after the ban of the Empire was published, they, according to the custom of that age, sent a herald to the Imperial camp, with a solemn declaration of war against Charles, to whom they no longer gave any other title than that of pretended Emperor, and renounced all allegiance, homage, or duty which he might claim, or which they had hitherto yielded to him. But previous to this formality, part of their troops had begun to act. The command of a considerable body of men raised by the city of Augsburg having been given to Sebastian Schertel, a soldier of fortune, who by the booty that he got when the Imperialists plundered Rome, together with the merit of long service, had acquired wealth and authority which placed him on a level with the chief of the German nobles: that gallant veteran resolved, before he joined the main body of the confederates, to attempt something suitable to his former fame, and to the expectation of his countrymen. As the Pope's forces were hastening towards Tyrol, in order to penetrate into Germany by the narrow passes through the mountains which run across that country, he advanced thither with the utmost rapidity, and seized Ehrenberg and Cufftein, two strong castles which commanded the principal defiles.

1546. They declare war against Charles.

Their first operations;

defiles. Without stopping a moment, he continued his march towards Infpruck, by getting poffeffion of which he would have obliged the Italians to ſtop ſhort, and with a ſmall body of men could have reſiſted all the efforts of the greateſt armies. Caſtlealto, the governor of Trent, knowing what a fatal blow this would be to the Emperor, all whoſe deſigns muſt have proved abortive if his Italian auxiliaries had been intercepted, raiſed a few troops with the utmoſt diſpatch, and threw himſelf into the town. Schertel, however, did not abandon the enterprize, and was preparing to attack the place, when the intelligence of the approach of the Italians, and an order from the Elector and Landgrave, obliged him to deſiſt. By his retreat the paſſes were left open, and the Italians entered Germany without any oppoſition, but from the garriſons which Schertel had placed in Ehrenberg and Cufffſtein, and theſe, having no hopes of being relieved, ſurrendered, after a ſhort reſiſtance [x] [*].

NOR

---

[x] Seckend. lib. ii. 70. Adriani Iſtoria di ſuoi Tempi, lib. 335.

[*] Seckendorf, the induſtrious author of the Commentarius Apologeticus de Lutheraniſmo, whom I have ſo long and ſafely followed as my guide in German affairs, was a deſcendant from Schertel. With the care and ſolicitude of a German, who was himſelf of noble birth, Seckendorf has publiſhed a long digreſſion concerning his anceſtor, calculated chiefly to ſhow how Schertel was ennobled, and his poſterity allied to many of the moſt ancient families in the Empire. Among other curious particulars, he gives us an account of his wealth, the chief ſource of which was the plunder he got

at

Nor was the recalling of Schertel the only error of which the confederates were guilty. As the supreme command of their army was committed, in terms of the league of Smalkalde, to the Elector of Saxony and Landgrave of Hesse with equal power, all the inconveniencies arising from a divided and co-ordinate authority, which is always of fatal consequence in the operations of war, were immediately felt. The Elector, though intrepid in his own person to excess, and most ardently zealous in the cause, was slow in deliberating, uncertain as well as irresolute in his determinations, and constantly preferred measures which were cautious and safe, to such as were bold or decisive. The Landgrave, of a more active and enterprising nature, formed all his resolutions with promptitude, wished to execute them with spirit, and uniformly preferred such measures as tended to bring the contest to a speedy issue. Thus their maxims, with regard to the conduct of the war, differed as widely as those by which they were influenced in preparing for it. Such perpetual contrariety in their sentiments gave rise, imperceptibly, to jealousy and the spirit of contention. These multiplied the dissensions flowing from the incompatibility of their natural tempers, and rendered them more

at Rome. His landed estate alone was sold by his grandsons for six hundred thousand florins. By this we may form some idea of the riches amassed by the *Condottieri*, or commanders of mercenary bands in that age. At the taking of Rome Schertel was only a captain. Seckend. lib. ii. 73.

violent. The other members of the league considering themselves as independent, and subject to the Elector and Landgrave, only in consequence of the articles of a voluntary confederacy, did not long retain a proper veneration for commanders who proceeded with so little concord; and the numerous army of the Protestants, like a vast machine whose parts are ill-compacted, and which is destitute of any power sufficient to move and regulate the whole, acted with no consistency, vigour, or effect.

The Pope's troops join the Emperor.

THE Emperor, who was afraid that, by remaining at Ratisbon, he might render it impossible for the Pope's forces to join him, having boldly advanced to Landshut on the Iser, the confederates lost some days in deliberating whether it was proper to follow him into the territories of the Duke of Bavaria, a neutral Prince. When at last they surmounted that scruple, and began to move towards his camp, they suddenly abandoned the design, and hastened to attack Ratisbon, in which town Charles could leave only a small garrison. By this time the Papal troops, amounting fully to that number which Paul had stipulated to furnish, had reached Landshut, and were soon followed by six thousand Spaniards of the veteran bands stationed in Naples. The confederates, after Schertel's spirited but fruitless expedition, seem to have permitted these forces to advance unmolested to the place of rendezvous, without any attempt to attack either them

or

or the Emperor feparately, or to prevent their junction[x]. The Imperial army amounted now to thirty-fix thoufand men, and was ftill more formidable by the difcipline and valour of the troops, than by their number. Avila, commendador of Alcantara, who had been prefent in all the wars carried on by Charles, and had ferved in the armies which gained the memorable victory at Pavia, which conquered Tunis, and invaded France, gives this the preference to any military force he had ever feen affembled[y]. Octavio Farnefe, the Pope's grandfon, affifted by the ableft officers formed in the long wars between Charles and Francis, commanded the Italian auxiliaries. His brother, the Cardinal Farnefe, accompanied him as Papal legate; and in order to give the war the appearance of a religious enterprize, he propofed to march at the head of the army, with a crofs carried before him, and to publifh indulgences wherever he came, to all who fhould give them any affiftance, as had anciently been the practice in the Crufades againft the Infidels. But this the Emperor ftrictly prohibited, as inconfiftent with all the declarations which he had made to the Germans of his own party; and the legate perceiving, to his aftonifhment, that the exercife of the Proteftant religion, the extirpation of which he confidered as the fole object of the war, was publicly permitted in the Imperial camp, foon returned in difguft to Italy[z].

[x] Adriani Iftoria de fuoi Tempi, lib. v. 340.
[y] Avila, 18. [z] F. Paul, 191.

THE arrival of these troops enabled the Emperor to send such a reinforcement to the garrison at Ratisbon, that the confederates, relinquishing all hopes of reducing that town, marched towards Ingoldstadt on the Danube, near to which Charles was now encamped. They exclaimed loudly against the Emperor's notorious violation of the laws and constitution of the Empire, in having called in foreigners to lay waste Germany, and to oppress its liberties. As in that age, the dominion of the Roman See was so odious to the Protestants, that the name of the Pope alone was sufficient to inspire them with horror at any enterprize which he countenanced, and to raise in their minds the blackest suspicions, it came to be universally believed among them, that Paul, not satisfied with attacking them openly by force of arms, had dispersed his emissaries all over Germany, to set on fire their towns and magazines, and to poison the wells and fountains of water. Nor did this rumour, which was extravagant and frightful enough to make a deep impression on the credulity of the vulgar, spread among them only; even the leaders of the party, blinded by their prejudices, published a declaration, in which they accused the Pope of having employed such Antichristian and diabolical arts against them [a]. These sentiments of the confederates were confirmed, in some measure, by the behaviour of the Papal troops, who, thinking nothing too rigorous towards

---

[a] Sleid. 399.

wards heretics anathematized by the church, were guilty of great excesses in the territories of the Lutheran States, and aggravated the calamities of war, by mingling with it all the cruelty of bigoted zeal.

The first operations in the field, however, did not correspond with the violence of those passions which animated individuals. The Emperor had prudently taken the resolution of avoiding an action with an enemy so far superior in number[b], especially as he foresaw that nothing could keep a body composed of so many and such dissimilar members from falling to pieces, but the pressing to attack it with an inconsiderate precipitancy. The confederates, though it was no less evident that to them every moment's delay was pernicious, were still prevented by the weakness or division of their leaders from exerting that vigour, with which their situation, as well as the ardour of their soldiers, ought to have inspired them. On their arrival at Ingoldstadt, they found the Emperor in a camp not remarkable for strength, and surrounded only by a slight entrenchment. Before the camp lay a plain of such extent, as afforded sufficient space for drawing out their whole army, and bringing it to act at once. Every consideration should have determined them to have seized this opportunity of attacking the Emperor; and their great superiority in numbers, the eagerness of their troops, together with the stability of the

The confederates advance towards the Imperial army.

August 29.

[b] Avila, 78, a.

German

German infantry in pitched battles, afforded them the moſt probable expectation of victory. The Landgrave urged this with great warmth, declaring that if the ſole command were veſted in him, he would terminate the war on that occaſion, and decide by one general action the fate of the two parties. But the Elector, reflecting on the valour and diſcipline of the enemy's forces, animated by the preſence of the Emperor, and conducted by the beſt officers of the age, would not venture upon an action, which he thought to be ſo doubtful, as the attacking ſuch a body of veterans on ground which they themſelves had choſen, and while covered by fortifications which, though imperfect, would afford them no ſmall advantage in the combat. Notwithſtanding his heſitation and remonſtrances, it was agreed to advance towards the enemy's camp in battle array, in order to make a trial whether by that inſult, and by a furious cannonade which they began, they could draw the Imperialiſts out of their works. But the Emperor had too much ſagacity to fall into this ſnare. He adhered to his own ſyſtem with inflexible conſtancy; and drawing up his ſoldiers behind their trenches, that they might be ready to receive the confederates if they ſhould venture upon an aſſault, calmly waited their approach, and carefully reſtrained his own men from any excurſions or ſkirmiſhes which might bring on a general engagement. He rode along the lines, and addreſſing the troops of the different nations in their own language, encouraged them not only by his words, but by the cheerfulneſs of his voice and

The Emperor declines a battle.

coun-

countenance; he expofed himfelf in places of greateft danger, and amidft the warmeft fire of the enemy's artillery, the moft numerous that had hitherto been brought into the field by any army. Roufed by his example, not a man quitted his ranks; it was thought infamous to difcover any fymptom of fear when the Emperor appeared fo intrepid; and the meaneft foldier plainly perceived, that their declining the combat at prefent was not the effect of timidity in their general, but the refult of a well-grounded caution. The confederates, after firing feveral hours on the Imperialifts, with more noife and terror than execution, feeing no profpect of alluring them to fight on equal terms, retired to their own camp. The Emperor employed the night with fuch diligence in ftrengthening his works, that the confederates, returning to the cannonade next day, found that, though they had now been willing to venture upon fuch a bold experiment, the opportunity of making an attack with advantage was loft [c].

After fuch a difcovery of the feeblenefs or irrefolution of their leaders, and the prudence as well as firmnefs of the Emperor's conduct, the confederates turned their whole attention towards preventing the arrival of a powerful reinforcement of ten thoufand foot, and four thoufand horfe, which the count de Buren was bringing to the Emperor from the Low-Countries. But though

The Flemifh troops join the Emperor.

[c] Sleid. 395. 397. Avila, 27, a. Lamb. Hortenf. ap. Scard. ii.

that general had to traverse such an extent of country; though his route lay through the territories of several states warmly disposed to favour the confederates; though they were apprized of his approach, and by their superiority in numbers might easily have detached a force sufficient to overpower him, he advanced with such rapidity, and by such well-concerted movements, while they opposed him with such remissness, and so little military skill, that he conducted this body to the Imperial camp without any loss [d].

Sept. 10.

Upon the arrival of the Flemings, in whom he placed great confidence, the Emperor altered, in some degree, his plan of operations, and began to act more upon the offensive, though he still avoided a battle with the utmost industry. He made himself master of Neuburg, Dillingen, and Donawert on the Danube; of Nordlingen, and several other towns, situated on the most considerable streams which fall into that mighty river. By this he got the command of a great extent of country, though not without being obliged to engage in several sharp encounters, of which the success was various, nor without being exposed, oftener than once, to the danger of being drawn into a battle. In this manner the whole autumn was spent; neither party gained any remarkable superiority over the other, and nothing was yet done towards bringing the war to a period. The Emperor had often foretold, with confidence,

State of both armies.

[d] Sleid. 403.

that

that discord and the want of money would compel the confederates to disperse that unwieldy body, which they had neither abilities to guide nor funds to support[e]. Though he waited with impatience for the accomplishment of his prediction, there was no prospect of that event being at hand. But he himself began to suffer from the want of forage and provisions; even the Catholic provinces being so much incensed at the introduction of foreigners into the Empire, that they furnished them with reluctance, while the camp of the confederates abounded with a profusion of all necessaries, which the zeal of their friends in the adjacent countries poured in with the utmost liberality and good will. Great numbers of the Italians and Spaniards, unaccustomed to the climate or food of Germany, were become unfit for service through sickness[f]. Considerable arrears were now due to the troops, who had scarcely received any money from the beginning of the campaign; the Emperor, experiencing on this, as well as on former occasions, that his jurisdiction was more extensive than his revenues, and that the former enabled him to assemble a greater number of soldiers, than the latter were sufficient to support. Upon all these accounts, he found it difficult to keep his army in the field; some of his ablest generals, and even the Duke of Alva

[e] Belli Smalkaldici Commentarius Græco sermone scriptus a Joach. Camerario, ap. Freherum, vol. iii. p. 479.
[f] Camerar. ap. Freher. 483.

himself, persevering and obstinate as he usually was in the prosecution of every measure, advising him to disperse his troops into winter-quarters. But as the arguments urged against any plan which he had adopted, rarely made much impression upon the Emperor, he paid no regard to their opinion, and determined to continue his efforts in order to weary out the confederates; being well assured that if he could once oblige them to separate, there was little probability of their uniting again in a body[g]. Still, however, it remained a doubtful point, whether his steadiness was most likely to fail, or their zeal to be exhausted. It was still uncertain which party, by first dividing its forces, would give the superiority to the other; when an unexpected event decided the contest, and occasioned a fatal reverse in the affairs of the confederates.

Schemes of Maurice of Saxony.

MAURICE of Saxony having insinuated himself into the Emperor's confidence, by the arts which have already been described, no sooner saw hostilities ready to break out between the confederates of Smalkalde and that monarch, than vast prospects of ambition began to open upon him. That portion of Saxony, which descended to him from his ancestors, was far from satisfying his aspiring mind; and he perceived with pleasure the approach of civil war, as, amidst the revolutions and convulsions occasioned by it, opportunities of

[g] Thuan. 83.

acquiring

acquiring additional power or dignity, which at other times are sought in vain, present themselves to an enterprising spirit. As he was thoroughly acquainted with the state of the two contending parties, and the qualities of their leaders, he did not hesitate long in determining on which side the greatest advantages were to be expected. Having revolved all these things in his own breast, and having taken his final resolution of joining the Emperor, he prudently determined to declare early in his favour; that by the merit of this, he might acquire a title to a proportional recompense. With this view, he had repaired to Ratisbon in the month of May, under pretext of attending the diet; and after many conferences with Charles or his ministers, he, with the most mysterious secrecy, concluded a treaty, in which he engaged to concur in assisting the Emperor as a faithful subject; and Charles, in return, stipulated to bestow on him all the spoils of the Elector of Saxony, his dignities as well as territories [h]. History hardly records any treaty that can be considered as a more manifest violation of the most powerful principles which ought to influence human actions. Maurice, a professed Protestant, at a time when the belief of religion, as well as zeal for its interests, took strong possession of every mind, binds himself to contribute his assistance towards carrying on a war which had mani-

His league with the Emperor.

[h] Haræi Annal. Brabant. vol. i. 638. Struvii Corp. 1048. Thuan. 84.

festly no other object than the extirpation of the Protestant doctrines. He engages to take arms against his father-in-law, and to strip his nearest relation of his honours and dominions. He joins a dubious friend against a known benefactor, to whom his obligations were both great and recent. Nor was the Prince who ventured upon all this, one of those audacious politicians, who, provided they can accomplish their ends, and secure their interest, avowedly disregard the most sacred obligations, and glory in contemning whatever is honourable or decent. Maurice's conduct, if the whole must be ascribed to policy, was more artful and masterly; he executed his plan in all its parts, and yet endeavoured to preserve, in every step which he took, the appearance of what was fair, and virtuous, and laudable. It is probable, from his subsequent behaviour, that, with regard to the Protestant religion at least, his intentions were upright, that he fondly trusted to the Emperor's promises for its security, but that, according to the fate of all who refine too much in policy, and who tread in dark and crooked paths, in attempting to deceive others, he himself was, in some degree, deceived.

His artifices in order to conceal his intentions.

His first care, however, was to keep the engagements into which he had entered with the Emperor closely concealed: and so perfect a master was he in the art of dissimulation, that the confederates, notwithstanding his declining all connexions with them, and his remarkable assiduity in paying court

court to the Emperor, seemed to have entertained no suspicion of his designs. Even the Elector of Saxony, when he marched at the beginning of the campaign to join his associates, committed his dominions to Maurice's protection, which he, with an insidious appearance of friendship, readily undertook [i]. But scarcely had the Elector taken the field, when Maurice began to consult privately with the King of the Romans how to invade those very territories, with the defence of which he was entrusted. Soon after, the Emperor sent him a copy of the Imperial ban denounced against the Elector and Landgrave. As he was next heir to the former, and particularly interested in preventing strangers from getting his dominions into their possession, Charles required him, not only for his own sake, but upon the allegiance and duty which he owed to the head of the Empire, instantly to seize and detain in his hands the forfeited estates of the Elector; warning him, at the same time, that if he neglected to obey these commands, he should be held as accessary to the crimes of his kinsman, and be liable to the same punishment [k].

This artifice, which it is probable Maurice himself suggested, was employed by him in order that his conduct towards the Elector might seem a matter of necessity but not of choice, an act of obedience to his superior, rather than a

[i] Struvii Corp. 1046.   [k] Sleid. 391. Thuan. 84.

voluntary invasion of the rights of his kinsman and ally. But in order to give some more specious appearance to this thin veil with which he endeavoured to cover his ambition, he, soon after his return from Ratisbon, had called together the states of his country; and representing to them that a civil war between the Emperor and confederates of Smalkalde was now become unavoidable, desired their advice with regard to the part which he should act in that event. They having been prepared, no doubt, and tutored before-hand, and being desirous of gratifying their Prince, whom they esteemed as well as loved, gave such counsel as they knew would be most agreeable; advising him to offer his mediation towards reconciling the contending parties; but if that were rejected, and he could obtain proper security for the Protestant religion, they delivered it as their opinion, that, in all other points, he ought to yield obedience to the Emperor. Upon receiving the Imperial rescript, together with the ban against the Elector and Landgrave, Maurice summoned the states of his country a second time; he laid before them the orders which he had received, and mentioned the punishment with which he was threatened in case of disobedience; he acquainted them that the confederates had refused to admit of his mediation, and that the Emperor had given him the most satisfactory declarations with regard to religion; he pointed out his own interest in securing possession of the electoral dominions, as well as the danger of allowing strangers

gers to obtain an establishment in Saxony; and
upon the whole, as the point under deliberation
respected his subjects no less than himself, he desired to know their sentiments, how he should
steer in that difficult and arduous conjuncture.
The states, no less obsequious and complaisant
than formerly, professing their own reliance on the
Emperor's promises as a perfect security for their
religion, proposed that, before he had recourse to
more violent methods, they would write to the
Elector, exhorting him, as the best means, not
only of appeasing the Emperor, but of preventing his dominions from being seized by foreign or
hostile powers, to give his consent that Maurice
should take possession of them quietly and without
opposition. Maurice himself seconded their arguments in a letter to the Landgrave, his father-in-law. Such an extravagant proposition was rejected
with the scorn and indignation which it deserved.
The Landgrave, in return to Maurice, taxed him
with his treachery and ingratitude towards a kinsman to whom he was so deeply indebted; he
treated with contempt his affectation of executing
the Imperial ban, which he could not but know
to be altogether void by the unconstitutional and
arbitrary manner in which it had been issued; he
besought him, not to suffer himself to be so far
blinded by ambition, as to forget the obligations
of honour and friendship, or to betray the Protestant religion, the extirpation of which out of
Germany, even by the acknowledgment of the

BOOK VIII.
1546.

He invades the territories of the Elector of Saxony.

November.

Pope himself, was the great object of the present war [1].

But Maurice had proceeded too far to be diverted from pursuing his plan by reproaches or arguments. Nothing now remained but to execute with vigour, what he had hitherto carried on by artifice and dissimulation. Nor was his boldness in action inferior to his subtlety in contrivance. Having assembled about twelve thousand men, he suddenly invaded one part of the electoral provinces, while Ferdinand, with an army composed of Bohemians and Hungarians, overran the other. Maurice, in two sharp encounters, defeated the troops which the Elector had left to guard his country; and improving these advantages to the utmost, made himself master of all the Electorate, except Wittemberg, Gotha, and Eisenach, which being places of considerable strength, and defended by sufficient garrisons, refused to open their gates. The news of these rapid conquests soon reached the Imperial and confederate camps. In the former, satisfaction with an event, which it was foreseen would be productive of the most important consequences, was expressed by every possible demonstration of joy. The latter was filled with astonishment and terror. The name of Maurice was mentioned with execration, as an apostate from religion, a

[1] Sleid. 405, &c. Thuan. 85. Camerar 484.

betrayer

betrayer of the German liberty, and a contemner of the moſt ſacred and natural ties. Every thing that the rage or invention of the party could ſuggeſt, in order to blacken and render him odious; invectives, ſatires, and lampoons, the furious declamations of their preachers, together with the rude wit of their authors, were all employed againſt him. While he, confiding in the arts which he had ſo long practiſed, as if his actions could have admitted of any ſerious juſtification, publiſhed a manifeſto, containing the ſame frivolous reaſons for his conduct, which he had formerly alleged in the meeting of his ſtates, and in his letter to the Landgrave[m].

The Elector, upon the firſt intelligence of Maurice's motions, propoſed to return home with his troops for the defence of Saxony. But the deputies of the league, aſſembled at Ulm, prevailed on him, at that time, to remain with the army, and to prefer the ſucceſs of the common cauſe before the ſecurity of his own dominions. At length the ſufferings and complaints of his ſubjects increaſed ſo much, that he diſcovered the utmoſt impatience to ſet out, in order to reſcue them from the oppreſſion of Maurice, and from the cruelty of the Hungarians, who, having been accuſtomed to that licentious and mercileſs ſpecies of war which was thought lawful againſt the Turks, committed, wherever they came, the wild-

The confederates make overtures of accommodation to the Emperor;

[m] Sleid. 409, 410.

est acts of rapine and violence. This desire of the Elector was so natural and so warmly urged, that the deputies at Ulm, though fully sensible of the unhappy consequences of dividing their army, durst not refuse their consent, how unwilling soever to grant it. In this perplexity, they repaired to the camp of the confederates at Giengen, on the Brenz, in order to consult their constituents. Nor were they less at a loss what to determine in this pressing emergence. But, after having considered seriously the open desertion of some of their allies; the scandalous lukewarmness of others, who had hitherto contributed nothing towards the war; the intolerable load which had fallen of consequence upon such members as were most zealous for the cause, or most faithful to their engagements; the ill success of all their endeavours to obtain foreign aid; the unusual length of the campaign; the rigour of the season; together with the great number of soldiers, and even officers, who had quitted the service on that account; they concluded that nothing could save them, but either the bringing the contest to the immediate decision of a battle, by attacking the Imperial army, or an accommodation of all their differences with Charles by a treaty. Such was the despondency and dejection which now oppressed the party, that of these two they chose what was most feeble and unmanly, empowering a minister of the Elector of Brandenburg to propound overtures of peace in their name to the Emperor.

No sooner did Charles perceive this haughty confederacy, which had so lately threatened to drive him out of Germany, condescending to make the first advances towards an agreement, than concluding their spirit to be gone, or their union to be broken, he immediately assumed the tone of a conqueror; and, as if they had been already at his mercy, would not hear of a negociation, but upon condition that the Elector of Saxony should previously give up himself and his dominions absolutely to his disposal[n]. As nothing more intolerable or ignominious could have been prescribed, even in the worst situation of their affairs, it is no wonder that this proposition should be rejected by a party, which was rather humbled and disconcerted than subdued. But though they refused to submit tamely to the Emperor's will, they wanted spirit to pursue the only plan which could have preserved their independence; and forgetting that it was the union of their troops in one body which had hitherto rendered the confederacy formidable, and had more than once obliged the Imperialists to think of quitting the field, they inconsiderately abandoned this advantage, which, in spite of the diversion in Saxony, would still have kept the Emperor in awe; and yielding to the Elector's entreaties, consented to his proposal of dividing the army. Nine thousand men were left in the dutchy of Wurtemberg, in order to protect that province,

[n] Hortensius, ap. Scard. ii. 485.

BOOK VIII.
1546.

as well as the free cities of Upper Germany; a considerable body marched with the Elector towards Saxony; but the greater part returned with their respective leaders into their own countries, and were dispersed there°.

Almost all the members of it submit to the Emperor.

THE moment that the troops separated, the confederacy ceased to be the object of terror; and the members of it, who, while they composed part of a great body, had felt but little anxiety about their own security, began to tremble when they reflected that they now stood exposed singly to the whole weight of the Emperor's vengeance. Charles did not allow them leisure to recover from their consternation, or to form any new schemes of union. As soon as the confederates began to retire, he put his army in motion, and though it was now the depth of winter, he resolved to keep the field, in order to make the most of that favourable juncture for which he had waited so long. Some small towns in which the Protestants had left garrisons, immediately opened their gates. Norlingen, Rotenberg, and Hall, Imperial cities, submitted soon after. Though Charles could not prevent the Elector from levying, as he retreated, large contributions upon the archbishop of Mentz, the abbot of Fulda, and other ecclesiastics [p], this was more than balanced by the submission of Ulm, one of the chief cities of Suabia, highly distinguished by its zeal for the Smalkaldic league,

° Sleid. 411.   P Thuan. 88.

league. As soon as an example was set of deserting the common cause, the rest of the members became instantly impatient to follow it, and seemed afraid lest others, by getting the start of them in returning to their duty, should, on that account, obtain more favourable terms. The Elector Palatine, a weak Prince, who, notwithstanding his professions of neutrality, had, very preposterously, sent to the confederates four hundred horse, a body so inconsiderable as to be scarcely any addition to their strength, but great enough to render him guilty in the eyes of the Emperor, made his acknowledgments in the most abject manner. The inhabitants of Augsburg, shaken by so many instances of apostacy, expelled the brave Schertel out of their city, and accepted such conditions as the Emperor was pleased to grant them.

The Duke of Wurtemberg, though among the first who had offered to submit, was obliged to sue for pardon on his knees; and even after this mortifying humiliation, obtained it with difficulty[q]. Memmingen, and other free cities in the circle of Suabia, being now abandoned by all their former associates, found it necessary to provide for their own safety, by throwing themselves on the Emperor's mercy. Strasburg and Frankfort on the Maine, cities far remote from the seat of danger, discovered no greater steadiness than

[q] Mem. de Ribier, tom. i. 589.

The rigorous conditions imposed by the Emperor.

those which lay more exposed. Thus a confederacy, lately so powerful as to shake the Imperial throne, fell to pieces, and was dissolved in the space of a few weeks; hardly any member of that formidable combination now remaining in arms, but the Elector and Landgrave, to whom the Emperor, having from the beginning marked them out as victims of his vengeance, was at no pains to offer terms of reconciliation. Nor did he grant those who submitted to him a generous and unconditional pardon. Conscious of his own superiority, he treated them both with haughtiness and rigour. All the Princes in person, and the cities by their deputies, were compelled to implore mercy in the humble posture of supplicants. As the Emperor laboured under great difficulties from the want of money, he imposed heavy fines upon them, which he levied with most rapacious exactness. The Duke of Wurtemberg paid three hundred thousand crowns; the city of Augsburg an hundred and fifty thousand; Ulm an hundred thousand; Frankfort eighty thousand; Memmingen fifty thousand; and the rest in proportion to their abilities, or their different degrees of guilt. They were obliged, besides, to renounce the league of Smalkalde; to furnish assistance, if required, towards executing the Imperial ban against the Elector and Landgrave; to give up their artillery and warlike stores to the Emperor; to admit garrisons into their principal cities and places of strength; and, in this disarmed and dependent situation, to expect the final award which the Emperor

peror should think proper to pronounce when the war came to an issue[r]. But, amidst the great variety of articles dictated by Charles on this occasion, he, in conformity to his original plan, took care that nothing relating to religion should be inserted; and to such a degree were the confederates humbled or overawed, that, forgetting the zeal which had so long animated them, they were solicitous only about their own safety, without venturing to insist on a point, the mention of which they saw the Emperor avoiding with so much industry. The inhabitants of Memmingen alone made some feeble efforts to procure a promise of protection in the exercise of their religion, but were checked so severely by the Imperial ministers, that they instantly fell from their demand.

The Elector of Cologne, whom, notwithstanding the sentence of excommunication issued against him by the Pope, Charles had hitherto allowed to remain in possession of the archiepiscopal see, being now required by the Emperor to submit to the censures of the church, this virtuous and disinterested prelate, unwilling to expose his subjects to the miseries of war on his own account, voluntarily resigned that high dignity. With a moderation becoming his age and character, he chose to enjoy truth, together with the exercise of his religion, in the retirement of a private life, rather than to disturb society by enga-

[r] Sleid. 411, &c. Thuan. lib. iv. p. 125. Mem. de Ribier, tom. i. 606.

ging in a doubtful and violent struggle in order to retain his office[s].

The Elector returns to Saxony, and recovers possession of it.

DURING these transactions, the Elector of Saxony reached the frontiers of his country unmolested. As Maurice could assemble no force equal to the army which accompanied him, he, in a short time, not only recovered possession of his own territories, but over-ran Misnia, and stripped his rival of all that belonged to him, except Dresden and Leipsic, which, being towns of some strength, could not be suddenly reduced. Maurice, obliged to quit the field, and to shut himself up in his capital, dispatched courier after courier to the Emperor, representing his dangerous situation, and soliciting him with the most earnest importunity to march immediately to his relief. But Charles, busy at that time in prescribing terms to such members of the league as were daily returning to their allegiance, thought it sufficient to detach Albert Marquis of Brandenburg-Anspach with three thousand men to his assistance. Albert, though an enterprising and active officer, was unexpectedly surprised by the Elector, who killed many of his troops, dispersed the remainder, and took him prisoner[t]. Maurice continued as much exposed as formerly; and if his enemy had known how to improve the opportunity which presented itself, his ruin must have been immediate and unavoidable. But the Elector, no less slow and di-

---
[s] Sleid. 418. Thuan. lib. iv. 128.
[t] Avila, 99. 6. Mem. de Ribier. tom. i. 620.

latory

latory when invested with the sole command, than he had been formerly when joined in authority with a partner, never gave any proof of military activity but in this enterprize, against Albert. Instead of marching directly towards Maurice, whom the defeat of his ally had greatly alarmed, he inconsiderately listened to overtures of accommodation, which his artful antagonist proposed with no other intention than to amuse him, and to slacken the vigour of his operations.

Such, indeed, was the posture of the Emperor's affairs, that he could not march instantly to the relief of his ally. Soon after the separation of the confederate army, he, in order to ease himself of the burden of maintaining a superfluous number of troops, had dismissed the count of Buren with his Flemings[u], imagining that the Spaniards and Germans, together with the papal forces, would be fully sufficient to crush any degree of vigour that yet remained among the members of the league. But Paul, growing wise too late, began now to discern the imprudence of that measure, from which the more sagacious Venetians had endeavoured in vain to dissuade him. The rapid progress of the Imperial arms, and the ease with which they had broken a combination that appeared no less firm than powerful, opened his eyes at length, and made him not only forget all the advantages which he had expected

The Emperor prevented from attacking the Elector and Landgrave.

[u] Avila, 83. 6. Mem. de Ribier, tom. i. 592.

from such a complete triumph over heresy, but placed, in the strongest light, his own impolitic conduct, in having contributed towards acquiring for Charles such an immense increase of power, as would enable him, after oppressing the liberties of Germany, to give law with absolute authority to all the states of Italy. The moment that he perceived his error, he endeavoured to correct it. Without giving the Emperor any warning of his intention, he ordered Farnese, his grandson, to return instantly to Italy with all the troops under his command, and at the same time recalled the licence which he had granted Charles, of appropriating to his own use, a large share of the church lands in Spain. He was not destitute of pretences to justify this abrupt desertion of his ally. The term of six months, during which the stipulations in their treaty were to continue in force, was now expired; the league, in opposition to which their alliance had been framed, seemed to be entirely dissipated; Charles, in all his negociations with the Princes and cities which had submitted to his will, had neither consulted the Pope, nor had allotted him any part of the conquests which he had made, nor had allowed him any share in the vast contributions which he had raised. He had not even made any provision for the suppression of heresy, or the reestablishment of the Catholic religion, which were Paul's chief inducements to bestow the treasures of the church so liberally in carrying on the war. These colours, however specious, did not conceal

conceal from the Emperor that secret jealousy which was the true motive of the Pope's conduct. But, as Paul's orders with regard to the march of his troops were no less peremptory than unexpected, it was impossible to prevent their retreat. Charles exclaimed loudly against his treachery, in abandoning him so unseasonably, while he was prosecuting a war undertaken in obedience to the papal injunctions, and from which, if successful, so much honour and advantage would redound to the church. To complaints he added threats and expostulations. But Paul remained inflexible; his troops continued their march towards the ecclesiastical state; and in an elaborate memorial, intended as an apology for his conduct, he discovered new and more manifest symptoms of alienation from the Emperor, together with a deep-rooted dread of his power [x]. Charles, weakened by the withdrawing of so great a body from his army, which was already much diminished by the number of garrisons that he had been obliged to throw into the towns which had capitulated, found it necessary to recruit his forces by new levies, before he could venture to march in person towards Saxony.

The fame and splendour of his success could not have failed of attracting such multitudes of soldiers into his service from all the extensive territories now subject to his authority, as must have

[x] F. Paul, 208. Pallavic. par. ii. p. 5. Thuan. 126.

soon put him in a condition of taking the field againſt the Elector; but the ſudden and violent eruption of a conſpiracy at Genoa, as well as the great revolutions which that event, extremely myſterious in its firſt appearances, ſeemed to portend, obliged him to avoid entangling himſelf in new operations in Germany, until he had fully diſcovered its ſource and tendency. The form of government which had been eſtabliſhed in Genoa, at the time when Andrew Doria reſtored liberty to his country, though calculated to obliterate the memory of former diſſenſions, and received at firſt with eager approbation, did not, after a trial of near twenty years, give univerſal ſatisfaction to thoſe turbulent and factious republicans. As the entire adminiſtration of affairs was now lodged in a certain number of noble families, many envying them that pre-eminence, wiſhed for the reſtitution of a popular government, to which they had been accuſtomed; and though all reverenced the diſintereſted virtue of Doria, and admired his talents, not a few were jealous of that aſcendant which he had acquired in the councils of the commonwealth. His age, however, his moderation, and his love of liberty, afforded ample ſecurity to his countrymen that he would not abuſe his power, nor ſtain the cloſe of his days by attempting to overturn that fabric, which it had been the labour and pride of his life to erect. But the authority and influence which in his hands were innocent, they eaſily ſaw would prove deſtructive, if uſurped by any citizen of greater ambition, or leſs virtue. A citizen of this

The object of the conſpirators.

this dangerous character had actually formed such pretenfions, and with fome profpect of fuccefs. Giannetino Doria, whom his grand uncle Andrew deftined to be the heir of his private fortune, aimed likewife at being his fucceffor in power. His temper haughty, infolent, and overbearing to fuch a degree as would hardly have been tolerated in one born to reign, was altogether infupportable in the citizen of a free ftate. The more fagacious among the Genoefe already feared and hated him as the enemy of thofe liberties for which they were indebted to his uncle. While Andrew himfelf, blinded by that violent and undifcerning affection which perfons in advanced age often contract for the younger members of their family, fet no bounds to the indulgence with which he treated him; feeming lefs folicitous to fecure and perpetuate the freedom of the commonwealth, than to aggrandize that undeferving kinfman.

But whatever fufpicion of Doria's defigns, or whatever diffatisfaction with the fyftem of adminiftration in the commonwealth, thefe circumftances might have occafioned, they would have ended, it is probable, in nothing more than murmurings and complaints, if John Lewis Fiefco count of Lavagna, obferving this growing difguft, had not been encouraged by it to attempt one of the boldeft actions recorded in hiftory. That young nobleman, the richeft and moft illuftrious fubject in the republic, poffeffed, in an eminent degree, all the qualities which win upon the human heart,

Fiefco count of Lavagna the head of the confpiracy.

BOOK
VIII.
~~~~~~
1547.

which command respect, or secure attachment. He was graceful and majestic in his person; magnificent even to profusion; of a generosity that anticipated the wishes of his friends, and exceeded the expectations of strangers; of an insinuating address, gentle manners, and a flowing affability. But under the appearance of these virtues, which seemed to form him for enjoying and adorning social life, he concealed all the dispositions which mark men out for taking the lead in the most dangerous and dark conspiracies; an insatiable and restless ambition, a courage unacquainted with fear, and a mind that disdained subordination. Such a temper could ill brook that station of inferiority, wherein he was placed in the republic; and as he envied the power which the elder Doria had acquired, he was filled with indignation at the thoughts of its descending, like an hereditary possession, to Giannetino. These various passions, preying with violence on his turbulent and aspiring mind, determined him to attempt overturning that domination to which he could not submit.

Intrigues and preparations of the conspirators.

As the most effectual method of accomplishing this, he thought at first of forming a connexion with Francis, and even proposed it to the French ambassador at Rome; and after expelling Doria, together with the Imperial faction, by his assistance, he offered to put the republic once more under the protection of that Monarch, hoping in return for that service to be entrusted with the principal

share

share in the administration of government. But having communicated his scheme to a few chosen confidents, from whom he kept nothing secret, Verrina, the chief of them, a man of desperate fortune, capable alike of advising and executing the most audacious deeds, remonstrated with earnestness against the folly of exposing himself to the most imminent danger, while he allowed another to reap all the fruits of his success; and exhorted him warmly to aim himself at that pre-eminence in his country, to which he was destined by his illustrious birth, was called by the voice of his fellow-citizens, and would be raised by the zeal of his friends. This discourse opened such great prospects to Fiesco, and so suitable to his genius, that abandoning his own plan, he eagerly adopted that of Verrina. The other persons present, though sensible of the hazardous nature of the undertaking, did not choose to condemn what their patron had so warmly approved. It was instantly resolved, in this dark cabal, to assassinate the two Dorias, as well as the principal persons of their party, to overturn the established system of government, and to place Fiesco on the ducal throne of Genoa. Time, however, and preparations were requisite to ripen such a design for execution; and while he was employed in carrying on these, Fiesco made it his chief care to guard against every thing that might betray his secret, or create suspicion. The disguise he assumed, was of all others the most impenetrable. He seemed to be abandoned entirely to pleasure and dissipation.

dissipation. A perpetual gaiety, diversified by the pursuit of all the amusements in which persons of his age and rank are apt to delight, engrossed, in appearance, the whole of his time and thoughts. But amidst this hurry of dissipation, he prosecuted his plan with the most cool attention, neither retarding the design by a timid hesitation, nor precipitating the execution by an excess of impatience. He continued his correspondence with the French ambassador at Rome, though without communicating to him his real intentions, that by his means he might secure the protection of the French arms, if hereafter he should find it necessary to call them in to his aid. He entered into a close confederacy with Farnese Duke of Parma, who being disgusted with the Emperor for refusing to grant him the investiture of that dutchy, was eager to promote any measure that tended to diminish his influence in Italy, or to ruin a family so implicitly devoted to him as that of Doria. Being sensible that, in a maritime state, the acquisition of naval power was what he ought chiefly to aim at, he purchased four gallies from the Pope, who probably was not unacquainted with the design which he had formed, and did not disapprove of it. Under colour of fitting out one of these gallies to sail on a cruise against the Turks, he not only assembled a good number of his own vassals, but engaged in his service many bold adventurers, whom the truce between the Emperor and Solyman had deprived of their usual occupation and subsistence.

WHILE

WHILE Fiefco was taking thefe important steps, he preferved fo admirably his ufual appearance of being devoted entirely to pleafure and amufement, and paid court with fuch artful addrefs to the two Dorias, as impofed not only on the generous and unfufpicious mind of Andrew, but deceived Giannetino, who, confcious of his own criminal intentions, was more apt to diftruft the defigns of others. So many inftruments being now prepared, nothing remained but to ftrike the blow. Various confultations were held by Fiefco with his confidents, in order to fettle the manner of doing it with the greateft certainty and effect. At firft, they propofed to murder the Dorias and their chief adherents, during the celebration of high mafs in the principal church; but as Andrew was often abfent from religious folemnities, on account of his great age, that defign was laid afide. It was then concerted that Fiefco fhould invite the uncle and nephew, with all their friends whom he had marked out as victims, to his houfe; where it would be eafy to cut them off at once without danger or refiftance; but as Giannetino was obliged to leave the town on the day which they had chofen, it became neceffary likewife to alter this plan. They at laft determined to attempt by open force, what they found difficult to effect by ftratagem, and fixed on the night between the fecond and third of January, for the execution of their enterprize. The time was chofen with great propriety; for as the Doge of the former year was to quit his office, according to custom, on the first of the month, and his successor could not be elected sooner than the fourth, the republic remained during that interval in a sort of anarchy, and Fiesco might with less violence take possession of the vacant dignity.

The conspirators assemble to execute their plan.

THE morning of that day Fiesco employed in visiting his friends, passing some hours among them with a spirit as gay and unembarrassed as at other times. Towards evening, he paid court to the Dorias with his usual marks of respect, and surveying their countenance and behaviour with the attention natural in his situation, was happy to observe the perfect security in which they remained, without the least foresight or dread of that storm which had been so long a gathering, and was now ready to burst over their heads. From their palace he hastened to his own, which stood by itself in the middle of a large court, surrounded by a high wall. The gates had been set open in the morning, and all persons, without distinction, were allowed to enter, but strong guards posted within the court suffered no one to return. Verrina, meanwhile, and a few persons trusted with the secret of the conspiracy, after conducting Fiesco's vassals, as well as the crews of his gallies, into the palace in small bodies, with as little noise as possible, dispersed themselves through the city, and, in the name of their patron, invited to an entertainment the principal citizens whom they knew to be disgusted with the admini-

EMPEROR CHARLES V. 377

administration of the Dorias, and to have inclination as well as courage to attempt a change in the government. Of the vast number of persons who now filled the palace, a few only knew for what purpose they were assembled; the rest, astonished at finding, instead of the preparations for a feast, a court crowded with armed men, and apartments filled with the instruments of war, gazed on each other with a mixture of curiosity, impatience, and terror.

WHILE their minds were in this state of suspense and agitation, Fiesco appeared. With a look full of alacrity and confidence, he addressed himself to the persons of chief distinction, telling them, that they were not now called to partake of the pleasure of an entertainment, but to join in a deed of valour, which would lead them to liberty and immortal renown. He set before their eyes the exorbitant as well as intolerable authority of the elder Doria, which the ambition of Giannetino, and the partiality of the Emperor to a family more devoted to him than to their country, was about to enlarge and to render perpetual. This unrighteous dominion, continued he, you have it now in your power to subvert, and to establish the freedom of your country on a firm basis. The tyrants must be cut off. I have taken the most effectual measures for this purpose. My associates are numerous. I can depend on allies and protectors if necessary. Happily, the tyrants are as secure as I have been provident.

Fiesco's exhortations to them.

vident. Their infolent contempt of their countrymen has banifhed the fufpicion and timidity which ufually render the guilty quick-fighted to difcern, as well as fagacious to guard againft the vengeance which they deferve. They will now feel the blow, before they fufpect any hoftile hand to be nigh. Let us then fally forth, that we may deliver our country by one generous effort, almoft unaccompanied with danger, and certain of fuccefs. Thefe words, uttered with that irrefiftible fervour which animates the mind when roufed by great objects, made the defired impreffion on the audience. Fiefco's vaffals, ready to execute whatever their mafter fhould command, received his difcourfe with a murmur of applaufe. To many whofe fortunes were defperate, the licence and confufion of an infurrection afforded an agreeable profpect. Thofe of higher rank and more virtuous fentimens, durft not difcover the furprife or horror with which they were ftruck at the propofal of an enterprize no lefs unexpected than atrocious; as each of them imagined the other to be in the fecret of the confpiracy, and faw himfelf furrounded by perfons who waited only a fignal from their leader to perpetrate the greateft crime. With one voice then all applauded, or feigned to applaud, the undertaking.

His interview with his wife.

FIESCO having thus fixed and encouraged his affociates, before he gave them his laft orders, he haftened for a moment to the apartment of his wife,

wife, a lady of the noble houſe of Cibo, whom he loved with tender affection, and whoſe beauty and virtue rendered her worthy of his love. The noiſe of the armed men who crowded the court and palace, having long before this reached her ears, ſhe concluded ſome hazardous enterprize to be in hand, and ſhe trembled for her huſband. He found her in all the anguiſh of uncertainty and fear; and as it was now impoſſible to keep his deſign concealed, he informed her of what he had undertaken. The proſpect of a ſcene ſo full of horror as well as danger, completed her agony; and foreboding immediately in her mind the fatal iſſue of it, ſhe endeavoured, by her tears, her entreaties, and her deſpair, to divert him from his purpoſe. Fieſco, after trying in vain to ſooth and to inſpire her with hope, broke from a ſituation into which an exceſs of tenderneſs had unwarily ſeduced him, though it could not ſhake his reſolution. "Farewell, he cried, as he quitted the apartment, you ſhall either never ſee me more, or you ſhall behold to-morrow every thing in Genoa ſubject to your power."

As ſoon as he rejoined his companions, he allotted each his proper ſtation; ſome were appointed to aſſault and ſeize the different gates of the city; ſome to make themſelves maſters of the principal ſtreets or places of ſtrength: Fieſco reſerved for himſelf the attack of the harbour where Doria's gallies were laid up, as the poſt of chief importance, and of greateſt danger. It was now

They attack the city.

now midnight, and the citizens slept in the security of peace, when this band of conspirators, numerous, desperate, and well-armed, rushed out to execute their plan. They surprised some of the gates, without meeting with any resistance. They got possession of others after a sharp conflict with the soldiers on guard. Verrina, with the galley which had been fitted out against the Turks, blocked up the mouth of the Darsena or little harbour where Doria's fleet lay. All possibility of escape being cut off by this precaution, when Fiesco attempted to enter the gallies from the shore, to which they were made fast, they were in no condition to make resistance, as they were not only unrigged and disarmed, but had no crew on board, except the slaves chained to the oar. Every quarter of the city was now filled with noise and tumult, all the streets resounding with the cry of *Fiesco* and *Liberty*. At that name, so popular and beloved, many of the lower rank took arms, and joined the conspirators. The nobles and partisans of the aristocracy, astonished or affrighted, shut the gates of their houses, and thought of nothing but of securing them from pillage. At last the noise excited by this scene of violence and confusion, reached the palace of Doria; Giannetino started immediately from his bed, and imagining that it was occasioned by some mutiny among the sailors, rushed out with a few attendants, and hurried towards the harbour. The gate of St. Thomas, through which he had to pass, was already in the possession of the conspi-

conspirators, who, the moment he appeared, fell upon him with the utmost fury, and murdered him on the spot. The same must have been the fate of the elder Doria, if Jerome de Fiesco had executed his brother's plan, and had proceeded immediately to attack him in his palace; but he, from the sordid consideration of preventing its being plundered amidst the confusion, having forbid his followers to advance, Andrew got intelligence of his nephew's death, as well as of his own danger; and mounting on horseback, saved himself by flight. Amidst this general consternation, a few senators had the courage to assemble in the palace of the republic[y]. At first, some of the most daring among them attempted to rally the scattered soldiers, and to attack a body of the conspirators; but being repulsed with loss, all agreed that nothing now remained, but to treat with the party which seemed to be irresistible. Deputies were accordingly sent to learn of Fiesco what were the concessions with which he would be satisfied, or rather to submit to whatever terms he should please to prescribe.

BUT by this time Fiesco, with whom they were empowered to negociate, was no more. Just as he was about to leave the harbour, where every thing had succeeded to his wish, that he might join his victorious companions, he heard some

Cause of their miscarriage.

[y] Il palazza della Signoria.

extra-

extraordinary uproar on board the Admiral galley. Alarmed at the noise, and fearing that the slaves might break their chains, and overpower his associates, he ran thither; but the plank which reached from the shore to the vessel happening to overturn, he fell into the sea, whilst he hurried forward too precipitately. Being loaded with heavy armour, he sunk to the bottom, and perished in the very moment when he must have taken full possession of every thing that his ambitious heart could desire. Verrina was the first who discovered this fatal accident, and foreseeing, at once, all its consequences, concealed it with the utmost industry from every one but a few leaders of the conspiracy. Nor was it difficult, amidst the darkness and confusion of the night, to have kept it secret, until a treaty with the senators should have put the city in the power of the conspirators. All their hopes of this were disconcerted by the imprudence of Jerome Fiesco, who, when the deputies of the senate inquired for his brother, the count of Lavagna, that they might make their proposal to him, replied with a childish vanity, " I am now the only person to whom that title belongs, and with me you must treat." These words discovered as well to his friends as to his enemies what had happened, and made the impression which might have been expected upon both. The deputies, encouraged by this event, the only one which could occasion such a sudden revolution as might turn to their advantage, assumed

assumed instantly, with admirable presence of mind, a new tone, suitable to the change in their circumstances, and made high demands. While they endeavoured to gain time by protracting the negociation, the rest of the senators were busy in assembling their partisans, and in forming a body capable of defending the palace of the republic. On the other hand, the conspirators, astonished at the death of a man whom they adored and trusted, and placing no confidence in Jerome, a giddy youth, felt their courage die away, and their arms fall from their hands. That profound and amazing secrecy with which the conspiracy had been concerted, and which had contributed hitherto so much to its success, proved now the chief cause of its miscarriage. The leader was gone; the greater part of those who acted under him, knew not his confidents, and were strangers to the object at which he aimed. There was no person among them whose authority or abilities entitled him to assume Fiesco's place, or to finish his plan; after having lost the spirit which animated it, life and activity deserted the whole body. Many of the conspirators withdrew to their houses, hoping that amidst the darkness of the night they had passed unobserved, and might remain unknown. Others sought for safety by a timely retreat; and before break of day, most of them fled with precipitation from a city, which, but a few hours before, was ready to acknowledge them as masters.

NEXT

BOOK VIII.
1547.
Tranquillity re-established in Genoa.

NEXT morning every thing was quiet in Genoa; not an enemy was to be seen; few marks of the violence of the former night appeared, the conspirators having conducted their enterprize with more noise than bloodshed, and gained all their advantages by surprise, rather than by force of arms. Towards evening, Andrew Doria returned to the city, being met by all the inhabitants, who received him with acclamations of joy. Though the disgrace as well as danger of the preceding night were fresh in his mind, and the mangled body of his kinsman still before his eyes, such was his moderation as well as magnanimity, that the decree issued by the senate against the conspirators, did not exceed that just measure of severity which was requisite for the support of government, and was dictated neither by the violence of resentment, nor the rancour of revenge [z].*

The Emperor alarmed at this conspiracy.

AFTER taking the necessary precautions for preventing the flame, which was now so happily

[z] Thuan. 93. Sigonii Vita Andræ Doriæ, 1196. La Conjuration du Compte de Fiesque, par Cardin. de Retz. Adriani Istoria, lib. vi. 369. Folietæ Conjuratio Jo. Lud. Fiesci, ap. Græv. Thes. Ital. i. 883.

* It is remarkable, that Cardinal de Retz, at the age of eighteen, composed a history of this conspiracy, containing such a discovery of his admiration of Fiesco and his enterprize, as render it not surprising that a minister, so jealous and discerning as Richlieu, should be led, by the perusal of it, to predict the turbulent and dangerous spirit of that young Ecclesiastic. Mem. de Retz, tom. i. p. 13.

extin-

extinguished, from breaking out anew, the first care of the senate was to send an ambassador to the Emperor, to give him a particular detail of what had happened, and to beg his assistance towards the reduction of Montobbio, a strong fort on the hereditary estate of the Fiesci, in which Jerome had shut himself up. Charles was no less alarmed than astonished at an event so strange and unexpected. He could not believe that Fiesco, how bold or adventurous soever, durst have attempted such an enterprize, but on foreign suggestion, and from the hope of foreign aid. Being informed that the Duke of Parma was well acquainted with the plan of the conspirators, he immediately supposed that the Pope could not be ignorant of a measure, which his son had countenanced. Proceeding from this to a farther conjecture, which Paul's cautious maxims of policy in other instances rendered extremely probable, he concluded, that the French King must have known and approved of the design; and he began to apprehend that this spark might again kindle the flame of war which had raged so long in Italy. As he had drained his Italian territories of troops on account of the German war, he was altogether unprovided for resisting any hostile attack in that country; and on the first appearance of danger, he must have detached thither the greatest part of his forces for its defence. In this situation of affairs, it would have been altogether imprudent in the Emperor to have advanced in person against the Elector,

<small>BOOK VIII.</small>

<small>1547.</small>

<small>Suspends his operations in Germany.</small>

Vol. III.   C c   until

until he should learn with some degree of certainty whether such a scene were not about to open in Italy, as might put it out of his power to keep the field with an army sufficient to oppose him.

THE HISTORY OF THE REIGN OF THE EMPEROR CHARLES V.

BOOK IX.

THE Emperor's dread of the hostile intentions of the Pope and French King did not proceed from any imaginary or ill-grounded suspicion. Paul had already given the strongest proofs both of his jealousy and enmity. Charles could not hope, that Francis, after a rivalship of so long continuance, would behold the great advantages which he had gained over the confederate Protestants, without feeling his ancient emulation revive. He was not deceived in this conjecture. Francis had observed the rapid progress of his arms with deep concern, and though hitherto prevented, by circumstances which have been mentioned, from interposing in order to check them, he was now convinced that, if he

1547. Francis jealous of the Emperor's power and success.

did

did not make some extraordinary and timely effort, Charles must acquire such a degree of power as would enable him to give law to the rest of Europe. This apprehension, which did not take its rise from the jealousy of rivalship alone, but was entertained by the wisest politicians of the age, suggested various expedients which might serve to retard the course of the Emperor's victories, and to form by degrees such a combination against him as might put a stop to his dangerous career.

<small>Negociates with the Protestants;</small>

WITH this view, Francis instructed his emissaries in Germany to employ all their address in order to revive the courage of the confederates, and to prevent them from submitting to the Emperor. He made liberal offers of his assistance to the Elector and Landgrave, whom he knew to be the most zealous as well as the most powerful of the whole body; he used every argument, and proposed every advantage, which could either confirm their dread of the Emperor's designs, or determine them not to imitate the inconsiderate credulity of their associates, in giving up their religion and liberties to his disposal. While he took this step towards continuing the civil war which raged in Germany, he endeavoured likewise to stir up foreign enemies against the Emperor.

<small>with Solyman;</small>

He solicited Solyman to seize this favourable opportunity of invading Hungary, which had been drained of all the troops necessary for its defence, in order to form the army against

against the confederates of Smalkalde. He exhorted the Pope to repair, by a vigorous and seasonable effort, the error of which he had been guilty in contributing to raise the Emperor to such a formidable height of power. Finding Paul, both from the consciousness of his own mistake, and his dread of its consequences, abundantly disposed to listen to what he suggested, he availed himself of this favourable disposition which the Pontiff began to discover, as an argument to gain the Venetians. He endeavoured to convince them that nothing could save Italy, and even Europe, from oppression and servitude, but their joining with the Pope and him, in giving the first beginning to a general confederacy, in order to humble that ambitious potentate, whom they had all equal reason to dread.

HAVING set on foot these negociations in the southern courts, he turned his attention next towards those in the north of Europe. As the King of Denmark had particular reasons to be offended with the Emperor, Francis imagined that the object of the league which he had projected would be highly acceptable to him; and lest considerations of caution or prudence should restrain him from joining in it, he attempted to overcome these, by offering him the young Queen of Scots in marriage to his son[a]. As the ministers who governed England in the name of Edward VI. had openly

[a] Mem. de Ribier, i. 600. 606.

declared themselves converts to the opinions of the Reformers, as soon as it became safe upon Henry's death to lay aside that disguise which his intolerant bigotry had forced them to assume, Francis flattered himself that their zeal would not allow them to remain inactive spectators of the overthrow and destruction of those who professed the same faith with themselves. He hoped, that notwithstanding the struggles of faction incident to a minority, and the prospect of an approaching rupture with the Scots, he might prevail on them likewise to take part in the common cause [b].

WHILE Francis employed such a variety of expedients, and exerted himself with such extraordinary activity, to rouse the different states of Europe against his rival, he did not neglect what depended on himself alone. He levied troops in all parts of his dominions; he collected military stores; he contracted with the Swiss cantons for a considerable body of men; he put his finances in admirable order; he remitted considerable sums to the Elector and Landgrave; and took all the other steps necessary towards commencing hostilities, on the shortest warning, and with the greatest vigour [c].

The Emperor greatly alarmed.

OPERATIONS so complicated, and which required the putting so many instruments in mo-

[b] Mem. de Ribier, i. 635.   [c] Ibid. 595.

tion, did not efcape the Emperor's obfervation. He was early informed of Francis's intrigues in the feveral courts of Europe, as well as of his domeftic preparations; and fenfible how fatal an interruption a foreign war would prove to his defigns in Germany, he trembled at the profpect of that event. The danger, however, appeared to him as unavoidable as it was great. He knew the infatiable and well-directed ambition of Solyman, and that he always chofe the feafon for beginning his military enterprifes with prudence equal to the valour with which he conducted them. The Pope, as he had good reafon to believe, wanted not pretexts to juftify a rupture, nor inclination to begin hoftilities. He had already made fome difcovery of his fentiments, by expreffing a joy altogether unbecoming the head of the church, upon receiving an account of the advantage which the Elector of Saxony had gained over Albert of Brandenburg; and as he was now fecure of finding, in the French King, an ally of fufficient power to fupport him, he was at no pains to conceal the violence and extent of his enmity[d]. The Venetians, Charles was well affured, had long obferved the growth of his power with jealoufy, which, added to the folicitations and promifes of France, might at laft quicken their flow counfels, and overcome their natural caution. The Danes and Englifh, it was evident, had both peculiar reafon to be difgufted, as well

[d] Mem. de Ribier, tom. i. 637.

as strong motives to act against him. But above all, he dreaded the active emulation of Francis himself, whom he considered as the soul and mover of any confederacy that could be formed against him; and, as that Monarch had afforded protection to Verina, who sailed directly to Marseilles upon the miscarriage of Fiesco's conspiracy, Charles expected every moment to see the commencement of those hostile operations in Italy, of which he conceived the insurrection in Genoa to have been only the prelude.

Entertains hope from the declining state of Francis's health.

But while he remained in this state of suspense and solicitude, there was one circumstance which afforded him some prospect of escaping the danger. The French King's health began to decline. A disease, which was the effect of his inconsiderate pursuit of pleasure, preyed gradually on his constitution. The preparations for war, as well as the negociations in the different courts, began to languish, together with the Monarch who gave spirit to both. The Genoese, during that interval, reduced Montobbio, took Jerome Fiesco prisoner, and putting him to death, together with his chief adherents, extinguished all remains of the conspiracy. Several of the Imperial cities in Germany, despairing of timely assistance from France, submitted to the Emperor. Even the Landgrave seemed disposed to abandon the Elector, and to bring matters to a speedy accommodation, on such terms as he could obtain. In the mean time, Charles waited with impa-

March.

impatience the issue of a distemper, which was to decide whether he must relinquish all other schemes, in order to prepare for resisting a combination of the greater part of Europe against him, or whether he might proceed to invade Saxony, without interruption or fear of danger.

THE good fortune, so remarkably propitious to his family, that some historians have called it the *Star of the House of Austria*, did not desert him on this occasion. Francis died at Rambouillet, on the last day of March, in the fifty-third year of his age, and the thirty-third of his reign. During twenty-eight years of that time, an avowed rivalship subsisted between him and the Emperor, which involved not only their own dominions, but the greater part of Europe, in wars, which were prosecuted with more violent animosity, and drawn out to a greater length, than had been known in any former period. Many circumstances contributed to this. Their animosity was founded in opposition of interest, heightened by personal emulation, and exasperated not only by mutual injuries, but by reciprocal insults. At the same time, whatever advantage one seemed to possess towards gaining the ascendant, was wonderfully balanced by some favourable circumstance peculiar to the other. The Emperor's dominions were of greater extent, the French King's lay more compact; Francis governed his kingdom with absolute power; that of Charles was limited, but he supplied the want of authority

Death of Francis, and reflections on his character and rivalship with Charles.

rity by address: the troops of the former were more impetuous and enterprising; those of the latter better disciplined, and more patient of fatigue. The talents and abilities of the two Monarchs were as different as the advantages which they possessed, and contributed no less to prolong the contest between them. Francis took his resolutions suddenly, prosecuted them at first with warmth, and pushed them into execution with a most adventurous courage; but being destitute of the perseverance necessary to surmount difficulties, he often abandoned his designs, or relaxed the vigour of pursuit, from impatience, and sometimes from levity. Charles deliberated long, and determined with coolness; but having once fixed his plan, he adhered to it with inflexible obstinacy, and neither danger nor discouragement could turn him aside from the execution of it. The success of their enterprises was suitable to the diversity of their characters, and was uniformly influenced by it. Francis, by his impetuous activity, often disconcerted the Emperor's best laid schemes; Charles, by a more calm but steady prosecution of his designs, checked the rapidity of his rival's career, and baffled or repulsed his most vigorous efforts. The former, at the opening of a war or of a campaign, broke in upon his enemy with the violence of a torrent, and carried all before him; the latter, waiting until he saw the force of his rival begin to abate, recovered in the end not only all that he had lost, but made new acquisitions. Few of the French Monarch's attempts

attempts towards conqueft, whatever promifing af-
fpect they might wear at firft, were conducted to an
happy iffue; many of the Emperor's enterprifes,
even after they appeared defperate and impracticable, terminated in the moft profperous manner.
Francis was dazzled with the fplendour of an undertaking; Charles was allured by the profpect of
its turning to his advantage.

The degree, however, of their comparative
merit and reputation has not been fixed either by
a ftrict fcrutiny into their abilities for government,
or by an impartial confideration of the greatnefs
and fuccefs of their undertakings; and Francis
is one of thofe Monarchs who occupies a higher
rank in the temple of Fame, than either his talents or performances entitle him to hold. This
pre-eminence he owed to many different circumftances. The fuperiority which Charles acquired
by the victory of Pavia, and which from that period he preferved through the remainder of his
reign, was fo manifeft, that Francis's ftruggle
againft his exorbitant and growing dominion was
viewed by moft of the other powers, not only with
the partiality which naturally arifes for thofe who
gallantly maintain an unequal conteft, but with
the favour due to one who was refifting a common enemy, and endeavouring to fet bounds to a
Monarch equally formidable to them all. The
characters of Princes, too, efpecially among their
contemporaries, depend not only upon their talents for government, but upon their qualities as
men.

men. Francis, notwithstanding the many errors conspicuous in his foreign policy and domestic administration, was nevertheless humane, beneficent, generous. He possessed dignity without pride; affability free from meanness; and courtesy exempt from deceit. All who had access to him, and no man of merit was ever denied that privilege, respected and loved him. Captivated with his personal qualities, his subjects forgot his defects as a Monarch, and admiring him as the most accomplished and amiable gentleman in his dominions, they hardly murmured at acts of male-administration, which, in a Prince of less engaging dispositions, would have been deemed unpardonable. This admiration, however, must have been temporary only, and would have died away, with the courtiers who bestowed it; the illusion arising from his private virtues must have ceased, and posterity would have judged of his public conduct with its usual impartiality; but another circumstance prevented this, and his name hath been transmitted to posterity with increasing reputation. Science and the arts had, at that time, made little progress in France. They were just beginning to advance beyond the limits of Italy, where they had revived, and which had hitherto been their only seat. Francis took them immediately under his protection, and vied with Leo himself, in the zeal and munificence with which he encouraged them. He invited learned men to his court, he conversed with them familiarly, he employed them in bufinefs, he raifed them to offices of dignity, and honoured them with his confidence. That order of men, not more prone to complain when denied the refpect to which they conceive themfelves entitled, than apt to be pleafed when treated with the diftinction which they confider as their due, thought they could not exceed in gratitude to fuch a benefactor, and ftrained their invention, and employed all their ingenuity in panegyric. Succeeding authors, warmed with their defcriptions of Francis's bounty, adopted their encomiums, and even added to them. The appellation of *Father of Letters* beftowed upon Francis, hath rendered his memory facred among hiftorians; and they feem to have regarded it as a fort of impiety to uncover his infirmities, or to point out his defects. Thus Francis, notwithftanding his inferior abilities, and want of fuccefs, hath more than equalled the fame of Charles. The good qualities which he poffeffed as a man, have entitled him to greater admiration and praife than have been beftowed upon the extenfive genius and fortunate arts of a more capable, but lefs amiable rival.

By his death a confiderable change was made in the ftate of Europe. Charles, grown old in the arts of government and command, had now to contend only with younger Monarchs, who could not be regarded as worthy to enter the lifts with him, who had ftood fo many encounters with Henry VIII. and Francis I. and come off with honour

Effects of Francis's death.

honour in all those different struggles. By this event, he was eased of all disquietude, and was happy to find that he might begin with safety those operations against the Elector of Saxony, which he had hitherto been obliged to suspend. He knew the abilities of Henry II. who had just mounted the throne of France, to be greatly inferior to those of his father, and foresaw that he would be so much occupied for some time in displacing the late King's ministers, whom he hated, and in gratifying the ambitious demands of his own favourites, that he had nothing to dread, either from his personal efforts, or from any confederacy which this unexperienced Prince could form.

Charles marches against the Elector of Saxony. April 13.

But as it was uncertain how long such an interval of security might continue, Charles determined instantly to improve it: and as soon as he heard of Francis's demise, he began his march from Egra on the borders of Bohemia. But the departure of the papal troops, together with the retreat of the Flemings, had so much diminished his army, that sixteen thousand men were all he could assemble. With this inconsiderable body he set out on an expedition, the event of which was to decide what degree of authority he should possess from that period in Germany: but as this little army consisted chiefly of the veteran Spanish and Italian bands, he did not, in trusting to them, commit much to the decision of chance; and even with so small a force he had reason to entertain the most sanguine hopes of success. The Elector had levied an army greatly

greatly superior in number; but neither the experience and discipline of his troops, nor the abilities of his officers, were to be compared with those of the Emperor. The Elector, besides, had already been guilty of an error, which deprived him of all the advantage which he might have derived from his superiority in number, and was alone sufficient to have occasioned his ruin. Instead of keeping his forces united, he detached one great body towards the frontiers of Bohemia, in order to facilitate his junction with the malecontents of that kingdom, and cantoned a considerable part of what remained in different places of Saxony, where he expected the Emperor would make the first impression, vainly imagining that open towns, with small garrisons, might be rendered tenable against an enemy.

The Emperor entered the southern frontier of Saxony, and attacked Altorf upon the Elster. The impropriety of the measure which the Elector had taken was immediately seen, the troops posted in that town surrendering without resistance; and those in all the other places between that and the Elbe, either imitated their example, or fled as the Imperialists approached. Charles, that they might not recover from the panic with which they seemed to be struck, advanced without losing a moment. The Elector, who had fixed his head-quarters at Meissen, continued in his wonted state of fluctuation and uncertainty. He even became more undetermined, in proportion as the danger

Progress of his arms.

danger drew near, and called for prompt and decisive resolutions. Sometimes he acted, as if he had resolved to defend the banks of the Elbe, and to hazard a battle with the enemy, as soon as the detachments which he had called in were able to join him. At other times, he abandoned this as rash and perilous, seeming to adopt the more prudent counsels of those who advised him to endeavour at protracting the war, and for that end to retire under the fortifications of Wittemberg, where the Imperialists could not attack him without manifest disadvantage, and where he might wait, in safety, for the succours which he expected from Mecklenburgh, Pomerania, and the Protestant cities on the Baltic. Without fixing upon either of these plans, he broke down the bridge at Meissen, and marched along the east bank of the Elbe to Muhlberg. There he deliberated anew, and, after much hesitation, adopted one of those middle schemes, which are always acceptable to feeble minds incapable of deciding. He left a detachment at Muhlberg to oppose the Imperialists, if they should attempt to pass at that place, and advancing a few miles with his main body, encamped there in expectation of the event, according to which he proposed to regulate his subsequent motions.

Passes the Elbe.

CHARLES, meanwhile, pushing forward incessantly, arrived the evening of the twenty-third of April on the banks of the Elbe, opposite to Muhlberg.

berg. The river, at that place, was three hundred paces in breadth, above four feet in depth, its current rapid, and the bank poffeffed by the Saxons was higher than that which he occupied. Undifmayed, however, by all thefe obftacles, he called together his general officers, and, without afking their opinions, communicated to them his intention of attempting next morning to force his paffage over the river, and to attack the enemy wherever he could come up with them. They all expreffed their aftonifhment at fuch a bold refolution; and even the Duke of Alva, though naturally daring and impetuous, and Maurice of Saxony, notwithftanding his impatience to crufh his rival the Elector, remonftrated earneftly againft it. But the Emperor, confiding in his own judgment or good fortune, paid no regard to their arguments, and gave the orders neceffary for executing his defign.

EARLY in the morning a body of Spanifh and Italian foot marched towards the river, and began an inceffant fire upon the enemy. The long heavy mufkets ufed in that age, did execution on the oppofite bank, and many of the foldiers, hurried on by a martial ardour in order to get nearer the enemy, rufhed into the ftream, and, advancing breaft-high, fired with a more certain aim, and with greater effect. Under cover of their fire, a bridge of boats was begun to be laid for the infantry; and a peafant having undertaken to conduct the cavalry through the river by a ford a ford with which he was well acquainted, they also were put in motion. The Saxons posted in Muhlberg endeavoured to obstruct these operations, by a brisk fire from a battery which they had erected; but as a thick fog covered all the low grounds upon the river, they could not take aim with any certainty, and the Imperialists suffered very little; at the same time the Saxons being much galled by the Spaniards and Italians, they set on fire some boats which had been collected near the village, and prepared to retire. The Imperialists perceiving this, ten Spanish soldiers instantly stript themselves, and holding their swords with their teeth, swam across the river, put to flight such of the Saxons as ventured to oppose them, saved from the flames as many boats as were sufficient to complete their own bridge, and by this spirited and successful action, encouraged their companions no less than they intimidated the enemy.

By this time, the cavalry, each trooper having a foot soldier behind him, began to enter the river, the light horse marching in the front, followed by the men at arms, whom the Emperor led in person, mounted on a Spanish horse, dressed in a sumptuous habit, and carrying a javelin in his hand. Such a numerous body struggling through a great river, in which, according to the directions of their guide, they were obliged to make several turns, sometimes treading on a firm bottom, sometimes swimming, presented to their companions,

nions, whom they left behind, a spectacle equally magnificent and interesting[d]. Their courage, at last, surmounted every obstacle, no man betraying any symptom of fear, when the Emperor shared in the danger no less than the meanest soldier. The moment that they reached the opposite side, Charles, without waiting the arrival of the rest of the infantry, advanced towards the Saxons with the troops which had passed along with him, who, flushed with their good fortune, and despising an enemy who had neglected to oppose them, when it might have been done with such advantage, made no account of their superior numbers, and marched on as to a certain victory.

During all these operations, which necessarily consumed much time, the Elector remained inactive in his camp; and from an infatuation which appears to be so amazing, that the best informed historians impute it to the treacherous arts of his generals who deceived him by false intelligence, he would not believe that the Emperor had passed the river, or could be so near at hand[e]. Being convinced, at last, of his fatal mistake, by the concurring testimony of eye-witnesses, he gave orders for retreating towards Wittemberg. But a German army, encumbered, as usual, with baggage and artillery, could not be put suddenly in

Ill conduct of the Elector.

[d] Avila, 115, a.
[e] Camerar. ap. Freher. iii. 493. Struv. Corp. Hist. Germ. 1047. 1049.

BOOK IX.

1547.

Battle of Mulhausen.

motion. They had juft begun to march when the light troops of the enemy came in view, and the Elector faw an engagement to be unavoidable. As he was no lefs bold in action than irrefolute in council, he made the difpofition for battle with the greateft prefence of mind, and in the moft proper manner; taking advantage of a great foreft to cover his wings, fo as to prevent his being furrounded by the enemy's cavalry, which were far more numerous than his own. The Emperor, likewife, ranged his men in order as they came up, and riding along the ranks, exhorted them with few but efficacious words to do their duty. It was with a very different fpirit that the two armies advanced to the charge. As the day, which had hitherto been dark and cloudy, happened to clear up at that moment, this accidental circumftance made an impreffion on the different parties correfponding to the tone of their minds; the Saxons, furprifed and difheartened, felt pain at being expofed fully to the view of the enemy; the Imperialifts, being now fecure that the Proteftant forces could not efcape from them, rejoiced at the return of fun-fhine, as a certain prefage of victory. The fhock of battle would not have been long doubtful, if the perfonal courage which the Elector difplayed, together with the activity which he exerted from the moment that the approach of the enemy rendered an engagement certain, and cut off all poffibility of hefitation, had not revived in fome degree the fpirit of his troops. They repulfed the Hungarian lighthorfe who began the attack, and received with firmnefs

firmnefs the men at arms who next advanced to the charge; but as thefe were the flower of the Imperial army, were commanded by experienced officers, and fought under the Emperor's eye, the Saxons foon began to give way, and the light troops rallying at the fame time and falling on their flanks, the flight became general. A fmall body of chofen foldiers, among whom the Elector had fought in perfon, ftill continued to defend themfelves, and endeavoured to fave their mafter by retiring into the foreft; but being furrounded on every fide, the Elector wounded in the face, exhaufted with fatigue, and perceiving all refiftance to be vain, furrendered himfelf a prifoner. He was conducted immediately towards the Emperor, whom he found juft returned from the purfuit, ftanding on the field of battle in the full exultation of fuccefs, and receiving the congratulations of his officers, upon this complete victory obtained by his valour and conduct. Even in fuch an unfortunate and humbling fituation, the Elector's behaviour was equally magnanimous and decent. Senfible of his condition, he approached his conqueror without any of the fullennefs or pride which would have been improper in a captive; and confcious of his own dignity, he defcended to no mean fubmiffion, unbecoming the high ftation which he held among the German Princes. "The fortune of war, faid he, has made me your prifoner, moft gracious Emperor, and I hope to be treated"——

BOOK IX.
1547.

The Elector defeated, and taken prifoner.

Here,

BOOK IX.

1547.
His harsh reception by the Emperor.

Here, Charles harshly interrupted him: "And am I then, at last, acknowledged to be Emperor? Charles of Ghent was the only title you lately allowed me. You shall be treated as you deserve." At these words he turned from him abruptly with an haughty air. To this cruel repulse, the King of the Romans added reproaches in his own name, using expressions still more ungenerous and insulting. The Elector made no reply; but, with an unaltered countenance, which discovered neither astonishment nor dejection, accompanied the Spanish soldiers appointed to guard him [f].

Charles's progress after his victory.

This decisive victory cost the Imperialists only fifty men. Twelve hundred of the Saxons were killed, chiefly in the pursuit, and a greater number taken prisoners. About four hundred kept in a body, and escaped to Wittemberg, together with the Electoral Prince, who had likewise been wounded in the action. After resting two days in the field of battle, partly to refresh his army, and partly to receive the deputies of the adjacent towns, which were impatient to secure his protection by submitting to his will, the Emperor began to move towards Wittemberg, that he might terminate the war at once, by the reduction of that city. The unfortunate Elector was

[f] Sleid. Hist. 426. Thuan. 136. Hortensius de Bello German. ap. Scard. vol. ii. 498. Descript. Pugnæ Mulberg. ibid. p. 509. P. Heuter. Rer. Austr. lib. xii. c. 13. p. 298.

carried

carried along in a fort of triumph, and expofed every where, as a captive, to his own fubjects; a fpectacle extremely afflicting to them, who both honoured and loved him; though the infult was fo far from fubduing his firm fpirit, that it did not even ruffle the wonted tranquillity and compofure of his mind.

As Wittemberg, the refidence, in that age, of the electoral branch of the Saxon family, was one of the ftrongeft cities in Germany, and could not be taken, if properly defended, without great difficulty, the Emperor marched thither with the utmoft difpatch, hoping that while the confternation occafioned by his victory was ftill recent, the inhabitants might imitate the example of their countrymen, and fubmit to his power, as foon as he appeared before their walls. But Sybilla of Cleves, the Elector's wife, a woman no lefs diftinguifhed by her abilities than her virtue, inftead of abandoning herfelf to tears and lamentations upon her hufband's misfortune, endeavoured, by her example as well as exhortations, to animate the citizens. She infpired them with fuch refolution, that, when fummoned to furrender, they returned a vigorous anfwer, warning the Emperor to behave towards their fovereign with the refpect due to his rank, as they were determined to treat Albert of Brandenburg, who was ftill a prifoner, precifely in the fame manner that he treated the Elector. The fpirit of the inhabitants, no lefs than the ftrength of the city, feemed now to render a fiege in form neceffary.

necessary. After such a signal victory it would have been disgraceful not to have undertaken it, though at the same time the Emperor was destitute of every thing requisite for carrying it on. But Maurice removed all difficulties by engaging to furnish provisions, artillery, ammunition, pioneers, and whatever else should be needed. Trusting to this, Charles gave orders to open the trenches before the town. It quickly appeared, that Maurice's eagerness to reduce the capital of those dominions, which he expected as his reward for taking arms against his kinsman, and deserting the Protestant cause, had led him to promise what exceeded his power to perform. A battering train was, indeed, carried safely down the Elbe from Dresden to Wittemberg; but as Maurice had not sufficient force to preserve a secure communication between his own territories and the camp of the besiegers, Count Mansfeldt, who commanded a body of electoral troops, intercepted and destroyed a convoy of provisions and military stores, and dispersed a band of pioneers destined for the service of the Imperialists. This put a stop to the progress of the siege, and convinced the Emperor, that as he could not rely on Maurice's promises, recourse ought to be had to some more expeditious as well as more certain method of getting possession of the town.

The Emperor's ungenerous treatment of the Elector.

THE unfortunate Elector was in his hands, and Charles was ungenerous and hard-hearted enough to take advantage of this, in order to make

make an experiment whether he might not bring about his defign, by working upon the tendernefs of a wife for her hufband, or upon the piety of children towards their parent. With this view, he fummoned Sybilla a fecond time to open the gates, letting her know that if fhe again refufed to comply, the Elector fhould anfwer with his head for her obftinacy. To convince her that this was not an empty threat, he brought his prifoner to an immediate trial. The proceedings againft him were as irregular as the ftratagem was barbarous. Inftead of confulting the ftates of the Empire, or remitting the caufe to any court, which, according to the German conftitution, might have legally taken cognizance of the Elector's crime, he fubjected the greateft Prince in the Empire to the jurifdiction of a court-martial, compofed of Spanifh and Italian officers, and in which the unrelenting Duke of Alva, a fit inftrument for any act of violence, prefided. This ftrange tribunal founded its charge upon the ban of the Empire which had been iffued againft the prifoner by the fole authority of the Emperor, and was deftitute of every legal formality which could render it valid. But the court-martial, prefuming the Elector to be thereby manifeftly convicted of treafon and rebellion, condemned him to fuffer death by being beheaded. This decree was intimated to the Elector while he was amufing himfelf in playing at Chefs with Erneft of Brunfwick his fellow-prifoner. He paufed for a moment, though without difcovering any fymptom either

1547.
The Elector's magnanimity.

either of surprize or terror; and after taking notice of the irregularity as well as injustice of the Emperor's proceedings: "It is easy, continued he, to comprehend his scheme. I must die, because Wittemberg will not surrender; and I shall lay down my life with pleasure, if, by that sacrifice, I can preserve the dignity of my house, and transmit to my posterity the inheritance which belongs to them. Would to God, that this sentence may not affect my wife and children more than it intimidates me! and that they, for the sake of adding a few days to a life already too long, may not renounce honours and territories which they were born to possess [g]!" He then turned to his antagonist, whom he challenged to continue the game. He played with his usual attention and ingenuity, and having beat Ernest, expressed all the satisfaction which is commonly felt on gaining such victories. After this, he withdrew to his own apartment, that he might employ the rest of his time in such religious exercises as were proper in his situation [h].

The distress of his family.

IT was not with the same indifference, or composure, that the account of the Elector's danger was received in Wittemberg. Sybilla, who had supported with such undaunted fortitude her husband's misfortunes, while she imagined that they could reach no farther than to diminish his power

[g] Thuan. i. 142.   [h] Struvii Corpus, 1050.

or territories, felt all her resolution fail as soon as his life was threatened. Solicitous to save that, she despised every other consideration; and was willing to make any sacrifice, in order to appease an incensed conqueror. At the same time, the Duke of Cleves, the Elector of Brandenburg, and Maurice, to none of whom Charles had communicated the true motives of his violent proceedings against the Elector, interceded warmly with him to spare his life. The first was prompted to do so merely by compassion for his sister, and regard for his brother-in-law. The two others dreaded the universal reproach that they would incur, if, after having boasted so often of the ample security which the Emperor had promised them with respect to their religion, the first effect of their union with him should be the public execution of a Prince, who was justly held in reverence as the most zealous protector of the Protestant cause. Maurice, in particular, foresaw that he must become the object of detestation to the Saxons, and could never hope to govern them with tranquillity, if he were considered by them as accessary to the death of his nearest kinsman, in order that he might obtain possession of his dominions.

While they, from such various motives, solicited Charles, with the most earnest importunity, not to execute the sentence; Sybilla, and his children, conjured the Elector, by letters as well as messengers, to scruple at no concession that would extricate

His treaty with Charles, by which he surrenders the Electorate;

extricate him out of the present danger, and deliver them from their fears and anguish on his account. The Emperor, perceiving that the expedient which he had tried began to prodcce the effect that he intended, fell by degrees from his former rigour, and allowed himself to soften into promises of clemency and forgiveness, if the Elector would shew himself worthy of his favour, by submitting to reasonable terms. The Elector, on whom the consideration of what he might suffer himself had made no impression, was melted by the tears of a wife whom he loved, and could not resist the intreaties of his family. In compliance with their repeated solicitations, he agreed to articles of accommodation, which he would otherwise have rejected with disdain. The chief of them were, that he should resign the Electoral dignity, as well for himself as for his posterity, into the Emperor's hands, to be disposed of entirely at his pleasure; that he should instantly put the Imperial troops in possession of the cities of Wittemberg and Gotha; that he should set Albert of Brandenburg at liberty without ransom; that he should submit to the decrees of the Imperial chamber, and acquiesce in whatever reformation the Emperor should make in the constitution of that court; that he should renounce all leagues against the Emperor or King of the Romans, and enter into no alliance for the future, in which they were not comprehended. In return for these important concessions, the Emperor not only promised to spare his life,

life, but to settle on him and his posterity the city of Gotha and its territories, together with an annual pension of fifty thousand florins, payable out of the revenues of the Electorate; and likewise to grant him a sum in ready money to be applied towards the discharge of his debts. Even these articles of grace were clogged with the mortifying condition of his remaining the Emperor's prisoner during the rest of his life[1]. To the whole, Charles had subjoined, that he should submit to the decrees of the Pope and council with regard to the controverted points in religion; but the Elector, though he had been persuaded to sacrifice all the objects which men commonly hold to be the dearest and most valuable, was inflexible with regard to this point; and neither threats nor intreaties could prevail to make him renounce what he deemed to be truth, or persuade him to act in opposition to the dictates of his conscience.

and remains a prisoner.

As soon as the Saxon garrison marched out of Wittemberg, the Emperor fulfilled his engagements to Maurice; and in reward for his merit in having deserted the Protestant cause, and having contributed with such success towards the dissolution of the Smalkaldic league, he gave him possession of that city, together with all the other towns in the Electorate. It was not without reluctance, however, that he made such a sacrifice;

Maurice put in possession of the Electoral dominions.

---

[1] Sleid. 427. Thuan. i. 142. Du Mont, Corps Diplom. iv. p. 11. 332.

BOOK IX.
1547.

the extraordinary succefs of his arms had begun to operate, in its usual manner, upon his ambitious mind, suggesting new and vast projects for the aggrandizement of his family, towards the accomplishment of which the retaining of Saxony would have been of the utmost consequence. But as this scheme was not then ripe for execution, he durst not yet venture to disclose it; nor would it have been either safe or prudent to offend Maurice, at that juncture, by such a manifest violation of all the promises, which had seduced him to abandon his natural allies.

Negociations with the Landgrave.

THE Landgrave, Maurice's father-in-law, was still in arms; and though now left alone to maintain the Protestant cause, was neither a feeble nor contemptible enemy. His dominions were of considerable extent; his subjects animated with zeal for the Reformation; and if he could have held the Imperialists at bay for a short time, he had much to hope from a party whose strength was still unbroken, whose union as well as vigour might return, and which had reason to depend, with certainty, on being effectually supported by the King of France. The Landgrave thought not of any thing so bold or adventurous; but being seized with the same consternation which had taken possession of his associates, he was intent only on the means of procuring favourable terms from the Emperor, whom he viewed as a conqueror, to whose will there was a necessity of submitting.

Maurice

Maurice encouraged this tame and pacific spirit, by magnifying, on the one hand, the Emperor's power; by boasting, on the other, of his own interest with his victorious ally; and by representing the advantageous conditions which he could not fail of obtaining by his intercession for a friend, whom he was so solicitous to save. Sometimes the Landgrave was induced to place such unbounded confidence in his promises, that he was impatient to bring matters to a final accommodation. On other occasions, the Emperor's exorbitant ambition, restrained neither by the scruples of decency, nor the maxims of justice, together with the recent and shocking proof which he had given of this in his treatment of the Elector of Saxony, came so full into his thoughts, and made such a lively impression on them, that he broke off abruptly the negociations which he had begun; seeming to be convinced that it was more prudent to depend for safety on his own arms, than to confide in Charles's generosity. But this bold resolution, which despair had suggested to an impatient spirit, fretted by disappointments, was not of long continuance. Upon a more deliberate survey of the enemy's power, as well as his own weakness, his doubts and fears returned upon him, and together with them the spirit of negociating, and the desire of accommodation.

MAURICE, and the Elector of Brandenburg, acted as mediators between him and the Emperor; *The conditions prescribed by the Emperor.*

peror; and after all that the former had vaunted of his influence, the conditions prescribed to the Landgrave were extremely rigorous. The articles with regard to his renouncing the league of Smalkalde, acknowledging the Emperor's authority, and submitting to the decrees of the Imperial chamber, were the same which had been imposed on the Elector of Saxony. Besides these, he was required to surrender his person and territories to the Emperor; to implore for pardon on his knees; to pay an hundred and fifty thousand crowns towards defraying the expences of the war; to demolish the fortifications of all the towns in his dominions except one; to oblige the garrison which he placed in it to take an oath of fidelity to the Emperor; to allow a free passage through his territories to the Imperial troops as often as it shall be demanded; to deliver up all his artillery and ammunition to the Emperor; to set at liberty, without ransom, Henry of Brunswick, together with the other prisoners whom he had taken during the war; and neither to take arms himself, nor to permit any of his subjects to serve, against the Emperor or his allies for the future [k].

To which he submits.

THE Landgrave ratified these articles, though with the utmost reluctance, as they contained no stipulation with regard to the manner in which he was to be treated, and left him entirely at the

[k] Sleid. 430. Thuan. l. iv. 146.

Emperor's mercy. Neceſſity, however, compelled him to give his aſſent to them. Charles, who had aſſumed the haughty and imperious tone of a conqueror, ever ſince the reduction of Saxony, inſiſted on unconditional ſubmiſſion, and would permit nothing to be added to the terms which he had preſcribed, that could in any degree limit the fulneſs of his power, or reſtrain him from behaving as he ſaw meet towards a Prince whom he regarded as abſolutely at his diſpoſal. But though he would not vouchſafe to negociate with the Landgrave, on ſuch a footing of equality, as to ſuffer any article to be inſerted among thoſe which he had dictated to him, that could be conſidered as a formal ſtipulation for the ſecurity and freedom of his perſon; he, or his miniſters in his name, gave the Elector of Brandenburg and Maurice ſuch full ſatisfaction with regard to this point, that they aſſured the Landgrave, that Charles would behave to him in the ſame way as he had done to the Duke of Wurtemberg, and would allow him, whenever he had made his ſubmiſſion, to return to his own territories. Upon finding the Landgrave to be ſtill poſſeſſed with his former ſuſpicions of the Emperor's intentions, and unwilling to truſt verbal or ambiguous declarations, in a matter of ſuch eſſential concern as his own liberty, they ſent him a bond ſigned by them both, containing the moſt ſolemn obligations, that if any violence whatſoever was offered to his perſon, during his interview with the Emperor, they would inſtantly ſurrender themſelves to to his sons, and remain in their hands to be treated by them in the same manner as the Emperor should treat him [1].

He repairs to the Imperial court.

This, together with the indispensable obligation of performing what was contained in the articles of which he had accepted, removed his doubts and scruples, or made it necessary to get over them. He repaired, for that purpose, to the Imperial camp at Hall in Saxony, where a circumstance occurred which revived his suspicions and increased his fears. Just as he was about to enter the chamber of presence, in order to make his public submission to the Emperor, a copy of the articles which he had approved of was put into his hands, in order that he might ratify them anew. Upon perusing them, he perceived that the Imperial ministers had added two new articles; one importing, that if any dispute should arise concerning the meaning of the former conditions, the Emperor should have the right of putting what interpretation upon them he thought most reasonable; the other, that the Landgrave was bound to submit implicitly to the decisions of the council of Trent. This unworthy artifice, calculated to surprise him into an approbation of articles, to which he had not the most distant idea of assenting, by proposing them to him at a time when his mind was engrossed and disquieted with the thoughts of

[1] Du Mont Corps Diplom. iv. p. 11. 336.

that humiliating ceremony which he had to perform, filled the Landgrave with indignation, and made him break out into all those violent expressions of rage to which his temper was prone. With some difficulty, the Elector of Brandenburg and Maurice prevailed at length on the Emperor's ministers to drop the former article as unjust, and to explain the latter in such a manner, that he could agree to it, without openly renouncing the Protestant religion.

The manner in which the Emperor received him.

THIS obstacle being surmounted, the Landgrave was impatient to finish a ceremony which, how mortifying soever, had been declared necessary towards his obtaining pardon. The Emperor was seated on a magnificent throne, with all the ensigns of his dignity, surrounded by a numerous train of the Princes of the Empire, among whom was Henry of Brunswick, lately the Landgrave's prisoner, and now, by a sudden reverse of fortune, a spectator of his humiliation. The Landgrave was introduced with great solemnity, and advancing towards the throne, fell upon his knees. His chancellor, who walked behind him, immediately read, by his master's command, a paper which contained an humble confession of the crime whereof he had been guilty; an acknowledgment that he had merited on that account the most severe punishment; an absolute resignation of himself and his dominions to be disposed of at the Emperor's pleasure; a submissive petition for pardon, his hopes of which

which were founded entirely on the Emperor's clemency; and it concluded with promises of behaving, for the future, like a subject whose principles of loyalty and obedience would be confirmed, and would even derive new force from the sentiments of gratitude which must hereafter fill and animate his heart. While the chancellor was reading this abject declaration, the eyes of all the spectators were fixed on the unfortunate Landgrave; few could behold a Prince, so powerful as well as high-spirited, suing for mercy in the posture of a supplicant, without being touched with commiseration, and perceiving serious reflections arise in their minds upon the instability and emptiness of human grandeur. The Emperor viewed the whole transaction with an haughty unfeeling composure; and preserving a profound silence himself, made a sign to one of his secretaries to read his answer; the tenor of which was, That though he might have justly inflicted on him the grievous punishment which his crimes deserved, yet, prompted by his own generosity, moved by the solicitations of several Princes in behalf of the Landgrave, and influenced by his penitential acknowledgments, he would not deal with him according to the rigour of justice, and would subject him to no penalty that was not specified in the articles which he had already subscribed. The moment the secretary had finished, Charles turned away abruptly, without deigning to give the unhappy suppliant any sign of compassion or reconcilement. He did not even desire

desire him to rise from his knees; which the
Landgrave having ventured to do unbidden, advanced towards the Emperor with an intention to
kiss his hand, flattering himself, that his guilt
being now fully expiated, he might presume to
take that liberty. But the Elector of Brandenburg, perceiving that this familiarity would be
offensive to the Emperor, interposed, and desired the Landgrave to go along with him and
Maurice to the Duke of Alva's apartments in
the castle.

HE was received and entertained by that nobleman with the respect and courtesy due to such a
guest. But after supper, while he was engaged in
play, the Duke took the Elector and Maurice
aside, and communicated to them the Emperor's
orders, that the Landgrave must remain a prisoner
in that place under the custody of a Spanish guard.
As they had not hitherto entertained the most distant suspicion of the Emperor's sincerity or rectitude of intention, their surprise was excessive, and
their indignation not inferior to it, on discovering
how greatly they had been deceived themselves,
and how infamously abused, in having been made
the instruments of deceiving and ruining their
friend. They had recourse to complaints, to arguments, and to intreaties, in order to save themselves from that disgrace, and to extricate him out
of the wretched situation into which he had been
betrayed by too great confidence in them. But
the Duke of Alva remained inflexible, and pleaded

He is detained a prisoner.

ed the neceſſity of executing the Emperor's commands. By this time it grew late, and the Landgrave, who knew nothing of what had paſſed, nor dreaded the ſnare in which he was entangled, prepared for departing, when the fatal orders were intimated to him. He was ſtruck dumb at firſt with aſtoniſhment, but after being ſilent a few moments, he broke out into all the violent expreſſions which horror, at injuſtice accompanied with fraud, naturally ſuggeſts. He complained, he expoſtulated, he exclaimed; ſometimes inveighing againſt the Emperor's artifices as unworthy of a great and generous Prince; ſometimes cenſuring the credulity of his friends in truſting to Charles's inſidious promiſes; ſometimes charging them with meanneſs in ſtooping to lend their aſſiſtance towards the execution of ſuch a perfidious and diſhonourable ſcheme; and in the end he required them to remember their engagements to his children, and inſtantly to fulfil them. They, after giving way for a little to the torrent of his paſſion, ſolemnly aſſerted their own innocence and upright intention in the whole tranſaction, and encouraged him to hope, that as ſoon as they ſaw the Emperor, they would obtain redreſs of an injury, which affected their own honour, no leſs than it did his liberty. At the ſame time, in order to ſoothe his rage and impatience, Maurice remained with him during the night, in the apartment where he was confined [m].

[m] Sleid. 433. Thuan. l. iv. 147. Struv. Corp. Hiſt. Germ. ii. 1052.

NEXT morning, the Elector and Maurice applied jointly to the Emperor, representing the infamy to which they would be exposed throughout Germany, if the Landgrave were detained in custody; that they would not have advised, nor would he himself have consented to an interview, if they had suspected that the loss of his liberty was to be the consequence of his submission; that they were bound to procure his release, having plighted their faith to that effect, and engaged their own persons as sureties for his. Charles listened to their earnest remonstrances with the utmost coolness. As he now stood no longer in need of their services, they had the mortification to find that their former obsequiousness was forgotten, and little regard paid to their intercession. He was ignorant, he told them, of their particular or private transactions with the Landgrave, nor was his conduct to be regulated by any engagements into which they had thought fit to enter; though he knew well what he himself had promised, which was not that the Landgrave should be exempt from all restraint, but that he should not be kept a prisoner during life*. Having

BOOK IX.

1547.
The Elector of Brandenburg and Maurice solicit in vain for his liberty.

---

* According to several historians of great name, the Emperor, in his treaty with the Landgrave, stipulated that he would not detain him in any prison. But in executing the deed, which was written in the German tongue, the Imperial ministers fraudulently substituted the word *ewiger*, instead of *einiger*, and thus the treaty, in place of a promise that he should

ing said this with a peremptory and decisive tone, he put an end to the conference; and they seeing no probability, at that time, of making any impression upon the Emperor, who seemed to have taken this resolution deliberately, and to be obstinately bent on adhering to it, were obliged to acquaint the unfortunate prisoner with the ill success of their endeavours in his behalf. The disappointment threw him into a new and more violent transport of rage, so that to prevent his proceeding to some desperate extremity, the Elector and Maurice promised that they would not quit the Emperor, until, by the frequency and fervour of their intercessions, they had extorted his consent to set him free. They accordingly renewed their solicitations a few days afterwards, but found Charles more haughty and intractable than before, and were warned that if

should not be detained in *any* prison, contained only an engagement that he should not be detained in *perpetual* imprisonment. But authors, eminent for historical knowledge and critical accuracy, have called in question the truth of this common story. The silence of Sleidan with regard to it, as well as its not being mentioned in the various memorials which he has published concerning the Landgrave's imprisonment, greatly favour this opinion. But as several books which contain the information necessary towards discussing this point with accuracy, are written in the German language, which I do not understand, I cannot pretend to inquire into this matter with the same precision wherewith I have endeavoured to settle some other controverted facts which have occurred in the course of this history. See Struv. Corp. 1052. Mosheim's Ecclef. Hist. vol. ii. p. 161, 162. Engl. edition.

they

they touched again upon a subject so disagreeable, and with regard to which he had determined to hear nothing farther, he would instantly give orders to convey the prisoner into Spain. Afraid of hurting the Landgrave by an officious or ill-timed zeal to serve him, they not only desisted, but left the court, and as they did not chuse to meet the first sallies of the Landgrave's rage upon his learning the cause of their departure, they informed him of it by a letter, wherein they exhorted him to fulfil all that he had promised to the Emperor, as the most certain means of procuring a speedy release.

BOOK IX.

1547.

WHATEVER violent emotions their abandoning his cause in this manner occasioned, the Landgrave's impatience to recover liberty made him follow their advice. He paid the sum which had been imposed on him, ordered his fortresses to be razed, and renounced all alliances which could give offence. This prompt compliance with the will of the conqueror produced no effect. He was still guarded with the same vigilant severity; and being carried about, together with the degraded Elector of Saxony, wherever the Emperor went, their disgrace and his triumph was each day renewed. The fortitude as well as equanimity, with which the Elector bore these repeated insults, were not more remarkable than the Landgrave's fretfulness and impatience. His active impetuous mind could ill brook restraint; and

His impatience under restraint.

and reflection upon the shameful artifices, by which he had been decoyed into that situation, as well as indignation at the injustice with which he was still detained in it, drove him often to the wildest excesses of passion.

The rigour of the Emperor's exactions in Germany.

THE people of the different cities, to whom Charles thus wantonly exposed those illustrious prisoners as a public spectacle, were sensibly touched with such an insult offered to the Germanic body, and murmured loudly at this indecent treatment of two of its greatest Princes. They had soon other causes of complaint, and such as affected them more nearly. Charles proceeded to add oppression to insult, and arrogating to himself all the rights of a conqueror, exercised them with the utmost rigour. He ordered his troops to seize the artillery and military stores belonging to such as had been members of the Smalkaldic league, and having collected upwards of five hundred pieces of cannon, a great number in that age, he sent part of them into the Low-Countries, part into Italy, and part into Spain, in order to spread by this means the fame of his success, and that they might serve as monuments of his having subdued a nation hitherto deemed invincible. He then levied, by his sole authority, large sums of money, as well upon those who had served him with fidelity during the war, as upon such as had been in arms against him; upon the former, as their contingent towards a war, which, having been undertaken, as he pretended,

tended, for the common benefit, ought to be car- BOOK IX.
ried on at the common charge; upon the latter,
as a fine by way of punifhment for their rebellion. 1547.
By thefe exactions, he amaffed above one million
fix hundred thoufand crowns, a fum which appeared prodigious in the fixteenth century. But fo
general was the confternation which had feized the
Germans upon his rapid fuccefs, and fuch their
dread of his victorious troops, that all implicitly
obeyed his commands; though, at the fame time,
thefe extraordinary ftretches of power greatly alarmed a people jealous of their privileges, and habitu-
ated, during feveral ages, to confider the Imperial
authority as neither extenfive nor formidable.
This difcontent and refentment, how induftrioufly
foever they concealed them, became univerfal; and
the more thefe paffions were reftrained and kept
down for the prefent, the more likely were they to
burft out foon with additional violence.

WHILE Charles gave law to the Germans like a   Ferdinand's
conquered people, Ferdinand treated his fubjects encroach-
                                                  ments on
in Bohemia with ftill greater rigour. That king- the liberties
                                                  of his Bo-
dom poffeffed privileges and immunities as exten- hemian fub-
                                                  jects.
five as thofe of any nation in which the feudal inftitutions were eftablifhed. The prerogative of
their Kings was extremely limited, and the crown
itfelf elective. Ferdinand, when raifed to the
throne, had confirmed their liberties with every
folemnity prefcribed by their exceffive folicitude
for the fecurity of a conftitution of government to
which

which they were extremely attached. He soon began, however, to be weary of a jurisdiction so much circumscribed, and to despise a sceptre which he could not transmit to his posterity; and notwithstanding all his former engagements, he attempted to overturn the constitution from its foundations; that, instead of an elective kingdom, he might render it hereditary. But the Bohemians were too high-spirited tamely to relinquish privileges which they had long enjoyed. At the same time, many of them having embraced the doctrines of the Reformers, the seeds of which John Huss and Jerome of Prague had planted in their country about the beginning of the preceding century, the desire of acquiring religious liberty mingled itself with their zeal for their civil rights; and these two kindred passions heightening, as usual, each other's force, precipitated them immediately into violent measures. They had not only refused to serve their sovereign against the confederates of Smalkalde, but having entered into a close alliance with the Elector of Saxony, they had bound themselves, by a solemn association, to defend their ancient constitution; and to persist, until they should obtain such additional privileges as they thought necessary towards perfecting the present model of their government, or rendering it more permanent. They chose Caspar Phlug, a nobleman of distinction, to be their general; and raised an army of thirty thousand men to enforce their petitions. But either from the weakness of their leader, or from

from the diffenfions in a great unwieldy body, which, having united haftily, was not thoroughly compacted, or from fome other unknown caufe, the fubfequent operations of the Bohemians bore no proportion to the zeal and ardour with which they took their firft refolutions. They fuffered themfelves to be amufed fo long with negociations and overtures of different kinds, that before they could enter Saxony, the battle of Muhlberg was fought, the Elector deprived of his dignity and territories, the Landgrave confined to clofe cuftody, and the league of Smalkalde entirely diffipated. The fame dread of the Emperor's power which had feized the reft of the Germans, reached them. As foon as their fovereign approached with a body of Imperial troops, they inftantly difperfed, thinking of nothing but how to atone for their paft guilt, and to acquire fome hope of forgivenefs by a prompt fubmiffion. But Ferdinand, who entered his dominions full of that implacable refentment which inflames Monarchs whofe authority has been defpifed, was not to be mollified by the late repentance and involuntary return of rebellious fubjects to their duty. He even heard, unmoved, the intreaties and tears of the citizens of Prague, who appeared before him in the pofture of fuppliants, and implored for mercy. The fentence which he pronounced againft them was rigorous to extremity; he abolifhed many of their privileges, he abridged others, and new-modelled the conftitution according to his pleafure. He

condemned

condemned to death many of those who had been most active in forming the late association against him, and punished still a greater number with confiscation of their goods, or perpetual banishment. He obliged all his subjects, of every condition, to give up their arms to be deposited in forts where he planted garrisons; and after disarming his people, he loaded them with new and exorbitant taxes. Thus, by an ill-conducted and unsuccessful effort to extend their privileges, the Bohemians not only enlarged the sphere of the royal prerogative, when they intended to have circumscribed it, but they almost annihilated those liberties which they aimed at establishing on a broader and more secure foundation [n].

Diet held at Augsburg.

THE Emperor, having now humbled, and, as he imagined, subdued the independent and stubborn spirit of the Germans by the terror of arms and the rigour of punishment, held a diet at Augsburg, in order to compose finally the controversies with regard to religion, which had so long disturbed the Empire. He durst not, however, trust the determination of a matter so interesting to the free suffrage of the Germans, broken as their minds now were to subjection. He entered the city at the head of his Spanish troops, and assigned them quarters there. The rest of his soldiers he cantoned in the adjacent villages; so that the mem-

[n] Sleid. 408. 419. 434.   Thuan. l. iv. 129. 150.   Struv. Corp. ii.

bers

bers of the diet, while they carried on their deliberations, were surrounded by the same army which had overcome their countrymen. Immediately after his public entry, Charles gave a proof of the violence with which he intended to proceed. He took possession by force of the cathedral, together with one of the principal churches; and his priests having, by various ceremonies, purified them from the pollution with which they supposed the unhallowed ministrations of the Protestants to have defiled them, they re-established with great pomp the rites of the Romish worship°.

THE concourse of members to this diet was extraordinary; the importance of the affairs concerning which it was to deliberate, added to the fear of giving offence to the Emperor by an absence which lay open to misconstruction, brought together almost all the Princes, nobles, and representatives of cities who had a right to sit in that assembly. The Emperor, in the speech with which he opened the meeting, called their attention immediately to that point, which seemed chiefly to merit it. Having mentioned the fatal effects of the religious dissensions which had arisen in Germany, and taken notice of his own unwearied endeavours to procure a general council, which alone could provide a remedy adequate to those evils, he exhorted them to recognise its authority, and to acquiesce in the deci-

The Emperor exhorts them to submit to the General Council.

Sleid. 435. 437.
6

BOOK IX.
1547.

Various revolutions in the council.

sions of an assembly to which they had originally appealed, as having the sole right of judgment in the case.

BUT the council, to which Charles wished them to refer all their controversies, had, by this time, undergone a violent change. The fear and jealousy, with which the Emperor's first successes against the confederates of Smalkalde had inspired the Pope, continued to increase. Not satisfied with attempting to retard the progress of the Imperial arms, by the sudden recal of his troops, Paul began to consider the Emperor as an enemy, the weight of whose power he must soon feel, and against whom he could not be too hasty in taking precautions. He foresaw that the immediate effect of the Emperor's acquiring absolute power in Germany, would be to render him entirely master of all the decisions of the council, if it should continue to meet in Trent. It was dangerous to allow a Monarch, so ambitious, to get the command of this formidable engine, which he might employ at pleasure to limit or to overturn the papal authority. As the only method of preventing this, he determined to remove the council to some city more immediately under his own jurisdiction, and at a greater distance from the terror of the Emperor's arms, or the reach of his influence. An incident fortunately occurred, which gave this measure the appearance of being necessary. One or two of the fathers of the council, together with some of their

their domestics, happening to die suddenly, the physicians, deceived by the symptoms, or suborned by the Pope's legates, pronounced the distemper to be infectious and pestilential. Some of the prelates, struck with a panic, retired; others were impatient to be gone; and after a short consultation, the council was translated to Bologna, a city subject to the Pope. All the bishops in the Imperial interest warmly opposed this resolution, as taken without necessity, and founded on false or frivolous pretexts. All the Spanish prelates, and most of the Neapolitan, by the Emperor's express command, remained at Trent; the rest, to the number of thirty-four, accompanying the legates to Bologna. Thus a schism commenced in that very assembly, which had been called to heal the divisions of Christendom; the fathers of Bologna inveighed against those who staid at Trent, as contumacious and regardless of the Pope's authority; while the other accused them of being so far intimidated by the fears of imaginary danger, as to remove to a place where their consultations could prove of no service towards re-establishing peace and order in Germany[p].

March 11. Translated from Trent to Bologna.

The Emperor, at the same time, employed all his interest to procure the return of the council to Trent. But Paul, who highly applauded his own sagacity in having taken a step which put it

Symptoms of disgust between the Pope and Emperor.

[p] F. Paul, 248, &c.

out of Charles's power to acquire the direction of that assembly, paid no regard to a request, the object of which was so extremely obvious. The summer was consumed in fruitless negociations with respect to this point, the importunity of the one and obstinacy of the other daily increasing. At last an event happened which widened the breach irreparably, and rendered the Pope utterly averse from listening to any proposal that came from the Emperor. Charles, as has been already observed, had so violently exasperated Peter Lewis Farnese, the Pope's son, by refusing to grant him the investiture of Parma and Placentia, that he had watched ever since that time with all the vigilance of resentment for an opportunity of revenging that injury. He had endeavoured to precipitate the Pope into open hostilities against the Emperor, and had earnestly solicited the King of France to invade Italy. His hatred and resentment extended to all those whom he knew that the Emperor favoured; he did every ill office in his power to Gonzaga, governor of Milan, and had encouraged Fiesco in his attempt upon the life of Andrew Doria, because both Gonzaga and Doria possessed a great degree of the Emperor's esteem and confidence. His malevolence and secret intrigues were not unknown to the Emperor, who could not be more desirous to take vengeance on him, than Gonzaga and Doria were to be employed as his instruments in inflicting it. Farnese, by the profligacy of his life, and by enormities of every kind, equal to those committed

by

by the worst tyrants who have disgraced human nature, had rendered himself so odious, that it was thought any violence whatever might be lawfully attempted against him. Gonzaga and Doria soon found, among his own subjects, persons who were eager, and even deemed it meritorious, to lend their hands in such a service. As Farnese, animated with the jealousy which usually possesses petty sovereigns, had employed all the cruelty and fraud, whereby they endeavour to supply their defect of power, in order to humble and extirpate the nobility subject to his government, five noblemen of the greatest distinction in Placentia combined to avenge the injuries which they themselves had suffered, as well as those which he had offered to their order. They formed their plan in conjunction with Gonzaga; but it remains uncertain whether he originally suggested the scheme to them, or only approved of what they proposed, and co operated in carrying it on. They concerted all the previous steps with such foresight, conducted their intrigues with such secrecy, and displayed such courage in the execution of their design, that it may be ranked among the most audacious deeds of that nature mentioned in history. One body of the conspirators surprised, at mid-day, the gates of the citadel of Placentia where Farnese resided, overpowered his guards, and murdered him. Another party of them made themselves masters of the town, and called upon their fellow-citizens to take arms, in order to recover their liberty. The multitude ran towards

BOOK IX.

1547.

Sept. 10.

The assassination of the Pope's son.

towards the citadel, from which three great guns, a signal concerted with Gonzaga, had been fired; and before they could guess the cause or the authors of the tumult, they saw the lifeless body of the tyrant hanging by the heels from one of the windows of the citadel. But so universally detestable had he become, that not one expressed any sentiment of concern at such a sad reverse of fortune, or discovered the least indignation at this ignominious treatment of a sovereign Prince. The exultation at the success of the conspiracy was general, and all applauded the actors in it, as the deliverers of their country. The body was tumbled into the ditch that surrounded the citadel, and exposed to the insults of the rabble; the rest of the citizens returned to their usual occupations, as if nothing extraordinary had happened.

The Imperial troops take possession of Placentia.

BEFORE next morning, a body of troops arriving from the frontiers of the Milanese, where they had been posted in expectation of the event, took possession of the city in the Emperor's name, and reinstated the inhabitants in the possession of their ancient privileges. Parma, which the Imperialists attempted likewise to surprise, was saved by the vigilance and fidelity of the officers whom Farnese had intrusted with the command of the garrison. The death of a son whom, notwithstanding his infamous vices, Paul loved with an excess of parental tenderness, overwhelmed him with the deepest affliction; and the loss of a city of such consequence as Placentia, greatly embittered his forrow. He accufed Gonzaga, in open confiftory, of having committed a cruel murder, in order to prepare the way for an unjuft ufurpation, and immediately demanded of the Emperor fatisfaction for both; for the former, by the punifhment of Gonzaga; for the latter, by the reftitution of Placentia to his grandfon Octavio, its rightful owner. But Charles, who, rather than quit a prize of fuch value, was willing, not only to expofe himfelf to the imputation of being acceffary to the crime which had given an opportunity of feizing it, but to bear the infamy of defrauding his own fon-in-law of the inheritance which belonged to him, eluded all his folicitations, and determined to keep poffeffion of the city, together with its territories [q].

This refolution, flowing from an ambition fo rapacious, as to be reftrained by no confideration either of decency or juftice, tranfported the Pope fo far beyond his ufual moderation and prudence, that he was eager to take arms againft the Emperor, in order to be avenged on the murderers of his fon, and to recover the inheritance wrefted from his family. Confcious, however, of his own inability to contend with fuch an enemy, he warmly folicited the French King and the republic of Venice to join in an offenfive league againft Charles. But Henry was intent at that time on other objects. His an-

The Pope courts the alliance of the French King and the Venetians.

---

[q] F. Paul, 257. Pallavic. 41, 42. Thuan. iv. 156. Mem. de Ribier, 59. 67. Natalis Comitis Hiftor. lib. iii. p. 64.

cient allies the Scots, having been defeated by the English in one of the greatest battles ever fought between these two rival nations, he was about to send a numerous body of veteran troops into that country, as well to preserve it from being conquered, as to gain the acquisition of a new kingdom to the French monarchy, by marrying his son the Dauphin to the young Queen of Scotland. An undertaking accompanied with such manifest advantages, the success of which appeared to be so certain, was not to be relinquished for the remote prospect of benefit from an alliance depending upon the precarious life of a Pope of fourscore, who had nothing at heart but the gratification of his own private resentment. Instead, therefore, of rushing headlong into the alliance proposed, Henry amused the Pope with such general professions and promises, as might keep him from any thoughts of endeavouring to accommodate his differences with the Emperor, but at the same time he avoided any such engagement as might occasion an immediate rupture with Charles, or precipitate him into a war for which he was not prepared. The Venetians, though much alarmed at seeing Placentia in the hands of the Imperialists, imitated the wary conduct of the French King, as it nearly resembled the spirit which usually regulated their own conduct [r].

[r] Mem. de Ribier, ii. 63. 71. 78. 85. 95. Paruta Istor. di Venez. 199. 203. Thuan. iv. 160.

BUT,

But, though the Pope found that it was not in his power to kindle immediately the flames of war, he did not forget the injuries which he was obliged for the prefent to endure; refentment fettled deeper in his mind, and became more rancorous in proportion as he felt the difficulty of gratifying it. It was while thefe fentiments of enmity were in full force, and the defire of vengeance at its height, that the diet of Augfburg, by the Emperor's command, petitioned the Pope, in the name of the whole Germanic body, to enjoin the prelates who had retired to Bologna to return again to Trent, and to renew their deliberations in that place. Charles had been at great pains in bringing the members to join in this requeft. Having obferved a confiderable variety of fentiments among the Proteftants with refpect to the fubmiffion which he had required to the decrees of the council, fome of them being altogether intractable, while others were ready to acknowledge its right of jurifdiction upon certain conditions, he employed all his addrefs in order to gain or to divide them. He threatened and overawed the Elector Palatine, a weak Prince, and afraid that the Emperor might inflict on him the punifhment to which he had made himfelf liable by the affiftance that he had given to the confederates of Smalkalde. The hope of procuring liberty for the Landgrave, together with the formal confirmation of his own electoral dignity, overcame Maurice's fcruples, or prevented him from oppofing what he knew would be agreeable to the Emperor.

Emperor. The Elector of Brandenburg, less influenced by religious zeal than any Prince of that age, was easily induced to imitate their example, in assenting to all that the Emperor required. The deputies of the cities remained still to be brought over. They were more tenacious of their principles, and though every thing that could operate either on their hopes or fears was tried, the utmost that they would promise was, to acknowledge the jurisdiction of the council, if effectual provision were made for securing to the divines of all parties free access to that assembly, with entire liberty of debate; and if all points in controversy were decided according to scripture and the usage of the primitive church. But when the memorial containing this declaration was presented to the Emperor, he ventured to put in practice a very extraordinary artifice. Without reading the paper, or taking any notice of the conditions on which they had insisted, he seemed to take it for granted that they had complied with his demand, and gave thanks to the deputies for their full and unreserved submission to the decrees of the council. The deputies, though astonished at what they had heard, did not attempt to set him right, both parties being better pleased that the matter should remain under this state of ambiguity, than to push for an explanation, which must have occasioned a dispute, and would have led, perhaps, to a rupture[*].

[*] F. Paul, 259. Sleid. 440. Thuan. tom. i. 155.

HAVING

HAVING obtained this seeming submission from the members of the diet to the authority of the council, Charles employed that as an argument to enforce their petition for its return to Trent. But the Pope, from the satisfaction which he felt in mortifying the Emperor, as well as from his own aversion to what was demanded, resolved, without hesitation, that his petition should not be granted; though, in order to avoid the imputation of being influenced wholly by resentment, he had the address to throw it upon the fathers at Bologna, to put a direct negative upon the request. With this view he referred to their consideration the petition of the diet, and they, ready to confirm by their assent whatever the legates were pleased to dictate, declared that the council could not, consistently with its dignity, return to Trent, unless the prelates who, by remaining there, had discovered a schismatic spirit, would first repair to Bologna, and join their brethren; and that, even after their junction, the council could not renew its consultations with any prospect of benefit to the church, if the Germans did not prove their intention of obeying its future decrees to be sincere, by yielding immediate obedience to those which it had already passed [r].

BOOK IX.

1547.
The Pope eludes the demand.

Decem. 20.

THIS answer was communicated to the Emperor by the Pope, who at the same time exhorted him to comply with demands which appeared to

The Emperor protests against the council of Bologna.

[r] F. Paul, 250. Pallav. ii. 49.

be

be so reasonable. But Charles was better acquainted with the duplicity of the Pope's character than to be deceived by such a gross artifice; he knew that the prelates of Bologna durst utter no sentiment but what Paul inspired; and, therefore, overlooking them as mere tools in the hand of another, he considered their reply as a full discovery of the Pope's intentions. As he could no longer hope to acquire such an ascendant in the council as to render it subservient to his own plan, he saw it to be necessary that Paul should not have it in his power to turn against him the authority of so venerable an assembly. In order to prevent this, he sent two Spanish lawyers to Bologna, who, in the presence of the legates, protested, That the translation of the council to that place had been unnecessary, and founded on false or frivolous pretexts; that while it continued to meet there, it ought to be deemed an unlawful and schismatical conventicle; that all its decisions ought of course to be held as null and invalid; and that since the Pope, together with the corrupt ecclesiastics who depended on him, had abandoned the care of the church, the Emperor, as its protector, would employ all the power which God had committed to him, in order to preserve it from those calamities with which it was threatened. A few days after, the Imperial ambassador at Rome demanded an audience of the Pope, and in presence of all the Cardinals, as well as foreign ministers, protested against the proceed-

proceedings of the prelates at Bologna, in terms equally harsh and disrespectful [u].

IT was not long before Charles proceeded to carry these threats, which greatly alarmed both the Pope and council at Bologna, into execution. He let the diet know the ill success of his endeavours to procure a favourable answer to their petition, and that the Pope, equally regardless of their entreaties, and of his services to the church, had refused to gratify them by allowing the council to meet again at Trent; that, though all hope of holding this assembly in a place, where they might look for freedom of debate and judgment, was not to be given up, the prospect of it was, at present, distant and uncertain; that, in the mean time, Germany was torn in pieces by religious dissensions, the purity of the faith corrupted, and the minds of the people disquieted with a multiplicity of new opinions and controversies formerly unknown among Christians; that, moved by the duty which he owed to them as their sovereign, and to the Church as its protector, he had employed some divines, of known abilities and learning, to prepare a system of doctrine, to which all should conform, until a council, such as they wished for, could be convocated. This system was compiled by Pflug, Helding, and Agricola, of whom the two former were dignitaries in the

The Emperor prepares a system, to serve as a rule of faith in Germany.

[u] F. Paul, 264. Pallav. 51. Sleid. 446. Goldasti Constit. Imperial. i. 561.

Romish church, but remarkable for their pacific and healing spirit; the last was a Protestant divine, suspected, not without reason, of having been gained, by bribes and promises, to betray or mislead his party on this occasion. The articles presented to the diet of Ratisbon in the year one thousand five hundred and forty-one, in order to reconcile the contending parties, served as a model for the present work. But as the Emperor's situation was much changed since that time, and he found it no longer necessary to manage the Protestants with the same delicacy as at that juncture, the concessions in their favour were not now so numerous, nor did they extend to points of so much consequence. The treatise contained a complete system of theology, conformable in almost every article to the tenets of the Romish church, though expressed, for the most part, in the softest words, or in scriptural phrases, or in terms of studied ambiguity. Every doctrine, however, peculiar to Popery, was retained, and the observation of all the rites, which the Protestants condemned as inventions of men introduced into the worship of God, was enjoined. With regard to two points only, some relaxation in the rigour of opinion as well as some latitude in practice were admitted. Such ecclesiastics as had married, and would not put away their wives, were allowed, nevertheless, to perform all the functions of their sacred office; and those provinces which had been accustomed to partake of the cup, as well as of the bread in the sacrament of the Lord's Supper,

Supper, were still indulged in the privilege of receiving both. Even these were declared to be concessions for the sake of peace, and granted only for a season, in compliance with the weakness or prejudices of their countrymen [x].

THIS system of doctrine, known afterwards by the name of the *Interim*, because it contained temporary regulations, which were to continue no longer in force than until a free general council could be held, the Emperor presented to the diet, with a pompous declaration of his sincere intention to re-establish tranquillity and order in the church, as well as of his hopes that their adopting these regulations would contribute greatly to bring about that desirable event. It was read in presence of the diet, according to form. As soon as it was finished, the archbishop of Mentz, president of the electoral college, rose up hastily, and, having thanked the Emperor for his unwearied and pious endeavours in order to restore peace to the church, he, in name of the diet, signified their approbation of the system of doctrine which had been read, together with their resolution of conforming to it in every particular. The whole assembly was amazed at a declaration so unprecedented and unconstitutional, as well as at the Elector's presumption in pretending to deliver the sense of the diet, upon a point which had not hitherto been the subject of consultation

This, which was called the Interim, he lays before the diet, May 15.

[x] F. Paul, 270. Pallav. ii. 60. Sleid. 453. 457. Struv. Corp. 1054. Goldast. Constit. Imper. i. 518.

or debate. But not one member had the courage to contradict what the Elector had said; some being overawed by fear, others remaining silent through complaisance. The Emperor held the archbishop's declaration to be a full constitutional ratification of the Interim, and prepared to enforce the observance of it, as a decree of the Empire [y].

During this diet, the wife and children of the Landgrave, warmly seconded by Maurice of Saxony, endeavoured to interest the members in behalf of that unhappy Prince, who still languished in confinement. But Charles, who did not chuse to be brought under the necessity of rejecting any request that came from such a respectable body, in order to prevent their representations, laid before the diet an account of his transactions with the Landgrave, together with the motives which had at first induced him to detain that Prince in custody, and which rendered it prudent, as he alleged, to keep him still under restraint. It was no easy matter to give any good reason for an action, incapable of being justified. But he thought the most frivolous pretexts might be produced in an assembly the members of which were willing to be deceived, and afraid of nothing so much as of discovering that they saw his conduct in its true colours. His account of his own conduct was accordingly admitted to be fully

[y] Sleid. 460. F. Paul, 273. Pallav. 63.

satisfactory, and after some feeble intreaties that he would extend his clemency to his unfortunate prisoner, the Landgrave's concerns were no more mentioned [z].

In order to counterbalance the unfavourable impression which this inflexible rigour might make, Charles, as a proof that his gratitude was no less permanent and unchangeable than his resentment, invested Maurice in the electoral dignity, with all the legal formalities. The ceremony was performed, with extraordinary pomp, in an open court, so near the apartment in which the degraded Elector was kept a prisoner, that he could view it from his windows. Even this insult did not ruffle his usual tranquillity; and turning his eyes that way, he beheld a prosperous rival receiving those ensigns of dignity of which he had been stripped, without uttering one sentiment unbecoming the fortitude that he had preserved amidst all his calamities [a].

Immediately after the dissolution of the diet, the Emperor ordered the Interim to be published in the German as well as Latin language. It met with the usual reception of conciliating schemes, when proposed to men heated with disputation; both parties declaimed against it with

The Interim equally disapproved of by Protestants and Papists.

---

[z] Sleid. 441.
[a] Thuan. Hist. lib. v. 176. Struv. Corp. 1054. Investitura Mauritii, a Mammerano Lucemburgo descripta, ap. Scardium, ii. 508.

equal violence. The Proteſtants condemned it as a ſyſtem containing the groſſeſt errors of Popery, diſguiſed with ſo little art, that it could impoſe only on the moſt ignorant, or on thoſe who, by wilfully ſhutting their eyes, favoured the deception. The Papiſts inveighed againſt it, as a work in which ſome doctrines of the church were impiouſly given up, others meanly concealed, and all of them delivered in terms calculated rather to deceive the unwary, than to inſtruct the ignorant, or to reclaim ſuch as were enemies to the truth. While the Lutheran divines fiercely attacked it, on one hand, the general of the Dominicans with no leſs vehemence impugned it on the other. But at Rome, as ſoon as the contents of the Interim came to be known, the indignation of the courtiers and eccleſiaſtics roſe to the greateſt height. They exclaimed againſt the Emperor's profane encroachment on the ſacerdotal function, in preſuming, with the concurrence of an aſſembly of laymen, to define articles of faith, and to regulate modes of worſhip. They compared this raſh deed to that of Uzziah, who, with an unhallowed hand, had touched the ark of God; or to the bold attempts of thoſe Emperors, who had rendered their memory deteſtable, by endeavouring to model the Chriſtian church according to their pleaſure. They even affected to find out a reſemblance between the Emperor's conduct and that of Henry VIII. and expreſſed their fear of his imitating the example of that apoſtate, by uſurping the

the title as well as jurisdiction belonging to the head of the church. All, therefore, contended with one voice, that as the foundations of ecclesiastical authority were now shaken, and the whole fabric ready to be overturned by a new enemy, some powerful method of defence must be provided, and a vigorous resistance must be made, in the beginning, before he grew too formidable to be opposed.

THE Pope, whose judgment was improved by longer experience in great transactions, as well as by a more extensive observation of human affairs, viewed the matter with more acute discernment, and derived comfort from the very circumstance which filled them with apprehension. He was astonished that a Prince of such superior sagacity as the Emperor, should be so intoxicated with a single victory, as to imagine that he might give law to mankind, and decide even in those matters, with regard to which they are most impatient of dominion. He saw that, by joining any one of the contending parties in Germany, Charles might have had it in his power to have oppressed the other, but that the presumption of success had now inspired him with the vain thought of his being able to domineer over both. He foretold that a system which all attacked, and none defended, could not be of long duration; and that, for this reason, there was no need of his interposing in order to hasten its fall; for as

The sentiments of the Pope with regard to it.

The Emperor enforces compliance with the Interim.

soon as the powerful hand which now upheld it was withdrawn, it would sink of its own accord, and be forgotten for ever [b].

THE Emperor, fond of his own plan, adhered to his resolution of carrying it into full execution. But though the Elector Palatine, the Elector of Brandenburg, and Maurice, influenced by the same considerations as formerly, seemed ready to yield implicit obedience to whatever he should enjoin, he met not every where with a like obsequious submission. John Marquis of Brandenburg Anspach, although he had taken part with great zeal in the war against the confederates of Smalkalde, refused to renounce doctrines which he held to be sacred; and reminding the Emperor of the repeated promises which he had given his Protestant allies, of allowing them the free exercise of their religion, he claimed, in consequence of these, to be exempted from receiving the Interim. Some other Princes, also, ventured to mention the same scruples, and to plead the same indulgence. But on this, as on other trying occasions, the firmness of the Elector of Saxony was most distinguished, and merited the highest praise. Charles, well knowing the authority of his example with all the Protestant party, laboured, with the utmost earnestness, to gain his approbation of the Interim, and by employing sometimes promises of setting him at liberty,

[b] Sleid. 468. F. Paul, 271. 277. Pallav. ii. 64.

some-

sometimes threats of treating him with greater harshness, attempted alternately to work upon his hopes and his fears. But he was alike regardless of both. After having declared his fixed belief in the doctrines of the Reformation, "I cannot now, said he, in my old age, abandon the principles, for which I early contended; nor, in order to procure freedom during a few declining years, will I betray that good cause, on account of which I have suffered so much, and am still willing to suffer. Better for me to enjoy, in this solitude, the esteem of virtuous men, together with the approbation of my own conscience, than to return into the world, with the imputation and guilt of apostacy, to disgrace and embitter the remainder of my days." By this magnanimous resolution, he set his countrymen a pattern of conduct, so very different from that which the Emperor wished him to have exhibited to them, that it drew upon him fresh marks of his displeasure. The rigour of his confinement was increased; the number of his servants abridged; the Lutheran clergymen, who had hitherto been permitted to attend him, were dismissed; and even the books of devotion, which had been his chief consolation during a tedious imprisonment, were taken from him[c]. The Landgrave of Hesse, his companion in misfortune, did not maintain the same constancy. His patience and fortitude were both so much exhausted by the length of his

[c] Sleid. 462.

confinement, that, willing to purchase freedom at any price, he wrote to the Emperor, offering not only to approve of the Interim, but to yield an unreserved submission to his will in every other particular. But Charles, who knew that whatever course the Landgrave might hold, neither his example nor authority would prevail on his children or subjects to receive the Interim, paid no regard to his offers. He was kept confined as strictly as ever; and while he suffered the cruel mortification of having his conduct set in contrast to that of the Elector, he derived not the smallest benefit from the mean step which exposed him to much deserved censure [d].

The free cities struggle against receiving the Interim.

But it was in the Imperial cities that Charles met with the most violent opposition to the Interim. These small commonwealths, the citizens of which were accustomed to liberty and independence, had embraced the doctrines of the Reformation when they were first published, with remarkable eagerness; the bold spirit of innovation being peculiarly suited to the genius of free government. Among them, the Protestant teachers had made the greatest number of proselytes. The most eminent divines of the party were settled in them as pastors. By having the direction of the schools and other seminaries of learning, they had trained up disciples, who were as well instructed in the articles of their faith, as they were zealous to defend them. Such persons were not to be guided

[d] Sleid. 462.

by example, or swayed by authority; but having been taught to employ their own understanding in examining and deciding with respect to the points in controversy, they thought that they were both qualified and entitled to judge for themselves. As soon as the contents of the Interim were known, they, with one voice, joined in refusing to admit it. Augsburg, Ulm, Strasburg, Constance, Bremen, Magdeburg, together with many other towns of less note, presented remonstrances to the Emperor, setting forth the irregular and unconstitutional manner in which the Interim had been enacted, and beseeching him not to offer such violence to their consciences, as to require their assent to a form of doctrine and worship, which appeared to them repugnant to the express precepts of the divine law. But Charles having prevailed on so many Princes of the Empire to approve of his new model, was not much moved by the representations of those cities, which, how formidable soever they might have proved, if they could have been formed into one body, lay so remote from each other, that it was easy to oppress them separately, before it was possible for them to unite.

IN order to accomplish this, the Emperor saw it to be requisite that his measures should be vigorous, and executed with such rapidity as to allow no time for concerting any common plan of opposition. Having laid down this maxim as the rule of his proceedings, his first attempt was

Compelled by violence to submit.

was upon the city of Augsburg, which, though overawed by the presence of the Spanish troops, he knew to be as much dissatisfied with the Interim as any in the Empire. He ordered one body of these troops to seize the gates; he posted the rest in different quarters of the city; and assembling all the burgesses in the town-hall, he, by his sole absolute authority, published a decree abolishing their present form of government, dissolving all their corporations and fraternities, and nominating a small number of persons, in whom he vested for the future all the powers of government. Each of the persons, thus chosen, took an oath to observe the Interim. An act of power so unprecedented as well as arbitrary, which excluded the body of the inhabitants from any share in the government of their own community, and subjected them to men who had no other merit than their servile devotion to the Emperor's will, gave general disgust; but as they durst not venture upon resistance, they were obliged to submit in silence[e]. From Augsburg, in which he left a garrison, he proceeded to Ulm, and new-modelling its government with the same violent hand, he seized such of their pastors as refused to subscribe the Interim, committed them to prison, and at his departure carried them along with him in chains[f]. By this severity he not only secured the reception of the Interim in two of the most

[e] Sleid. 469. [f] Ibid. 472.

powerful

powerful cities, but gave warning to the reft what fuch as continued refractory had to expect. The effect of the example was as great as he could have wifhed; and many towns, in order to fave themfelves from the like treatment, found it neceffary to comply with what he enjoined. This obedience, extorted by the rigour of authority, produced no change in the fentiments of the Germans, and extended no farther than to make them conform fo far to what he required, as was barely fufficient to fcreen them from punifhment. The Proteftant preachers accompanied thofe religious rites, the obfervation of which the Interim prefcribed, with fuch an explication of their tendency, as ferved rather to confirm than to remove the fcruples of their hearers with regard to them. The people, many of whom had grown up to mature years fince the eftablifhment of the reformed religion, and had never known any other form of public worfhip, beheld the pompous pageantry of the popifh fervice with contempt or horror; and in moft places the Romifh ecclefiaftics who returned to take poffeffion of their churches, could hardly be protected from infult, or their miniftrations from interruption. Thus, notwithftanding the apparent compliance of fo many cities, the inhabitants being accuftomed to freedom, fubmitted with reluctance to the power which now oppreffed them. Their underftanding as well as inclination revolted againft the doctrines and ceremonies impofed on them; and though,

though, for the prefent, they concealed their difguft and refentment, it was evident that thefe paffions could not always be kept under reftraint, but would break out at laft in effects proportional to their violence [g].

The Pope difmiffes the Council affembled at Bologna.

CHARLES, however, highly pleafed with having bent the ftubborn fpirit of the Germans to fuch general fubmiffion, departed for the Low-Countries, fully determined to compel the cities, which ftill ftood out, to receive the Interim. He carried his two prifoners, the Elector of Saxony and Landgrave of Heffe, along with him, either becaufe he durft not leave them behind him in Germany, or becaufe he wifhed to give his countrymen the Flemings this illuftrious proof of the fuccefs of his arms, and the extent of his power.

Sept. 17.

Before Charles arrived at Bruffels, he was informed that the Pope's legates at Bologna had difmiffed the council by an indefinite prorogation, and that the prelates affembled there had returned to their refpective countries. Neceffity had driven the Pope into this meafure. By the feceffion of thofe who had voted againft the tranflation, together with the departure of others, who grew weary of continuing in a place where they were not fuffered to proceed to bufinefs, fo few and fuch inconfiderable members remained, that the pompous appellation of a General Council could not, with decency, be beftowed any longer

[g] Mem. de Ribier, ii. 218. Sleid. 491.

upon

upon them. Paul had no choice but to diffolve an affembly which was become the object of contempt, and exhibited to all Chriftendom a moft glaring proof of the impotence of the Romifh See. But unavoidable as the meafure was, it lay open to be unfavourably interpreted, and had the appearance of withdrawing the remedy, at the very time when thofe for whofe recovery it was provided, were prevailed on to acknowledge its virtue, and to make trial of its efficacy. Charles did not fail to put this conftruction on the conduct of the Pope; and by an artful comparifon of his own efforts to fupprefs herefy, with Paul's fcandalous inattention to a point fo effential, he endeavoured to render the Pontiff odious to all zealous Catholics. At the fame time, he commanded the prelates of his faction to remain at Trent, that the Council might ftill appear to have a being, and might be ready, whenever it was thought expedient to refume its deliberations for the good of the church [h].

The motive of Charles's journey to the Low-Countries, befide gratifying his favourite paffion of travelling from one part of his dominions to another, was to receive Philip his only fon, who was now in the twenty-firft year of his age, and whom he had called thither, not only that he might be recognized by the States of the Ne-

The Emperor receives his fon Philip in the Low-Countries.

[h] Pallav. p. 11. 72.

therlands

therlands as heir-apparent, but in order to facilitate the execution of a vast scheme, the object of which, and the reception it met with, shall be hereafter explained. Philip, having left the government of Spain to Maximilian, Ferdinand's eldest son, to whom the Emperor had given the Princess Mary his daughter in marriage, embarked for Italy, attended by a numerous retinue of Spanish nobles [i]. The squadron which escorted him, was commanded by Andrew Doria, who, notwithstanding his advanced age, insisted on the honour of performing, in person, the same duty to the son, which he had often discharged towards the father. He landed safely at Genoa; from thence he went to Milan, and proceeding through Germany, arrived at the Imperial court in Brussels. The States of Brabant, in the first place, and those of the other provinces in their order, acknowledged his right of succession in common form, and he took the customary oath to preserve all their privileges inviolate [k]. In all the towns of the Low-countries through which Philip passed, he was received with extraordinary pomp. Nothing that could either express the respect of the people, or contribute to his amusement, was neglected; pageants, tournaments, and public spectacles of every kind, were exhibited with that expensive magnificence which commercial

[i] Ochoa, Carolea, 362.
[k] Haraei Annal. Brabant. 652.

nations

nations are fond of displaying, when, on any occasion, they depart from their usual maxims of frugality. But amidst these scenes of festivity and pleasure, Philip's natural severity of temper was discernible. Youth itself could not render him agreeable, nor his being a candidate for power form him to courtesy. He maintained a haughty reserve in his behaviour, and discovered such manifest partiality towards his Spanish attendants, together with such an avowed preference to the manners of their country, as highly disgusted the Flemings, and gave rise to that antipathy, which afterwards occasioned a revolution fatal to him in that part of his dominions [1].

Charles was long detained in the Netherlands by a violent attack of the gout, which returned upon him so frequently, and with such increasing violence, that it had broken, to a great degree, the vigour of his constitution. He nevertheless did not slacken his endeavours to enforce the Interim. The inhabitants of Strasburg, after a long struggle, found it necessary to yield obedience; those of Constance, who had taken arms in their own defence, were compelled not only to conform to the Interim, but to renounce their privileges as a free city, to do homage to Ferdinand as Archduke of Austria,

[1] Mem. de Ribier, ii. 29. L'Evesque Mem. de Card. Granvelle, i. 21.

and,

and, as his vaffals, to admit an Auftrian governor and garrifon^m. Magdeburg, Bremen, Hamburg, and Lubeck, were the only Imperial cities of note that ftill continued refractory.

^m Sleid. 474. 491.

END OF THE THIRD VOLUME.